Essentials of Consumer Behavior

T0334650

This thoroughly updated second edition of *Essentials of Consumer Behavior* offers a concise alternative to traditional textbooks with a practice-based approach.

Stephens emphasizes that consumer behavior does not simply equate to buyer behavior. She examines the thoughts, feelings, and behaviors that shape consumers' attitudes and motivations in relation to brands, products, and marketing messages. The new edition of this concise guide to the discipline offers comprehensive coverage of issues including:

- Technology now integrated into all chapters
- Consumer vulnerability, expanded beyond young consumers and persons with disabilities to include the economically disadvantaged and those marginalized because of ethnicity and gender
- Consumers' roles in the lives of nonhuman animals, with extensive discussion of the consumer journey toward acquiring an animal companion and the impact of pet ownership on consumers' non-pet-related purchases

Suitable for marketing and consumer behavior students at advanced undergraduate and postgraduate levels, this clearly written and thorough textbook will keep students engaged and help them to become savvier marketers. Online resources include links to videos and podcasts, further reading, questions, and exercises. Instructor supplements include PowerPoint slides and chapter quizzes.

Debra L. Stephens is Associate Professor of Marketing at the University of Portland, USA. She has published in leading journals, including the *Journal of Consumer Research*, the *Journal of Public Policy and Marketing*, and the *Journal of Business Ethics*.

"After years of preparation, pursuing a broadly interdisciplinary perspective, Stephens has created a carefully constructed and beautifully written treatise that covers the conventional decision-oriented information-processing approach to buyer choices and the traditional methods of data-driven research, but that also branches into such newer areas as ethnography and netnography, the impact of social media, and the special needs of vulnerable consumers – including the disabled, children, other marginalized groups, and even animals. Stephens provides plentiful real-world examples and an engaging style throughout, perhaps most of all when she delves into the world of pet ownership and tells tales of her own beloved Gounguroo."

– **Morris B. Holbrook**, *W. T. Dillard Professor Emeritus of Marketing, Graduate School of Business, Columbia University*

"One of the strengths of this textbook is the author's use of vivid examples to clarify the nature of the concepts being introduced. Further, the examples do a good job of demonstrating the nature of their interface with society. This text provides an interesting and somewhat unique perspective of consumer behavior."

– **James W. Gentry**, *Emeritus Professor of Marketing, University of Nebraska-Lincoln*

"This consumer behavior book is a rare offering that goes beyond the stale structure that focuses on selling soap to include a more humanistic approach that recognizes the vagaries of everyday life. If you want your students to have a deeper understanding of our material environments, you should direct them to this wholistic understanding of the intersection of people and markets in a most profound way. Few, if any, other options provide a similar academic journey."

– **Ron Hill**, *Dean's Professor of Marketing and Public Policy, Kogod School of Business, Marketing Department Chair, Vice President of Publications, American Marketing Association*

"Debra Stephens has crafted an easy-to-read, comprehensive textbook on consumer behavior that brings key concepts to life through examples and cases. In particular, I appreciate the integration of vulnerability into the study of consumer behavior, as it facilitates a deeper understanding of the realities of today's marketplace. Kudos to Debra for her outstanding work!"

– **Andrew S. Gallan**, *PhD, Assistant Professor, Department of Marketing, College of Business, Florida Atlantic University*

Essentials of Consumer Behavior

An Applied Approach

Second Edition

Debra L. Stephens

Routledge
Taylor & Francis Group

NEW YORK AND LONDON

Cover image: wildpixel/Getty Images

Second edition published 2023
by Routledge
605 Third Avenue, New York, NY 10158

and by Routledge
4 Park Square, Milton Park, Abingdon, Oxon, OX14 4RN

Routledge is an imprint of the Taylor & Francis Group, an informa business

© 2023 Taylor & Francis

The right of Debra L. Stephens to be identified as author of this work has been asserted in accordance with sections 77 and 78 of the Copyright, Designs and Patents Act 1988.

First edition published by Routledge 2016

Library of Congress Cataloging-in-Publication Data
Names: Stephens, Debra L., author.
Title: Essentials of consumer behavior:
an applied approach / Debra L. Stephens.
Description: 2nd Edition. | New York, NY: Routledge, 2023. |
Revisededition of the author's Essentials of consumer behavior, 2017. |
Includes bibliographical references and index.
Identifiers: LCCN 2022042009 | ISBN 9780367426880 (hardback) |
ISBN 9780367426866 (paperback) | ISBN 9780367426897 (ebook)
Subjects: LCSH: Consumer behavior. | Consumers—Research.
Classification: LCC HF5415.32.S7395 2023 |
DDC658.8/342—dc23/eng/20220908
LC record available at https://lccn.loc.gov/2022042009

ISBN: 978-0-367-42688-0 (hbk)
ISBN: 978-0-367-42686-6 (pbk)
ISBN: 978-0-367-42689-7 (ebk)

DOI: 10.4324/9780367426897

Typeset in Bembo
by codeMantra

Access the Support Material: https://www.routledge.com/9780367426880

This book is dedicated to my cat companions, with thanks for their wisdom, grace, and affection.

Contents

PART 4
Shifts in Technology and Consumer Values 187

Figures and Tables

Acknowledgments

This book would not have been written were it not for the many students who have enriched my understanding of consumer behavior, marketing, and generational changes. There is no greater impetus to deepen one's understanding of a concept than to teach it to others.

Thanks to the editors at Routledge and my colleagues at the University of Portland for their support and encouragement.

I am grateful and indebted to Judy Ferguson, Vimal Jairath, and Elizabeth Martin, who listened patiently and provided feedback and moral support throughout the years of research and writing.

Part 1
Fundamental Concepts in Consumer Behavior

1 Introduction to Consumer Behavior

Objectives

1. To show how understanding consumer behavior can benefit marketers, public policy makers, consumer advocates, and consumers themselves.
2. To specify the parameters of the study of consumer behavior.
3. To explore the interdisciplinary underpinnings of the study of consumer behavior.

Benefits of Studying Consumer Behavior

What's the first thing you do when you get up in the morning? Jump into the shower, pour a bit of body wash into your hand, and reach for your loofa? Stumble sleepily toward the kitchen to pour your first cup of coffee from the coffeemaker with the timer that ensures that your coffee is wafting its fragrance toward your bedroom when you first open your eyes? Throw on your sweats and start stretching for your morning run? Take the dog for a walk, feed the cat, change your toddler's diaper?

Each of these small, seemingly insignificant actions involves purchased products, most of which you chose from a vast array of alternatives. Many mundane actions strung together constitute your morning routine, a scripted performance you've memorized without trying to, the goal of which is to get your day started. The products you use to ease the transition from waking to being ready to face the world are, if they are working right, virtually invisible after so many repeat performances; it's how they help you and those you love that matters. After the novelty wears off, you may stop noticing the fragrance of your shower gel, the aroma of your morning coffee, the stretchy comfort and warmth of your sweats, the environmental friendliness of your toddler's diaper brand.

For marketers of the body wash, the coffee, the yoga pants, and the diaper, understanding your routine and the mental processes underlying it means their

DOI: 10.4324/9780367426897-2

livelihood. What made you choose one brand of body wash over all the others? Did you research product ingredients or reach for it unthinking, by force of habit? If you twisted off the cap to take a little sniff, did the fragrance remind you of something pleasant or make you feel energized, attractive, nostalgic? Or did your sweetheart, who shops for the two of you, select it?

The highly successful 2010 Old Spice campaign ("The Man Your Man Could Smell Like") was, according to the 2011 Effie Award Case Study, based on the consumer insight that women purchased three of every five men's body washes, coupled with the awareness that body washes were "low-involvement," unexciting products that seldom inspired consumer conversation (Effie Awards, 2011). Based on these insights, advertising agency Wieden+Kennedy created commercials and a social media campaign that appealed to women with its attractive spokesperson, former NFL wide receiver Isaiah Mustafa, and to both genders with its tongue-in-cheek humor. It got people talking, revitalized the Old Spice brand, and most important, led to a significant increase in sales of Old Spice ("Creative Marketer of the Year: Procter & Gamble," 2010). The campaign was updated in January 2020 to appeal to younger viewers. The original actor Isaiah Mustafa is joined by a son character and the slogan has been changed to "Smell like your own man, man." The son tells Mustafa that he is his own man with his own scent and grooming preferences (Beer, 2020). And in a post-pandemic move to increase its share of younger consumers and the Hispanic market, Old Spice's parent company Procter & Gamble has struck a multiyear advertising and sponsorship deal with Major League Soccer (Kaplan, 2021).

Does your morning coffee stream into your mug from a Keurig or other single-serve brewer?

In 2019, more than four of ten U.S. consumers owned a single-cup coffee brewing system. Starbucks and Dunkin' Donuts now produce their own single-cup coffee capsules to compete with Keurig and private label brands (Conway, 2021; Ridder, 2022).

K-cups cost an estimated two to nine times more than ground coffee (Scott, 2021). How can so many of us convince ourselves to spend that much on coffee, no matter the convenience? The answer: Keurig creator Green Mountain Coffee found that we don't calculate our coffee expenditures based on price per pound; Starbucks taught us to calculate cost by the cup, and K-cups are considerably cheaper than the Starbucks coffees they replace. The Great Recession and coffee pod marketers helped us break our habit of grabbing a coffee on the way to work, and we are indeed saving money – just not as much as we could!

The article below describes how our coffee consumption patterns changed during the COVID-19 pandemic and how they are returning to pre-COVID patterns (National Coffee Association, 2021):

NEW YORK, April 1, 2021/PRNewswire/ – COVID-19 drove record coffee consumption at home, with 85% of coffee drinkers having at least one cup at home (up 8% since January 2020) and average daily consumption steady at nearly 2 cups per capita.

A majority of Americans (nearly 60%) choose coffee each day rather than any other beverage, including tap water, according to the Spring 2021 National Coffee Data Trends (NCDT) survey conducted by Dig Research and released today (Thursday) by the National Coffee Association (NCA).

While COVID-19 restrictions and closures continue to crimp coffee preparation away from home (workplace coffee preparation is down 55% since January 2020), on-the-go options are flourishing – drive through and app-based ordering are both up 30%.

The Spring 2021 NCDT was for the first time conducted with the support of the Specialty Coffee Association (SCA), allowing us to bring this exclusive market research to more members of the coffee community than ever before at a critical time in our industry's COVID-19 recovery.

NCA President and CEO William "Bill" Murray commented:

"The COVID-19 pandemic has kept many people at home for the better part of a year, and the latest 'Atlas of American Coffee' shows they took their coffees with them. In fact, we've seen Americans embracing their new coffee routines, experimenting with new coffees, and even trying to replicate their favorite beverages at home.

Now, with light at the end of the pandemic tunnel, many Americans are also returning to their favorite coffee businesses or plan to do so within the next month."

More than 40% of Americans bought types of coffee they had never tried before during the pandemic, and nearly one third tried to replicate a favorite coffee shop beverage at home. One-quarter of Americans purchased new coffee formats, and nearly one-quarter purchased a new home coffee machine.

While enjoying new home coffee routines, about 35% of Americans miss their favorite coffee businesses and beverages. Nearly half of Americans (48%) are already returning to coffee shops or plan to within the next month.

As some Americans return to work, they are getting more comfortable using shared coffee stations and returning to local coffee businesses – compared to September 2020, 23% fewer have decreased use of shared coffee stations because of the pandemic, and 17% more have returned to local coffee shops.

So what's the lesson? It's our perceptions and beliefs rather than a fully informed rational analysis that shape many of our purchase decisions. Marketers can't assume they know what we think or feel; they have to ask us repeatedly, over time and in different ways, to deeply understand our decisions to buy their brand or another, or an entirely different product, or nothing at all.

But marketers are not the only ones who benefit from understanding our motives for buying and our ways of using and disposing of products. So do the government agencies charged with ensuring product safety, fair business practices, truth in advertising, clear labelling – all concerned with our remaining safe from defective products, free from discriminatory business practices, and well-informed about our choices in the marketplace. More information is given below on regulatory agencies in the US and Europe.

U.S. agencies concerned with consumer protection include:

• The Consumer Product Safety Commission (CPSC)

CPSC is charged with protecting consumers from "unreasonable risks of injury or death associated with the use of the thousands of types of consumer products under the agency's jurisdiction." The agency works with manufacturers and businesses to develop voluntary safety standards, issues and enforces mandatory product safety standards, obtains product recalls, researches potential product hazards, and provides product safety information to consumers, manufacturers, and foreign, state, and local governments (Consumer Product Safety Commission (n.d.), www.cpsc.gov/aboutus).

During the pandemic, many consumers embarked upon home workout regimens as gyms closed and work-from-home orders proliferated. Peloton, a brand of high-end cardio equipment, was the subject of an urgent warning issued by the CPSC on April 17, 2021:

> *Urgent Warning Comes After Agency Finds One Death and Dozens of Incidents of Children Being Sucked Beneath the Tread+ (Formerly Known as the Tread)*
>
> WASHINGTON, D.C. – The U.S. Consumer Product Safety Commission (CPSC) is warning consumers about the danger of popular Peloton Tread+ exercise machine after multiple incidents of small children and a pet being injured beneath the machines. The Commission has found that the public health and safety requires this notice to warn the public quickly of the hazard.
>
> The urgent warning comes less than a month after Peloton itself released news of a child's death by a Peloton Tread+ and CPSC's announcement of an investigation into that incident.
>
> (Consumer Product Safety Commission, April 17, 2021)

The CPSC urges consumers with small pets or children to stop using the treadmill. If they choose to continue using the product, they are advised to do so only in a locked room to prevent children and pets from accessing it while it is in use. When the treadmill is not in use, CPSC strongly recommends that it be unplugged (CPSC, April 17, 2021). Notably, the company did not issue a recall of the product until May 5, 2021, a full two and a half weeks after this warning (CPSC, 2021).

Other agencies involved with consumer protection include:

• Bureau of Alcohol, Tobacco, and Firearms (www.atf.gov/), ("Bureau of Alcohol, Tobacco, Firearms, and Explosives," n.d.).

- Federal Trade Commission (www.ftc.gov/).
- Food and Drug Administration (www.fda.gov/).

European directives concerned with consumer protection are described in the General Product Safety Directive (12/03/2001) on the European Commission's website (European Commission, 2001).

Insights into how consumers make choices could and should shape agency directives aimed at ensuring our safety and our access to the information we need in order to choose wisely. The U.S. Food and Drug Administration mandates nutritional labelling on most packaged foods, but ingredients potentially harmful to increasingly large consumer segments have many legal disguises (Food and Drug Administration, n.d.). For diabetics, it is critically important to evaluate sugar content and this is difficult without knowledge of the many words for sugar commonly used by marketers. While our health concerns motivate us to consult these labels, few of us have the time or knowledge of chemistry to interpret them accurately.

The Federal Trade Commission (FTC) mandates that marketing communications (advertisements, company web sites, etc.) be truthful as interpreted by a "reasonable" person. The agency developed many of its directives based on consumer research (Federal Trade Commission, n.d.). For example, the FTC may argue that a marketing communication is misleading even if it does not contain a blatant falsehood, but rather is likely to mislead by implication. Below are two examples of FTC actions against companies attempting to mislead and exploit consumers who are seeking protection from COVID-19 (first article) or facing pandemic-related financial difficulties (second article).

The letters highlight specific claims made by the companies or their participants in social media posts and videos posted online, including claims made in Spanish.

The claims addressed in the letters include:

- A Spanish-language social media post promoting Vivri USA, LLC that said:

   Take care of your health, your body, avoid many diseases many viruses, since this virus and many others are here to stay, coronavirus, influenza, flu, we should nourish our cells, our immune systems, reinforce it with the best nutrition system in the world …

- A social media post that said, "#VIRUS_CORONA Worried? I've been boosting my immune system for several years with high-quality Plexus supplements. You can too! #Plexus provides excellent all-natural supplements that truly work. Be sensible – not fearful. Scientifically formulated & doctor-approved! Ask me!"
- A video promoting The Juice Plus Company that said:

   There are a lot of people out there who have lost income … You may want to build a side income, you know, make $500 a month, $1,000 a month or more.

FTC Sends Second Round of Warning Letters to Multilevel Marketers Regarding Coronavirus Related Health and Earnings Claims
June 5, 2020

Letters to Six Companies Target Deceptive Claims in Response to Pandemic

The FTC today announced it has sent six letters warning multilevel marketing (MLM) companies to remove and address claims about their products' ability to treat or prevent coronavirus 2019 (COVID-19) or about the earnings people who have recently lost income can make, or both. This is the second set of warning letters to MLMs the FTC has announced as part of its ongoing efforts to protect consumers from COVID-19 scams.

> There's no ceiling on this. It's whatever you want it to be … What would you like this do to for you? … Maybe it could cover one of your bills, like a car payment. Or enjoy more time and financial freedom. I can tell you those are both possible at the same time because I've been living that for the past eight years, and it's wonderful to be able to offer that to other people.

In letters alleging unsubstantiated health claims, the FTC states that one or more of the efficacy claims made by the companies are unsubstantiated because they are not supported by scientific evidence, and therefore violate the FTC Act (FTC, June 5, 2020).

Understanding consumer perceptions and motives informs the actions of consumer advocacy organizations as well. The Center for Science in the Public Interest together with the Berkeley Media Studies Group convened the Food Marketing Workgroup:

> a network of more than 225 organizations and academic experts who are concerned about the proliferation of marketing of unhealthful foods and beverages that targets children and adolescents. This national network, convened by the Center for Science in the Public Interest (CSPI) and Berkeley Media Studies Group (BMSG), is dedicated to eliminating harmful food marketing—particularly marketing aimed at those who are most vulnerable to obesity and other nutrition-related diseases—by actively identifying, investigating, and advocating changes to marketing practices that undermine health.
>
> (The Food Marketing Workgroup, n.d.)

As important as it is for marketers, policy makers, and consumer advocates to delve into our motives to find our purchase "triggers" and understand our quandaries about what to buy, it is essential for us as consumers to know what drives us, to develop the ability and then habit of observing our own foibles and vulnerabilities, and honoring our future selves while relishing the compelling, playful, and hedonistic marketplace experience.

What Is Consumer Behavior?

The American Marketing Association defines consumer behavior as follows: "The dynamic interaction of affect and cognition, behavior, and the environment by which human beings conduct the exchange aspects of their lives" (Bennett, 1995).

Notice that this definition specifies the three aspects of consumer processes: cognitions or thoughts, affect or feelings, and behaviors. But cognitions and affect are not directly observable, so we must rely on people to articulate their thoughts and feelings. As we'll see in Chapter 2, researchers have developed methods for obtaining accurate self-reports from consumers, as well as very clever experiments from which they can infer what participants are thinking or feeling.

Behavior, on the other hand, is directly observable; we can watch consumers as they shop, make purchases, use products, and share experiences with other consumers both online and offline. Consumers' interactions with one another are as important to understand as consumers' responses to marketing; increasingly, we rely on user reviews to make purchase decisions and on user advice to resolve product malfunctions.

Notice also that the phrase "exchange aspects" encompasses not only product acquisition, purchase, and usage, but also product disposition, that is, disposal. What we do with things we're done using is of increasing concern as our landfills overflow, our oceans become choked with human detritus, and the recyclers who disassemble our electronic discards are sickened by the toxic materials inside them.

The last thing to notice about the definition of consumer behavior is its reference to products and services. We can claim ownership of any object, physical or metaphorical, and we can objectify anything including other sentient beings. In its broad sense, "products" may include goods, people, nonhuman animals, and even ideas. And while we cannot own services, we can and do consume them.

We see that consumer behavior encompasses many if not most of our daily activities. Even when we sleep, we are using beds and bed linens, and an increasing numbers of people are using sleep tracking devices. While products and brands are usually not protagonists in our life narratives, they are part of the context, some, like the tablet on which this book is being written, facilitating our daily work; others, like the suit you might wear to a job interview, identifying your role to all concerned; still others, like a long-anticipated trip abroad, lending exotic color, fun, and adventure to our stories.

Our consumer behavior is shaped in part by forces beyond our control, and it is essential that marketers and consumer advocates stay abreast of our responses to these forces, including new technologies, lifestyle and life stage transitions, fluctuations in the economy, and new regulations governing product marketing and consumption. The COVID-19 pandemic is another type of force, an "ad hoc" one, akin to a natural disaster or major conflict. The excerpt below, which is from the prominent market research company Mintel, describes how our consumer health priorities and values have changed as a result of the pandemic and offers examples of innovative branding:

> Consumers are in search of a wellbeing experience through an entirely new lens, seeking total integration into nearly all aspects of their lives. This new outlook is built around a sense of uncertainty as to when life will translate back into more balanced routines, and this is driving demand for comfort and structure.
>
> As brands aim to set a new tone and new structures, an opportunity exists to return to a mindset where being active and taking mental breaks feels more like a curious adventure and playtime rather than hard work. ...
>
> Just as kids learn to express and deal with emotions, adults need a new framework for processing emotions and mental health concerns. The stage of simply openly talking about mental health is expanding into creation of an actual structure for talking about it, and brands have the opportunity to lead that conversation.
>
> Globally, the pandemic has put health at the forefront of consumers' daily lives. As consumers move forward beyond the pandemic, they will experience a new type of gratitude for what it means to have a healthy body. Brands can lead with that note of positivity and gratitude and shift the conversation away from aesthetics and body image.
>
> Wellbeing has traditionally focused on the 'why' factor or a tangible end goal. The end goal for working out once revolved solely around weight loss. Now, the desire for working out is multifaceted. This means that brands need to focus on their own 'why' in order to fully support consumers in new ways.
>
> **Innovative Brands**
>
> **An outdoor reset (US)**
>
> The North Face's new campaign encourages consumers to 'reset' their lives through exploration, and the company is dedicating $7 million to initiatives to make the outdoors more inclusive.
>
> **Eat your veggies (Argentina)**
>
> Argentinian chef Narda Lepes has partnered with Microsoft and local start-up Shifta to create Comé + Plantas (Eat More Vegetables), an app designed to provide useful information about vegetables and promote healthy eating practices.
>
> **Painfully funny (South Korea)**
>
> Ketotop, a brand of over-the-counter pain relief patches, has created cartoons that explain conditions such as 'binge-watching pain' and 'new dad pain.'
>
> (Mintel, 2021)

Which Disciplines Inform the Study of Consumer Behavior?

As an area of study, consumer behavior draws from several decades of research in social sciences, including economics, psychology, sociology, and anthropology. More recent advances in neuroscience knowledge and methods of study have also attracted consumer behavior researchers seeking evermore concrete and definitive ways of modifying marketing stimuli to elicit predictably positive responses from consumers. Each of these disciplines provides a lens through which a different aspect of consumer behavior becomes visible.

The traditional economist views consumer behavior as a reason-driven quest to maximize utility, that is, value for the money, with each purchase. While that perspective has fallen out of favor from time to time, it has merit in a world of skeptical consumers who have ready access to evermore product and company information. It also captures the goal-oriented nature of our cognitive processes and consequent behaviors. In the book *Absolute Value: What Really Influences Customers in the Age of (Nearly) Perfect Information,* authors Itamar Simonson and Emanuel Rosen (2014) argue that consumers can now choose brands based on their objective attributes rather than having to rely on marketing hyperbole. In other words, our access to nearly "perfect" information should enable us to act more rationally.

In the 1950s, as Freudian psychoanalysis gained greater acceptance in the US and Europe, branding and sheer numbers of brands also rose. These two apparently unrelated trends enabled marketers to wonder, perhaps for the first time ever, whether we choose brands based on powerful unconscious motives rather than rational analysis. Fueling this argument were some puzzling consumer behaviors that economists couldn't readily explain in terms of utility maximization. New and more convenient food products like cake mixes, instant coffee, and canned pie fillings were not generating the excitement or sales marketers had predicted based on the considerable time and effort they saved purchasers. Marketing researchers employing projective techniques, adapted from psychoanalysis hence especially effective for uncovering unconscious motives and biases, discovered that the target consumers, married women with children, associated these time-saving products with laziness and neglect of home and family. After the marketers of these brands changed their ad campaigns to show how homemakers could use the time saved to care for their families in other ways, these new brand forms flew off the shelves. (See Spry & Pich, 2021, for a recent example of the insights projective techniques offer.)

Motivational psychologists' claim that unconscious motives and emotions profoundly affect our choices and judgments has garnered support from an unexpected source: neurosciences. As neuroscientists develop more accurate measures of brain function, they are amassing evidence that our self-reported emotional responses to external stimuli frequently do not match the emotions reflected in areas of the brain that are activated. Furthermore, the latter are often better predictors of our choices, judgments, and memory content. For an overview of neuromarketing research methods and examples of findings, see Plassman (2019).

Neuromarketing research has proven especially useful in evaluating the impact of package design and message content on consumers' choices. In one study, participants viewed six chocolate bar communications and product pictures while their brains were scanned using functional magnetic resonance imaging technology. Then they were asked to state their brand and message preferences. The messages were subsequently posted in supermarkets and sales were tracked. The researchers found that the message preferences indicated by brain activity had a higher correlation with sales than did the messages participants stated that they preferred (Kuhn et al., 2016).

The traditional economic view of the rational consumer stands in stark contrast to the motivational researcher's portrayal of a consumer beset by unresolved fears and unfulfilled yearnings. Enter social psychologists. Like economists, they posited that our overt behaviors are driven by mental processes we can readily report if asked. But they went on to deconstruct these mental processes in order to determine their role in shaping behavior. Martin Fishbein and Isek Ajzen, in their seminal 1975 book *Belief, Attitude, Intention and Behavior,* theorized that in order to explain or predict behavior, researchers must measure not only our attitudes toward the action in question, but also our perceptions of what others will think of us if we act as we are inclined. In a consumer context, our attitude (beliefs, feelings, evaluation) toward a brand plays a major role in our decision whether to purchase it, but social norms may either put the brakes on or support our choice. Most of us adults have learned to temper our impulses in order to please people significant to us. For example, your favorite pizza may be Dominos, but if a friend you respect seems appalled at your "bad taste" ("If you must eat pizza, at least buy gourmet!"), you may begin purchasing a brand less tasty to you but more acceptable in your friend's eyes. We may not always buy the brand we prefer because of powerful social influences.

Social psychology reigned supreme in our study of consumer behavior until the 1980s, when computer models of the brain became popular. The field of cognitive psychology emerged, dramatically enriching our approach to studying consumer behavior. The computational model of brain function enabled consumer behavior researchers to investigate how we make sense of, or process, information we encounter in the marketplace. Cognitive research revealed that our memories are vast networks of interconnected concepts, linked with one another based on what we believe as well as what we feel. Our memories of familiar brands include many associative links to factual information, feelings, and experiences we have had while using the brand. And new information from marketing or other sources may reinforce or dramatically alter those associations which in turn shape our purchase decisions.

For example, when a favorite brand has a crisis, how do consumers integrate the new and negative information into their positive mental representation of the brand? The company's response to the crisis largely determines the long-term effects on consumer memory and brand attitude. Chipotle restaurant, known for its fresh, locally sourced food, was associated with an outbreak of *E. coli* and

Norovirus in 2015–2016. While none of the food analyzed was found to be tainted, the restaurant was the only common link among the people who became ill. The company became a leader in food safety practices, and made a strong recovery with the help of revamped advertising and a partnership with DoorDash, a leading food delivery app (Yaffe-Bellany, 2019). Chipotle currently ranks first among QSRs (quick service restaurants) for its COVID-19 safety practices, according to data from global market research firm Ipsos' Consumer Health & Safety Index (Kelso, 2020).

Complementing the internal individual focus of cognitive psychology, sociologists have contributed much to the study of consumer behavior by specifying the ways in which groups and individuals important to us influence our purchase decisions. In addition, using network analysis they can trace the path of an innovative product or idea from the individual(s) who first adopt or purchase it and tell others about it, to the very last ones to adopt it. With the speed of digital communication and the multiplicity of social networking media, it is essential for marketers to understand and capitalize upon these patterns of influence that crisscross the globe.

Sociologists also brought to consumer behavior the concept of homophily, i.e., we associate with others who are similar in some meaningful way. Geodemographic market segmentation is based on this important premise. Recent research suggests that homophily helps explain why children who perceive themselves as similar to others in a brand community are more likely to perceive the brand positively ("I'm like you, you're like me, we make a great brand community!" Similarity and children's brand community participation). Homophily also strengthens the popularity of beauty product vloggers and increases the likelihood that consumers who perceive themselves as similar to a vlogger are more likely to purchase the recommended brand (Ladhari et al., 2020).

As brands continued to proliferate up to and well beyond the turn of the century, marketers seeking an edge turned to anthropologists for insights into how their products fit into consumers' daily lives. Retail anthropologist Paco Underhill characterized the current jostling for consumers' attention in a marketplace teeming with competition as a "bar brawl," requiring a deep and detailed analysis of how we navigate retail settings and interact with brands after we get them home. Other anthropologists who study consumer behavior explore the roles of products and brands in our holiday rituals, rites of passage (weddings, birthdays, retirement, etc.), and rituals focusing on products themselves. For example, an anthropologist might attend a Harley Davidson motorcyclists' rally to learn more about how groups of Harley owners form a collective identity based on their shared love of riding and aspiration to emulate the Hollywood-created archetypal rebel. From consumer anthropologists, we have learned that people often form such brand communities – online and offline – some so cohesive and distinct from mainstream culture as to be considered subcultures. Even Nutella, beloved by many from childhood, has a passionate following on Facebook and other social media sites (see Lee, 2016).

We started this section by describing the classical economist's view of the consumer as a rational being whose goal is to maximize utility. We end it with a discussion of how *behavioral economists* have deepened our understanding of consumer behavior by exploring the systematic biases in our thinking that result in judgments and choices that are *not* rational. Three of the most influential scholars in this area are Dan Ariely, who described how biases affect consumer behavior in his popular book *Predictably Irrational* (2010); Richard Thaler, whose book *Nudge* (Thaler & Sunstein, 2008) took a prescriptive approach showing how we can improve our decisions; and Daniel Kahneman, author of *Thinking Fast and Slow* (2011), an eloquent and highly readable treatise on the nature, pervasiveness, and effects of our perceptual and cognitive biases on many aspects of our lives. An experiment reported in the *New York Times* (Carey, 2008) and published in the *Journal of the American Medical Association* demonstrates how profoundly bias may affect consumer experience. Given a choice of two "pain relievers" (actually placebos), one costing $2.50 per pill and the other "discounted" to $0.10 per pill, participants who received the more expensive one reported significantly less pain from mild electric shocks than those given the "discount" tablet. The conviction that the more expensive tablet had greater efficacy actually affected consumers' experiences of pain!

To get a clearer idea on how this broad array of disciplines helps interested stakeholders understand consumer behavior, let's revisit our discussion of coffee consumption.

- A traditional economist might inquire whether the relatively high price of single-serve pods compared to ground coffee might make the pods more of an "affordable luxury" in the eyes of the many consumers who choose them.
- A motivational psychologist would wonder why avid coffee drinkers care so deeply about how their coffee is prepared.
- A social psychologist might ask about how friends, family, and colleagues influence consumers' coffee preferences and purchases. S/he might go on to inquire how these coffee consumption patterns fit with the norms of the town or city in which a consumer resides.
- A cognitive psychologist might ask an avid coffee drinker to verbalize her thoughts and feelings before, during, and after the purchase and consumption. S/he might also ask the consumer to specify and assign importance weights to her criteria for choosing from among the alternatives. Further, s/he might inquire whether the immediate sensory context of the retailer/web site and the place where coffee consumption occurs help shape the consumer's thoughts and feelings about the coffee selected.
- A sociologist might delve into the demographics of consumers of different forms and varieties of coffee. Regional, age, and social class variations in usage would likely be of particular interest.
- An anthropologist would want to learn more about the occasions (rites and rituals) during which it is appropriate or desirable for a consumer of a specific age, social stature, or subculture to consume coffee.

- A behavioral economist might inquire whether the coffee consumer's purchase decision is influenced by the way the alternatives are presented in the retail environment.

A marketer would have an interest in the answers to all of these questions. As a good that varies widely in price, quality, and convenience, a coffee brand or form may fetch a higher price if its exclusivity is emphasized by its retailers and e-tailers. The reasons why finding just the right coffee matters so much to many consumers would inform a barista's or retail employee's interactions with them as they consider the wide array of choices. Understanding friends'/colleagues' influence on consumers' decisions would also inform these interactions. Knowing the regional, social, and cultural contexts that help shape coffee preferences would enable retailers in different regions to choose appropriate brands, forms, flavors, and quantities of coffee to stock for different occasions. Knowledge of the coffee consumer's decision process and the many sensory factors that help shape it could inform store design and location, merchandise presentation, and salesperson behavior.

Organization of Book

This book takes an interdisciplinary approach to exploring the many important facets of consumer behavior. It is organized as follows. In Chapter 2 we explain the major consumer research methods and the contexts in which each is most appropriate; we also point readers to excellent sources of secondary consumer research. We distinguish between self-report and direct observation and discuss the differences between qualitative and quantitative research methods, emphasizing that they are complementary, each uncovering insights the other cannot.

Chapter 3, "Why We Buy," examines how our product purchases are related to our goals and core values. We describe the research method that may be used to reveal and further analyze these connections between products and goals or values. The chapter also discusses our varying levels and types of cognitive and emotional involvement with different products and brands.

Chapter 4, "The Consumer's Journey," incorporates moments of truth (MOTs) and purchase journey mapping into a discussion of the consumer's progression from brand awareness to brand advocacy. The chapter explores how the purchase journey changes depending on how the consumer thinks and feels (i.e., forms attitudes) about the product, brand, and purchase itself, for example, whether it is carefully considered or routine.

Part 2 (Chapters 5 through 7) explores how consumers create meaning from a chaotic bombardment of information, ranging from persuasive pleas to dire warnings, from arcane technical specifications to fun factoids.

Chapter 5, "Memory and Priming," describes how we form, organize, and retrieve brand- and product-related memories, both cognitive and emotional, whether semantic or episodic. The chapter explains how incidental brand exposure may prime related memories and behaviors.

Chapter 6, "Sensory Perception in a Consumption Context," investigates sensory perception with an emphasis on the retail context, one of the richest and most complex consumer environments. We describe how consumers respond cognitively, emotionally, and behaviorally to a variety of marketer-created sensory stimuli.

In Chapter 7, "Sociocultural and Interpersonal Influences on Consumer Behavior," we explore how others influence our consumption goals, desires, and practices, collectively and anonymously through cultural and social norms and constraints; and individually, through the important reference groups in our lives. The chapter examines how others help shape our brand perceptions and choices and discusses the power and mechanisms of word of mouth influence on our consumer behavior.

Part 3 (Chapters 8 through 10) focuses on consumers not typically given prominence in a consumer behavior text. Chapter 8 explores the consumer experiences of marginalized people, many of whom are impeded in their attempts to access the information, products, and services that should be available to all consumers.

Chapter 9, "Children and Adolescents as Consumers," focuses on the impact of brain development and socialization on consumer behavior and discusses implications for marketing ethically to young consumers.

Chapter 10 explores consumers' relationships with pets, characterized here as special possessions that themselves shape purchase behavior.

In Part 4 (Chapter 11), we discuss how consumption practices are changing in response to technology and shifting societal values. Chapter 11 focuses on the rise of collaborative consumption, fueled by near-ubiquitous digital media, a do-it-yourself mindset, and economic challenges. We explore similarities and differences between traditional consumer-brand relationships and collaborative consumption communities like Airbnb and Etsy.

I wrote this book to educate, but also to engage and intrigue readers so that they will continue to learn about this fascinating and important area, and about their own consumer behavior, wise and unwise, considered and impulsive, but never mundane or trivial.

References

Ariely, D. (2010). *Predictably Irrational*. London: Harper Perennial.

Beer, J. (2020). "The old spice guy celebrates its 10th anniversary-as an embarrassing old spice guy". Fast Company. Retrieved from: www.fastcompany.com/90454029/old-spice-guy-celebrates-its-10th-anniversary-as-an-embarrassing-old-spice-dad.

Bennett, P. D. (Ed.) (1995). *AMA Dictionary of Marketing Terms* (2nd edn). New York: McGraw Hill.

Bureau of Alcohol, Tobacco, Firearms and Explosives (n.d.). "About the bureau of alcohol, tobacco, firearms and explosives". Retrieved from: www.atf.gov.

Carey, B. (2008, March 5). "More expensive placebos bring more relief". *New York Times*. Retrieved from: www.nytimes.com/2008/03/05/health/research/05 placebo.html.

Conway, J. (2021, July 14). "Key brands market share of single-cup coffee in the U.S. 2021". Statista. Retrieved from: www.sstatista.com/sstatistics/315036/market-share-of-single-cup-coffee-in-the-us-by-leading-brand/.

Consumer Product Safety Commission (n.d.). "About CPSC". Retrieved from: www.cpsc.gov.

Consumer Product Safety Commission (2021, April 17). "CPSC warns consumers to stop using the Peloton Tread +". Retrieved from: www.cpsc.gov/Newsroom/News-Releases/2021/CPSC-Warns-Consumers-Stop-Using-the-Peloton-Tread.

Consumer Product Safety Commission (2021, May 5). "CPSC and Peloton announce: Recall of Tread+ treadmills after one child death and 70 incidents". Retrieved from: www.cpsc.gov/Newsroom/News-Releases/2021/CPSC-and-Peloton-Announce-Recall-of-Tread-Plus-Treadmills-After-One-Child-Death-and-70-Incidents-Recall-of-Tread-Treadmills-Due-to-Risk-of-Injury.

"Creative Marketer of the Year: Proctor & Gamble" (2010, December 17). *SHOOT* 10559825 *51*(10).

Effie Awards (2011). "The man your man could smell like". 2011 Gold Effie Winner. Available at: www.current.effie.org/downloads/2011_Grand_NA_OldSpice.pdf.

European Commission (2001, December 3). "General product safety directive".

Federal Trade Commission (n.d.). "About the FTC". Retrieved from: www.ftc.gov/.

Federal Trade Commission (2020, June 5). "FTC coronavirus warning letters to companies". Retrieved from: www.ftc.gov/legal-library/browse/warning-letters.

Fishbein, M., & Ajzen, I. (1975). *Belief, Attitude, Intention and Behavior.* Reading, MA: Addison-Wesley.

Food and Drug Administration (n.d.). "About FDA". Retrieved from: www.fda.gov/.

Food Marketing Workgroup (n.d.). "About the food marketing workgroup". Retrieved from: www.foodmarketing.org/about/.

Kahneman, D. (2011). *Thinking Fast and Slow.* New York: Farrar, Straus and Giroux.

Kaplan, D. (2021). "As sports return Proctor Gamble kicks off multiyear partnership with major league soccer". Adweek. Retrieved from: www.adweek.com/brand-marketing/as-sports-return-procter-gamble-kicks-off-multiyear-partnership-with-major-league-soccer/.

Kelso, A. (2020, June 24). "Chipotle ranks among QSRs for covid19 safety measures, report says". *Dive Brief.* Retrieved from: www.resurantdive.com/news/chipotle-ranks-no-1-for-covid-19-safety-measures--report-says/580407/.

Kuhn, S., Strelow, E., & Gallinat, J. (2016). "Multiple 'buy buttons' in the brain: Forecasting chocolate sales at point-of-sale based on functional brain activation using fMRI". *Neuroimage.* https://pubmed.mcbi.nim.nih.gov/27173762/dx.doi.org/10.1016/j neuroimage.2016.05.021.

Ladhari, R., Massa, E., & Skandrani, H. (2020). "YouTube vloggers popularity and influence: The roles of homophily, emotional attachment, and expertise". *Journal of Retailing and Consumer Services, 54.* https://doi.org/10.1016/j.retconser. 2019.102027.

Lee, A. (2016, March 7). "How Nutella became the world's favorite 'breakfast spread'". ReferralCandy (blog). Retrieved from: www.referralcandy.com/blog/nutella-word-of-mouth-marketing/.

Mintel Group Ltd. (2021). "2021 global consumer trends". Retrieved from: www.downloads.mintel.com/private/Syng1/files/853243/.

National Coffee Association (2021, April 1). "Covid-19 drives record at-home coffee drinking, on-the-go ordering. 2021 national coffee data trends report". Retrieved from: www.prnewswire.com/news-releases/covid-19-drives-record-at-home-coffee-drinking-on-the-go-ordering-2021-national-coffee-data-trends-report-301260248.html.

Plassmann, H. (2019). "A non-scientist's guide to the neuromarketing toolkit." Marketing blog. Retrieved from: https://knowledge.insead.edu/blog/insead-blog/a-non-scientists-guide-to-the-neuromarketing-toolkit-11721.

Ridder, M. (2022, January 13). "Key brands market share of single cup coffee in the U.S. 2021". Retrieved from: www.statista.com.

Scott, C. (2021). "How do the cost of K-cups really compare to drip coffee?". *Smart Family Money*. Retrieved from: www.smartfamilymoney.com/cost-of-k-cup-vs-drip-coffee/.

Simonson, I., & Rosen, E. (2014). *Absolute Value: What Really Influences Customers in the Age of (Nearly) Perfect Information*. New York: HarperCollins.

Spry, L., & Pich, C. (2021). "Enhancing data collection methods with qualitative projective techniques in the exploration of a university's brand identity and brand image". *International Journal of Market Research, 63*(2). https://doi.org/10.1177/1470785320943045.

Thaler, R., & Sunstein, C. (2008). *Nudge: Improving Decisions about Health, Wealth, and Happiness*. New Haven, CT: Yale University Press.

Yaffe-Bellany, D. (2019, July 23). "Chipotle, with food-safety issues behind it, recovers strongly". *New York Times*. Retrieved from: www.nytimes.com/2019/07/23/business/chipotle-stock-earnings.html.

2 Consumer Research Methods

Objectives

1. To explore a range of methods of investigating consumers' cognitions (thoughts), affects (feelings), and behaviors.
2. To clarify what we can and cannot conclude based on different research methods.
3. To describe how to construct a clear and answerable research question.

Introduction

The scene is a busy street in Manhattan. A well-dressed 30-something man is hurrying down the sidewalk, jostling the pedestrians around him. He has a mobile phone – an early, bricklike model – plastered to his ear and wears a smug smile as he shouts into the phone, "You're fired!" As he is putting the phone away in his coat pocket, an enormous truck grill appears right in front of him. He shouts as the scene fades. The next scene looks like a lot of us would envision heaven: fluffy white clouds drifting around our protagonist, angelic voices singing – and a plate of gigantic cookies. "Mmmm, heaven!" he says, very smugly indeed now that he has, he assumes, been accepted into paradise, where his every want will be anticipated. After eagerly munching a delicious-looking cookie, he opens an enormous refrigerator filled with cartons of milk. Eagerly the thirsty cookie consumer grabs a carton and tilts it toward his mouth, expecting the cold, refreshing milk as a welcome contrast to those rich, sweet chocolate chips. Feeling how light the carton is, he shakes it to make sure it is empty and tosses it aside. He grabs carton after carton, hurling each away as he finds it empty. Very thirsty and frustrated, he shouts, "Arghhh!" Then, as the terrible truth dawns on him, "Wait a minute; where am I?" The scene fades into the words "Got Milk?" Flames lick at the letters as a sinister voice asks the question (Goodby, Silverstein & Partners, 1995).

The foregoing describes a television commercial in the long-running "Got Milk?" marketing campaign, which Goodby Silverstein created for the California

DOI: 10.4324/9780367426897-3

Milk Fluid Processors' Board to reverse a decade-long decline in U.S. milk consumption (Goodby, Silverstein & Partners, 1995). Throughout the 1980s milk consumption was on the decline for several reasons. First, scientists had discovered what they thought was clear evidence of the perils of fat consumption, and many milk drinkers preferred to forego milk entirely rather than resort to drinking the nonfat version (then called "skim" milk). Second, new beverage brands and flavors of established brands were flooding the marketplace. So-called "New Age" beverages abounded, including ready-to-drink cold teas Snapple and Arizona, and bottled water brands ranging from expensive European imports such as Perrier and Pellegrino to lower-priced American brands like Coca-Cola's Dasani and PepsiCo's Aquafina. The third reason for milk's popularity decline was that as more women entered the workplace, busy dual-income families consumed more meals on the go and menus featured soft drinks more prominently than milk.

In short, Goodby Silverstein faced a daunting task. How could any marketing campaign possibly reverse a sales decline driven by such significant social and market trends? The first thing they did was look at milk advertising worldwide. They quickly discovered that almost all these ads focused on the purported health benefits of drinking milk. Since that appeal was clearly no longer effective, the agency needed a new perspective on milk consumption. They sought insights from an innovative research paradigm called "gluttony deprivation." Focus group participants were recruited from among regular consumers of milk. They were instructed not to have any milk in the refrigerator for one whole week prior to the focus group interview, and to keep a journal during that week, recording everything they ate and drank, along with accompanying feelings.

By the time these milk-deprived individuals made it to their research appointments, they were frustrated and ready to talk about the trials of going without milk. Focus group interviews revealed the insight that shaped the Got Milk? campaign: We view milk as an accompaniment to the food we choose to eat. We elect to have cereal for breakfast, not cereal and milk. We ask for coffee, not milk and coffee. We cannot resist those fragrant cookies fresh out of the oven, with which we drink milk. We choose the food and assume the milk will be there. Milk, while secondary to the food, completes the consumption experience. During that week without milk, the participants could not enjoy their morning bowl of crunchy corn flakes or cheerios, or get reenergized by that coffee laced with half-and-half, or even guiltily guzzle a glass of cold milk to wash down those late-night Oreos.

In addition to finding that consumers choose what to eat and then get milk if it "goes with" the food, Goodby Silverstein's research revealed that people don't usually even think about milk until, cereal in the bowl or cookie in hand, they open the refrigerator and find an almost empty carton or none at all.

In terms of the consumer responses we seek to understand, measure, and ultimately influence, the research behind the "Got Milk?" campaign unearthed valuable insights into all three types, that is, thoughts, feelings, and behaviors, related to milk. It showed that people don't usually have any thoughts about milk until they want to eat a food that "requires" it. Not thinking about milk can result in running out of it and not noticing until the food it complements is already on the table. Then, finding no milk in the refrigerator leads to feelings of frustration and disappointment. If there is enough milk to accompany the food in question, the consumer still doesn't so much think about the milk itself as feel pleasure in the behavior of consuming the food that milk makes even more delicious, or in some instances merely palatable.

The very successful and long-lived "Got Milk?" marketing campaign arose from this innovative research. The campaign objective was to change consumers' behavior, that is, to motivate them to buy more milk, in part by increasing consumption of foods that need milk and in part by reminding people to pick up some milk while they were out doing other things. The agency developed a series of television commercials (one of which is described above) using humor to show the frustration consumers experience when they are deprived of milk and have just eaten – or are about to eat – something that requires it. To jog memory at the point of purchase, the agency developed in-store deals offering discounts on milk purchased along with well-known brands of dry cereal, peanut butter, cookies, and other foods that "need" milk. As added reminders to pick up milk on the way home from work, billboards showing delicious cupcakes and cookies, thirsty children and eager kittens clamoring for milk, were placed near access roads to supermarkets.

The result? The "Got Milk?" campaign was the first in many years to do more than enhance consumers' attitudes toward milk; it dramatically increased sales as well. We'll return to Goodby Silverstein's landmark research later when we discuss qualitative methods.

(For more contextual information, Daddona (2018) converses with key players in the creation of this two-decade-long campaign.)

Methods of Investigating Consumer Cognitions, Affect, and Behavior

There are two broad categories of research methods – qualitative and quantitative – and which one we choose depends on the questions we want to answer. In brief, qualitative research is excellent for delving into the "why's" of consumer behavior, while quantitative research is well-suited to answering the "who, what, and how much" questions. Below are examples that will further clarify what we can learn using each of these methods.

Quantitative Research

Quantitative research is so named because it is used to quantify aspects of the object of study; this means it requires data that is either numerical or may be coded as such. Examples include frequencies and rates of occurrence (e.g., numbers of ice cream purchases during summer versus winter), ratings and rankings (e.g., online consumer ratings, top ten lists), magnitudes or counts (e.g., sales, number of people who click on an ad), answers to questions with specific alternatives (e.g., yes-no and multiple-choice questions). The following list, though not exhaustive, gives an idea how extensively quantitative methods are used and the kinds of questions they enable us to answer.

Consumer Demographics and Lifestyles

Demographic data such as that collected in the decennial U.S. Census can answer many questions of interest to marketers, public policy makers, and consumer advocates. Among the many sources of international data are the U.S. Census Bureau's International Database (2021), the Population Reference Bureau (n.d.), Euromonitor International (2022), and Statista (n.d.). One of the thousands of questions this data may be used to answer is: What is the average household size and composition and how will it change over the next two, five, ten years?

The answers are important to marketers of a variety of products ranging from groceries to real estate to lawn care and home repair. The Häagen-Dazs lover who is one of the growing numbers of consumers who live alone can now enjoy a perfectly sized one-half cup serving of her favorite flavor without worry about succumbing to the temptation of finishing the entire carton (Euromonitor International, 2020a). The more nutritionally vigilant consumer can now buy a personal-size watermelon or a single gluten- and preservative-free black bean burrito made by Amy's Kitchen.

While one-person households are on the increase across the globe, so are multi-generational ones: our lengthening life expectancy is swelling the numbers of Baby Boomers taking care of elderly parents, and increasing numbers of "boomerang kids," underemployed or unemployed 25–34 year-olds, live with their parents (Cohn & Passel, 2018). Young adults without a college degree are more likely to live at home than are those who have graduated from college. The latter are more likely to reside in their own home, alone or with a spouse or partner. Homebuilders have seized the opportunity to market houses built with additions or even separate structures for elderly parents, who may wish to retain their privacy and some measure of independence while enjoying the safety and intimacy proximity affords them. For their adult children, the close but separate quarters for their parents give them peace of mind, relative convenience should the elders need help, and the tranquility their own privacy provides (Curtis, 2020). For a global perspective, see "Living Arrangements of Older Persons around the World" (United Nations – Department of Economic and Social Affairs – Population Division, 2019).

Compared to our demographic identities, our lifestyles shape many more of our product and brand preferences. For example, Portland, Oregon with its natural beauty and proximity to the beach, mountains, and even desert is a haven for outdoor enthusiasts who spend much of their free time hiking, running, or rock climbing; skateboarding, skiing, or snowboarding; surfing, kayaking, or rafting; and those who embrace this lifestyle will happily pay premium prices for high-performance sports apparel and equipment. The metro area can thus sustain several top-notch outdoor products brands and retailers, including Columbia Sportswear, North Face, Patagonia, REI, and Nike. Many of these retailers' customers are not particularly fond of outdoor pursuits but purchase the apparel because it represents an aspirational lifestyle of adventure, closeness to nature, and for some, physical prowess. In addition, many consumers are revamping their wardrobes to be "more casual and less bloated," part of a larger trend toward more sustainably oriented consumption practices (Schiffer, 2019).

Lifestyle research involves compiling data from a variety of sources, including consumer surveys, ad networks, and traditional media companies that track, respectively, consumers' online and offline media usage; loyalty cards; and public records. All this data is combined in statistical analyses to create categories or segments of consumers based on their geographical locations, demographics such as age, income, education, and occupation, their leisure activities and interests, media choices, and purchase patterns. Nielsen, a leading lifestyle research provider market, has identified more than 60 distinct lifestyle segments in the US, enabling its client companies to identify, describe, locate, and communicate with current and potential customers (Claritas, 2022). Custom reports are readily available; Nielsen (2022) explains: "We might not have ready-made data on motorcycle moms from Georgia who jet ski, but if that's who you need to reach, we'll find the best way." Sources of global lifestyle data include Marketresearch.com (2022), Euromonitor International (2020b), and Nielsen Holdings (2022).

Consumers' Self-reported Thoughts, Feelings, and Behaviors

Large-scale, regularly occurring surveys track a wide variety of trends (social, economic, technology, etc.), many of interest to marketers and consumer advocates and policy makers. For example, those who market to children would find it useful to know how much money their young consumers get to decide how to spend. A survey of kids' allowances provides a partial answer to this question. Seven of ten children receive an allowance, and the survey average by age varies from USD 3.80 for four-year-olds to USD 12.51. Overall, parents believe that older children should get a larger one. The survey finds that very few children save any of their money (T. Rowe Price, 2019).

Advocates against marketing to children, for example, Fairplay, could use this information about parents' attitudes toward allowances to encourage family discussions and activities focused on teaching children the value and meaning of money, and the anticipation and ultimate satisfaction that comes from saving for something chosen with care and forethought rather than acquiescing unquestioningly to marketing messages and peer pressure to own the latest, most popular sneakers or video game (Fairplay, n.d.).

Surveys may also address topics of interest to specific industries or organizations; an example is the annual J. D. Power's survey of customer satisfaction and its determinants across many industries and brands. Marketers need to track not only overall satisfaction with their industry and brands, but also customers' ratings of their performance on factors that determine satisfaction. For example, J. D. Power annually tracks customers' satisfaction with a number of industries and brands, including North American airlines. The North America Airline Satisfaction Study measures both business and leisure passengers' satisfaction with North American airlines based on performance on eight factors: aircraft, baggage, boarding, check-in, cost and fees, flight crew, in-flight services, and reservations. The 2021 survey revealed that during the pandemic, health and safety measures (empty middle seats, mask requirements), flight crew attentiveness, and waivers of change fees were central to customer satisfaction as the industry confronted pandemic fears (J. D. Power, 2021).

If a survey has a large enough sample to permit proper statistical analysis, the researcher can be comfortable assuming the findings are generalizable to the entire population of people like the respondents in ways that matter in the research. One longstanding debate in testing of new pharmaceuticals is whether results found in the many all-male samples in clinical trials can be generalized to females, who until very recently were much less frequently included. For marketing research firms like Nielsen and IRiWorldwide, the ability to generalize findings to an entire consumer market segment is essential; hence the large, well-incentivized consumer panels.

Consumer Behaviors Directly Measured

We want to measure actual behavior like purchases and media usage because self-reports of some behaviors may not be accurate. Can you list the items you bought on your most recent trip to the grocery store or recite the list of web sites you visited in the past seven days? Your lists might be mostly accurate if you just write down your habitual purchases or favorite web sites. But could you recall package sizes and prices or the pages you explored on a web site? While tracking actual behavior may be more expensive or time-consuming than having consumers complete a retrospective survey, the added knowledge and tactical improvements it leads to may be well worth the investment.

Product and brand purchases may be tracked using retail scanner data. Nielsen Holdings (2022) and IriWorldwide (Information Resources, 2022) are market research firms that provide their marketer clients such "store data," which includes store-level brand and product sales volume, pricing, promotions at the point of sale, and distribution across individual store locations. These data enable a marketer to determine whether price changes, special promotions, and/or locations of stores carrying their brands are correlated with changes in sales volume. Nielsen obtains longitudinal household-level sales data from more than 250,000 households in 25 countries by incentivizing participants in ongoing Consumer Panels to use a handheld in-home scanner to track all of their purchases that are identified with a Universal Product Code (NielsenIQ, 2022). This type of data is especially useful for tracking brand loyalty and switching in response to the client's own and competitors' promotions (e.g., coupons, contests, special end-of-aisle displays), packaging or product modifications, price changes, and other marketing tactics. For example, when the price of sugar rises, a candy bar marketer has two choices for keeping its costs constant: pass the price increase on to consumers or sell a smaller bar for the same price. The only way to determine which strategy works better is to try both and track sales or units (bars) sold. An ongoing consumer panel enables the sugary treat seller to do just that. Note, however, that these portable scanners do not work for unpackaged fresh produce or bulk items.

In addition to tracking purchases, marketers must stay current with consumers' media choices and habits because they need to know where to place their advertising and other communications so as to reach those mostly likely to purchase their products, that is, their target market. Two major trends make ad placement decisions especially challenging: first, our media choices are growing exponentially with advances, and second, we are adept at and able to avoid marketing messages. Google Analytics makes it easy for marketers large and small to track online consumer behaviors including product, brand, and other keyword searches, visits to company sites, and clicks on ads (Google LLC, n.d.). Facebook, Twitter, and other social media sites enable marketers to target and track responses of specific consumer groups defined by demographics, interests, and online presence. Thanks to these tracking capabilities and automated marketer responses, you may feel at times as if someone is looking over your shoulder, either a virtual nosy neighbor or a helpful friend, depending on your perspective on privacy. If you shop on one site for a baby car seat, your screen will immediately and for some time thereafter carry ads for car seats, cribs and bassinets, and other baby paraphernalia, all a click away.

A marketer like iTunes or Amazon compiles data over time and many consumer searches and purchases to arrive at recommended lists of songs, movies, books, and other products for you based on your searches and purchases. The algorithms used are complex and proprietary, but the basic idea is that these marketers can use data amassed from millions of consumers to estimate how likely you are to buy, say, the Twilight or Harry Potter series, given your book purchases and searches up to now. The algorithms developed recognize patterns of purchases and searches and make predictions about yours by finding other consumers with the same patterns and identifying their additional purchases as the ones most likely to interest you. Hence the Amazon recommendations: People who browsed (purchased) these books also browsed (purchased) the following ones. With every bit of new data, the algorithm learns to make more accurate predictions.

Finely honed online marketing research and consumer message targeting are exciting new business capabilities but make many consumers uncomfortable with this new world in which every keystroke and click communicates an aspect of identity. What causes more consternation among consumers and privacy advocates are that large data brokers like Acxiom (Acxiom, 2022) regularly collect and sell every morsel of data they can find without consumers' knowledge or permission. "What Are Data Brokers—And What Is Your Data Worth," an infographic by WebFX (2020), reveals the magnitude of this "big data" brokering and its potential impact on consumers.

For businesses and regulators, tracking and attempting to understand consumer behavior that is unsafe for or harmful to the consumer herself or others is also an important focus of consumer research, so that we can develop effective prevention or deterrence measures. For an example of this type of behavior tracking, we return to the airline industry.

As the pandemic wanes in the US, air travel is increasing – and so is passenger misbehavior. The Federal Aviation Administration (FAA), which oversees and tracks compliance with airline safety rules, has noted:

> a "disturbing increase" in the number of unruly passengers who have returned to the skies with the easing of pandemic restrictions….the F.A.A. said that it had received more than 1,300 unruly-passenger reports from airlines since February. In the previous decade, the agency said, it took enforcement actions against 1,300 passengers total.
>
> (Vigdor, 2020)

The FAA states that "Interfering with the duties of a crewmember" violates federal law and that passengers who assault, threaten, or otherwise interfere with crewmember duties may face substantial fines or prosecution on criminal charges (Federal Aviation Administration, 2021).

Incidents of passenger misbehavior range from refusal to adhere to the airline's mandate to wear a mask, to physical assaults of crewmembers and other passengers. It is possible that the prospect of a fine or imprisonment may deter some potential miscreants from flouting regulations and putting others at risk.

Involuntary Physiological Consumer Responses

How can we capture consumers' attention and emotional responses to branding and messaging without directly asking them? As we observed earlier in the chapter, consumers' responses to surveys and comments in in-depth interviews or focus groups are under the participants' voluntary control, hence subject to self-censorship. Most of us want to please the interviewer and to make a favorable impression on others. *Neuromarketing research* circumvents our self-editing tendencies by employing advanced technology to measure our *involuntary physiological responses* to brands and messaging. An article entitled "A Non-Scientist's Guide to the Neuromarketing Toolkit" provides an overview of measures commonly used (Plassmann & Ling, 2019):

1. *Functional magnetic resonance imaging* (fMRI) measures blood oxygenation in the brain. Changes in blood oxygenation correlate with changes in neural activity. An fMRI scanner can thus pinpoint where a change in neural activity occurs when a consumer, for example, evaluates willingness-to-pay (WTP) for a product.

2. *Electroencephalography* (EEG) records changes in brain activity nanosecond by nanosecond via sensors affixed to the scalp. EEG signals (reflect) different characteristics such as memory processing, attention, and emotional engagement. EEG can trace very fast neural activity (~one millisecond) in real time.

    [However], there are differing schools of thought on how to interpret EEG signals.

3. *Functional near-infrared spectroscopy* (fNIRS) uses light that penetrates the scalp and brain tissue (up to two to three centimeters) and is then absorbed by the blood due to changes in neural activity. Differences in absorption are employed to trace changes in regional neural activity of the cortex relatively fast (~100 milliseconds). With its limited penetrative power, fNIRS can pick up activity of the surface cortex associated with attention, valuation, and cognitive control, but cannot study deeper brain regions linked with memories, motivation, and emotions.

4. *Eye-tracking* devices can measure consumers' visual attention. For example, a lab at Clemson University in the US simulates a supermarket environment where study participants can browse the aisles as they would at a real store while wearing eye-tracking spectacles that capture which products catch their eye and how they visually engage with branded packaging.

5. *Skin conductance response* (SCR) captures changes in the skin's electrical resistance stemming from increased engagement and arousal, as reflected in sweat gland activity. It can pick up relatively slow changes (~four seconds), but not whether this feeling is positive or negative. Using SCR and eye-tracking, Italian digital marketing company **The Sixth W** tested two ways for customers to queue at a movie theater's concession stand. It found consumers were more drawn to unhealthy food – and more likely to purchase unhealthy snacks – when there was a single long queue rather than shorter, counter-specific queues.

6. *Facial affect recording* (FAR) analyses facial muscle configurations to recognize different basic emotions such as anger, disgust, fear, happiness, sadness, and surprise. The goal is to extract consumer thoughts and sentiments that may otherwise go unexpressed. According to our experience with this software, it reliably captures how positive or negative an emotion is, but it is less adept at distinguishing and decoding different negative emotions.

    Keep in mind that your question should dictate which technique you choose, and that neuromarketing research complements but cannot replace other research methods.

Qualitative Research Methods

In contrast to quantitative research, qualitative studies are well-suited to questions when too little is known about the potential answers to construct closed-ended survey questions sporting lists of well-specified alternatives or when the object of study is not readily quantifiable. Examples include complex, emotionally fraught topics such as how we think and feel about the idea of luxury, the nature of our relationships with our animal companions, and how we go about planning a significant cultural rite like a wedding or christening.

Goodby Silverstein researchers gleaned their insights into consumers' milk-related thoughts, feelings, and behaviors from qualitative (as opposed to quantitative) self-reported (rather than directly observed) data which they collected from consumers' journals and subsequent focus group interviews. Unlike quantitative research, which must be designed to meet the stringent requirements for meaningful statistical analysis, qualitative research must meet a different but equally rigorous set of standards for thematic analysis. Other examples of qualitative investigations of consumer behavior include one-on-one in-depth interviews, ethnographic research in which the researcher simultaneously participates in and observes people using brands in their daily lives (recall Harley Owners' Groups described in Chapter 1), and "netnography," which is the study of online consumer communities that have sprung up as people who deeply appreciate and enjoy a particular brand, product, or lifestyle find one another.

Focus Groups

When a marketer needs to find out how target consumers feel about a product, service, or advertising message, focus groups may be appropriate. These are typically small group sessions lasting one to two hours, during which a moderator hired by the brand client or ad agency facilitates an extended discussion of a topic among a small group (usually about eight to 12) of consumers recruited based on client-specified characteristics of their demographics, interests, product experiences, etc., and paid for their time.

In-depth Interviews

If the research topic is sensitive or private or requires a deep understanding of a personal narrative or account of an experience, one-on-one interviews may be the method of choice. A luxury automaker wanted to gain fresh insights into its customers' experiences, in which the flagship vehicle played a role, for the purpose of creating more compelling advertising messages. To that end, the automaker's ad agency conducted in-depth interviews with a number of the car's owners, each of whom was instructed to create a collage beforehand consisting of anything – pictures from magazines, personal photos, even objects – that reflected their feelings about the car. The idea behind having participants make collages is that many people find it difficult to put their feelings into words but can readily point to pictorial or other concrete metaphors that capture the feelings. The interviewer uses the collage to draw out the interviewee; in explaining the collage, s/he expresses and reflects on his/her feelings about the topic of focus. One female participant attached a sparkly, expensive stiletto-heeled shoe to her collage, describing it as representing the freedom and hedonism she felt when driving the car.

In qualitative research, sample sizes tend to be small for two reasons: (a) These methods are costly in time and labor, and (b) the philosophy underlying them is that when new themes stop emerging with each additional informant, there is no need for further sampling. The themes uncovered are not assumed to be generalizable beyond the sample informants; a follow-up quantitative study with an appropriately large sample would be required to generalize findings.

Ethnography

A source of qualitative as well as quantitative data is direct observations and videos of consumer behavior in retail, home, and other settings of interest. As the coronavirus pandemic has accelerated consumer adoption of online shopping, digital anthropologists can advise companies on how to best serve customers in a digital environment. Here is a discussion of what a digital anthropologist can offer.

Traditional ethnography is qualitative and is premised on the assumption that in order to access and understand an experience, whether it is a lifestyle or a discrete occurrence, online or offline, the researcher must simultaneously participate in and observe her own and other participants' responses as the experience unfolds. While ethnographic research is time-consuming, it may yield rich insights into consumer behavior. In "Invisible brands: An ethnography of households and the brands in their kitchen pantries," Coupland (2005) wanted to investigate how consumers interact with brands in the supermarket on their regular shopping excursions, and at home, storing, preparing, and serving the food. One of her more surprising findings was that some shoppers strip the food of its packaging as they are putting it away in the cupboards and refrigerator, in essence "unbranding" it. While the function of this unpackaging may be to save space, the result is that in a household with children, there are no brands for which they can develop early and strong brand loyalty. This is good or bad depending on whether you are a marketer trying to reach young consumers, a parent who wants to teach their offspring to be wise consumers through exposure and reflection on marketing tactics, or a parent or advocate who believes children should not be targets of marketers' efforts to persuade and that there is too much branding of children's products already. However we look at the findings, an ethnographic approach is ideal for getting to this level of intimate knowledge of consumer behavior.

During the COVID-19 pandemic, many ethnographic studies were implemented using digital research methods because COVID-19 made in-person meetings infeasible. The following article by Stassopoulous (2020) explains how digital ethnography may actually yield more insights than in-person research:

Digital ethnography: Understanding people not only in a COVID World

Updated: Nov 17, 2020

Source: Third Eye, InsightAsia, Trinetra

Ethnography during COVID is digital rather than physical. That started out as a necessity, with social distancing making consumers' home visits unfeasible, but in certain contexts it has given us an even better read of consumers and their lives.

We find that Emerging Market consumers are happy to share their lives and their stories online – and over the past months, we have been working with ethnographic consultants on the use of digital media to shape the techniques and processes we employ in classical ethnography.

A simple way to translate traditional research methodology into a digital environment is to hold video conferences with EM consumers. They can stream through their smartphones using WhatsApp or Instagram, like they would with their friends. With this sort of session, we can follow conversations with the facilitator...as well as ask questions, and even get a virtual tour of the house.

New tools allow communication beyond a typical two-hour study of a persons' life. In recent years, we have been setting up WhatsApp groups with respondents. Communication continues long after the visit, and we still get updates from some respondents three years after our Immersion visits.

Working with Third Eye in India, for example, we've explored digital processes that could provide more sustained contact with people, and better context around what's happening to them during the COVID-19 pandemic. One such technique is to set up a virtual panel on WhatsApp with several respondents. Panel members would, over a period of a week, be asked to complete 2–3 daily assignments, recording it with text, audio, or video. Some of the assignments could for example be recording their new disinfection rituals or their new cooking routines, or describing situations where they had specific feelings, such as frustration or anxiety.

This ongoing digital engagement with people we meet on Immersions studies, both real and virtual, creates the ability to capture consumers' changing habits, live and longitudinally. The online medium allows us to have continuous conversations with them and makes the engagement more dynamic and interactive.

An important type of ethnography is *netnography*. Netnography is research using participant observation to gain insights into online communities that are formed in the normal course of consumers' sharing their interests in specific brands, products, and activities. Robert Kozinets, who coined the term, states that the term *netnography* refers to "a specific set of online ethnographic procedures characterized by a particular methodology, including an epistemological background, analytic frameworks, and a consistent and evolving set of guidelines for entree, observation, data analysis, ethics, and so on" (2013).

Brands that have given rise to such communities range from Mini Coopers to Nutella, from Apple's Newton (a long-defunct, early forerunner of the Blackberry) to Nike+, a very popular system integrating an iPod-type data collection device into Nike running shoes that enables runners to monitor their performance over time. To conduct netnographic research, the investigator must become a participant observer in the community, and in offline gatherings or encounters as well. These multiple sources of data deepen and enrich the researcher's experience and understanding of the brand's meaning to the community and inform her perspective on how the community itself functions and the value individual members derive from it. A study by Schau, Muñiz, and Arnould (2009) of a thriving online Mini Cooper community revealed that "newbies," the proud Mini purchasers who are awaiting their production and delivery, are welcomed warmly and their new vehicles anticipated eagerly by established community members. Owners name and customize their vehicles, wave at other Mini drivers they encounter on the road, and take immense pleasure in discussing the car. The insights netnography can uncover fascinate academic researchers and inform branding and marketing practitioners as they create campaigns and sponsored events that will capture the hearts and minds of current and aspiring Mini owners.

Should We Use Qualitative or Quantitative Methods?

How do we go about deciding whether to use quantitative or qualitative methods? In general, quantitative methods require that we know precisely the content and order of the questions we want to ask, as well as most if not all possible answers. If we do not have this knowledge or if we are looking for rich insights that may be difficult to articulate, qualitative research is the better choice.

For example, most of us do not spend much time reflecting on what our pets mean to us and how their presence affects our lives and even our relationships with other humans. And depending on our immediate cultural milieu, we may be embarrassed to admit how much – or how little – they mean to us. But how we view our animal companion directly affects the decision we make as their guardians. How much money are we willing to spend on pet food, supplies, and medical care? Do we buy them what we want or what we have reason to believe they want or need? How attuned are we to changes in their physical and emotional well-being? Consumers who regard their animals as "children with fur" will likely spend more on veterinary care than owners whose pets are child substitutes or "practice" children, and those who take the position that animals are "just animals" are likely to spend least of all on pet care and supplies. Can't we just ask pet owners to complete a survey question like the following?

Which of the following best describes the role your pet plays in your life?

a.   S/he is my child, no different from a human child.
b.   S/he is giving me experience taking care of someone besides myself.
c.   S/he is helping teach my children responsibility.
d.   S/he is just a pet.

e.   S/he does work for me (please specify) _____.
f.   Other (please specify) _____.

There is nothing wrong with this approach. But we would deepen and enrich our understanding of these different perspectives if we also sat face-to-face with a few pet owners, one at a time, and asked them some open-ended questions like the following:

a.   What motivated you to adopt an animal?
b.   How did you go about searching for the animal?
c.   What made you choose this animal over the others?
d.   How would you describe your pet's place in the household?
e.   How would you describe your relationship with your pet?
f.   What does a typical day look like for you and your pet?
g.   How, if at all, does your pet affect your relationships with other people?

An interview gives you the flexibility to delve more deeply into any of the areas the questions cover if the interviewee gives an ambiguous or very general answer that needs clarifying or completing, and affords the interviewee an opportunity to learn and share something new about herself because she is able to reflect and elaborate on her answers. If we interview pet owners with a variety of perspectives on animals, we will come away with a treasure trove of pet-related feelings, thoughts, memories, and associations. How do we make sense of this embarrassment of riches? We can look for themes that emerge as we continue to interview owners. A recent study by Blouin (2015), conducted using in-depth interviews to explore people's perspectives on their dog companions, revealed three distinct views: dominionistic (it's just an animal), humanistic (the dog is regarded as a surrogate human), and protectionistic (high regard for all species, not just companion animals). In short, our attachments to our animal companions are complex, and the more completely veterinarians and animal welfare advocates understand them, the greater their capacity to empathize with, and work to help, animals and humans alike.

As we introduce more consumer behavior research with each new chapter, you will get a clearer idea of the vast and fascinating array of questions that quantitative and qualitative research can work in concert to answer.

References

Acxiom (2022). "Data, identity solution & people-based marketing solutions". Retrieved from: www.acxiom.com/.
Blouin, D. D. (2015). "Are dogs children, companions, or just animals? Understanding variations in people's orientations toward animals". *Anthrozoös*, 26(2), 279–294. https://doi.org/10.2752/175303713X13636846944402.
Claritas LLC (2022). "Segment details". Retrieved from: https://claritas360.claritas.com/mybestsegments/#segDetails.

Cohn, D. V., & Passel, J. S. (2018, April 5). "A record 64 million Americans live in multigenerational households". Pew Research Center. Retrieved from: https://pewrsr.ch/2JjKACu.

Coupland, J. C. (2005). "Invisible brands: An ethnography of households and the brands in their kitchen pantries". *Journal of Consumer Research, 32*(1), 106–118. https://doi.org/10.1086/429604.

Curtis, J. (2020, August 18). "8 ways to design multigenerational homes". MYMOVE. Retrieved from: www.mymove.com/home-inspiration/decoration-design-ideas/multigenerational-homes/.

Daddona, M. (2018, June 13). "Got milk? How the iconic campaign came to be, 25 years ago". Fast Company. Retrieved from: www.fastcompany.com/40556502/got-milk-how-the-iconic-campaign-came-to-be-25-years-ago.

Euromonitor International (2020a, January). "Innovation in food packaging for single-person households". Retrieved from: www.euromonitor.com/innovation-in-food-packaging-for-single-person-households/report.

Euromonitor International (2020b). "Top 10 global consumer trends 2020". Retrieved from: https://go.euromonitor.com/white-paper-EC-2020-Top-10-Global-Consumer-Trends.html.

Euromonitor International (2022). "Market research – United States". Retrieved from: www.euromonitor.com/usa.

Fairplay (n.d.). "Fairplay (formerly known as campaign for a commercial-free childhood)". Accessed at: https://fairplayforkids.org/.

Federal Aviation Administration (2021, October 19). "Unruly passengers". Retrieved from: www.faa.gov/data_research/passengers_cargo/unruly_passengers/.

Goodby, Silverstein & Partners (1995). "Got milk? Where am I? Heaven or hell" [Video]. Commercial for the California Milk Processor Board. Youtube. Retrieved from: https://youtu.be/hnIjgw5A-iI.

Google LLC (n.d.). "Analytics tools & solutions for your business – Google analytics". Retrieved from: https://marketingplatform.google.com/about/analytics/.

Information Resources, Inc. (2022). "IRI – delivering growth for CPG, retail, and healthcare". Retrieved from: www.iriworldwide.com/en-us.

J. D. Power (2021, May 12). "Attentive flight crews, flexible fares and charges during pandemic drive record high customer satisfaction with North American airlines, J.D. Power finds". Press release. Retrieved from: www.jdpower.com/sites/default/files/file/2021-05/2021046a%20N.A.%20Airline%20Satisfaction.pdf.

Kozinets, R. (2013, April). "Is netnography just a synonym for online ethnography? Brand new worlds – perspectives of a marketing anthropologist". Retrieved from: https://kozinets.net/archives/475.

MarketResearch.com (2022). "Global lifestyle market research reports & analysis". Retrieved from: www.marketresearch.com/seek/Lifestyle-Global/134/1407/1.html.

Nielsen Holdings Inc. (2022). "Audience Is Everything®". Retrieved from: https://global.nielsen.com/global/en/.

NielsenIQ (2022). "Homescan". Retrieved from: https://nielseniq.com/global/en/solutions/homescan/.

Plassmann, H., & Ling, A. (2019, June 10). "A non-scientist's guide to the neuromarketing toolkit". Marketing Blog. INSEAD. Retrieved from: https://knowledge.insead.edu/blog/insead-blog/a-non-scientists-guide-to-the-neuromarketing-toolkit-11721.

Population Reference Bureau (n.d.). "Data sheets". Retrieved from: www.prb.org/collections/data-sheets/.

Schau, H. J., Muñiz, A. M., & Arnould, E. J. (2009). "How brand community practices create value". *Journal of Marketing, 73*(5), 30–51. https://doi.org/10.1509/jmkg.73.5.30.

Schiffer, J. (2019, June 10). "Behind fashion's obsession with outdoor gear". Vogue Business. Retrieved from: www.voguebusiness.com/consumers/outdoor-gear-athleisure-luxury-brands-patagonia-north-face.

Stassopoulous, T. (2020, July 27). "Digital ethnography: Understanding people not only in a COVID world". Trinetra. Retrieved from: www.trinetra-im.com/post/digital-ethnography.

Statista (n.d.). "The statistics portal for market data, market research and market studies". Retrieved from: www.statista.com/.

T. Rowe Price (2019). "11th annual parents, kids & money survey". SlideShare. Retrieved from: www.slideshare.net/TRowePrice/t-rowe-prices-11th-annual-parents-kids-money-survey.

United Nations – Department of Economic and Social Affairs – Population Division (2019, April). "Living arrangements of older persons around the world". Retrieved from: www.un.org/en/development/desa/population/publications/pdf/popfacts/PopFacts_2019-2.pdf.

United States Census Bureau (2021, 8 October). "International data base (IDB)". Retrieved from: www.census.gov/programs-surveys/international-programs/about/idb.html.

Vigdor, N. (2021, May 10). "Cases of unruly airline passengers are soaring, and so are federal fines". *The New York Times*. Retrieved from: www.nytimes.com/2021/05/10/travel/faa-unruly-airline-passenger-fines.html.

WebFX (2020, March 16). "What are data brokers—and what is your data worth?". Infographic. Retrieved from: www.webfx.com/blog/internet/what-are-data-brokers-and-what-is-your-data-worth-infographic/.

3 Why We Buy

Objectives

1. To explore the means-end theory of how products help us achieve our goals.
2. To delineate differences among the product features we can readily evaluate for ourselves and those we cannot.
3. To investigate the dimensions of product involvement and how they color our preferences and choices.

Introduction

It's been a stressful day at work, and you are ready to relax. You:

a. Meet friends for happy hour at your favorite microbrewery.
b. Call your massage therapist for a last-minute appointment.
c. Go home, order a pizza, and watch the latest game in the World Series.
d. Fetch your yellow lab puppy from home to go running with you.
e. Slip into a warm foamy bubble bath for a long soak.
f. Other (please specify).

Whatever relaxes you probably involves using a product or service that you or someone else has purchased for that very reason. Consumer research over the decades provides ample evidence that we buy many products, not as ends in themselves, but rather as means of achieving goals, for example, relaxation. In alternative (a), the bar you go to and the beer you buy are integral to your unwinding with friends, and your feelings about both include your recollections of these relaxing, convivial times. The pizza retailer and the pizza itself in alterative (c) are strongly associated with the pleasure you derive from watching the game and add to the game experience. And while the puppy in alternative (d) is not a product, s/he is legally a possession, the playful and loving companion who makes your run a welcome respite from the demands of your job. The beer, the pizza, the

DOI: 10.4324/9780367426897-4

puppy – all are more than the sum of their attributes (features) and any may be a means of relaxing.

Why Do We Purchase Products?

Our lives are filled with our efforts to meet goals, some basic, instinctive, short-term (to satisfy hunger or quench thirst, to rest and sleep), others more abstract and longer-term (to advance professionally, have a community, love and be loved). As shown in the example above, we often seek help from products or services in our efforts to achieve our goals. According to *means-end chain* (MEC) *theory*, we choose products that possess the specific attributes (features) we associate with the outcomes (*consequences* or *benefits*) we seek when we use the product. These consequences are, in turn, linked to our larger goals and values. Zhou et al. (2020) observe that consumers:

> often are not aware of how their product preferences and usage behaviors are linked with their own needs and values, nor are they conscious about the influence of the marketing messages that they are exposed to … The MEC theory provides a useful solution for marketing researchers and practitioners to discover consumers' underlying needs and values.

A structured interview or survey method termed "laddering" is used to unearth MECs, which are connections among product attributes, consequences, and values. Laddering is widely used in market research to guide managerial decisions about market segmentation, product planning, and promotional strategy. Here are examples of hypothetical MECs:

MEC for pizza retailer in alternative (c) above:

Attribute: Delivers

Brand use **consequence(s)** of that attribute: Convenience (I don't have to cook or brave rush hour traffic to pick up carryout on the way home from work).

Goal that the consequence helps the consumer achieve: I can make it home in time to watch the game and relax and unwind while I wait for the pizza delivery.

Even if there is another pizza retailer that offers better-tasting pizza, if the store does not deliver, it will not help the consumer achieve her goal in this example.

MEC for puppy in alternative (d) above:

Attribute: Loves to run

Consequence of that attribute when owner interacts with puppy: Her love of running helps motivate me to run farther and more frequently.

Second-order consequences resulting from running farther and more frequently:

Goal 1. I'm at my optimal weight.

Goal 2. I'm self-disciplined about exercise.

Value 1 that underlies Goal 1: Physical and mental well-being.

Value 2 that underlies Goal 2: Self-respect.

Notice that the product attribute exists even if the product is never bought or used, and the goals and values reside exclusively in the consumer's mind. It is the consequence alone that embodies the consumer's interaction with the product. Marketing a brand based on its features (attributes) might appeal to expert users, as they can quickly translate the attributes into consequences and corresponding goals. In most cases, however, a message that shows the consequences of using a brand and at least alludes to goals and values will be more effective at arousing consumer interest and building brand preference.

You may be wondering how we define values here. Social psychologist Milton Rokeach, in his book *The Nature of Human Values* (1973), defined value as "an enduring belief that a specific mode of conduct or end state of existence is personally or socially preferable to an opposite or converse mode of conduct or end state of existence." While many of the values Rokeach identified have readily recognized relevance to consumer behavior, several – for example, national security, a world at peace, obedience, forgiveness – do not. One of the most widely used lists of values in consumer research is the List of Values (LOV) developed by Kahle and Kennedy (1988). It is based in part on Maslow's hierarchy of needs and proposes that the following nine values or "desired end-states" are common across cultures and demographic segments. We give brand message examples for each value:

Self-Respect – L'Oreal Paris: "Because you're worth it"

Excitement – Tesla: "Lay rubber where your carbon footprint used to be"

Security – Brinks Home Security: "Peace of mind"; MetLife: "Trust MetLife to protect the ones you love"

Warm Relationships with Others – Pampers: "Welcome to a world of love, sleep, and play"; Cheerios: "A family favorite for over 70 years"

Sense of Accomplishment – Lenovo: "For those who do"; Microsoft Windows XP: "Yes you can"

Self-Fulfillment – Nike: "Just Do It"; Red Bull "gives you wings"

Being Well Respected by Others – Dos Equis: "The only name he drops is his own"; Crossfit: "Forging elite fitness"

Sense of Belonging – Coca-Cola: "Share a coke with friends"

Fun and Enjoyment in Life – Nissan Leaf: "100% electric. 100% fun"; Disney: "Where dreams come true"

We can research MECs for brands or products using an in-depth interview technique called *laddering*. Through structured sequences of questions, we ascend from product attributes that are important to the interviewee, to the consequences of using a product with that attribute, to the goal or core value each consequence helps the consumer fulfill. Let's look at an example of a laddering interview for "athleisure" wear from Zhou et al. (2020), which discusses athletic apparel that is worn not just for working out, but also as a fashion statement:

Donna (interviewee): Let's say I'm wearing a pair of black yoga pants and a co-ordinated grey razor back. And then I would wear a pink sports bra, so it sorts of stands out. *Researcher*: Why do you want to wear something that stands out?

Donna: I think it looks nice. Because I can't really accentuate much with my bottom. I do it with my top. I think it's because I want to stand out.

Researcher: Why do you want to stand out?

Donna: I do it more to boost my own self-confidence. There are days when I'm extremely stressed out, but when I pick these really colorful things and wear them, and then I feel better about myself.

In this case, Donna's perceptions of activewear were linked to the attribute of color, the consequence of standing out, and the end state value of self-confidence. The example illustrates how the researchers probed participants to talk about the important attributes, consequences and values of wearing active wear.

The following are the MECs the researchers found, with an illustrative quote below each one.

Attribute – Perceived Consequence(s) – Goal or Core Value

Fit – physical appearance – self-respect
You feel like you look good (when wearing tight pants). And it is always better to go in a workout already thinking that you look good than being like, "Oh, I'm so bloated and fat." I think putting on a pair of tight capris makes you feel good about yourself.

Fit – physical comfort-task facilitation – sense of accomplishment
I prefer a tighter fit activewear because I want to feel so comfortable that I don't even have to think about it. I can appreciate what my body does for me and what I am doing at the moment.

Color and pattern – physical appearance–task facilitation – sense of accomplishment
It makes you feel better doing the exercise when you wear the colorful top, as opposed to the duller, solid ones. Dark colors make me feel like "I have a chore to do, and this is my chore clothes." If it is a bright color, it looks good and it makes me feel I am doing something great for my body, helping my body to be leaner and healthier.

Color and pattern – physical appearance–social relationship – self-respect
It (the pattern) was something that was different enough but not too different. (I don't like an obvious pattern because) I don't want to be perceived as a crazy person. You are still around people (when you exercise) and you want to present yourself well.

Stylish design – physical appearance – self-respect
Before I had kids, I did my hair and makeup every day. Now that I have kids, it (doing hair and makeup) is not always possible. By wearing activewear, I feel like I am making an effort on myself. It makes me feel presentable, not just a mom.

Stylish design – fun and enjoyment
I think it is really a matter of fun. The first thing in the morning I do when I get out of bed is I am going to put on my workout clothes. When it is something nice, it is just more fun. Maybe I don't even plan to work out, but I've got my really nice shirt and sneakers. It is just more enticing to put on than other clothes.

Functional design – physical comfort–task facilitation – self-respect
(W)hen I go to the gym, I don't like to use the locker. I typically would just bring my car key and I need a pocket for that.

Fabric – physical comfort–task facilitation – sense of accomplishment
It (an activewear) is more than something that covers my body. If I am lifting weights, I need to wear a firmer fabric that can protect my knees. If I do more intense exercises, I will wear something stretchy because I don't want to keep pulling my pants up when I work out.

The athleisure study illustrates several important aspects of MECs for a given product:

1. Any one attribute may be linked to more than one consequence, and any consequence may be linked to more than one end-state value.
2. An attribute may link directly to a value.
3. A consequence may link to another consequence.

A hotly debated question is whether marketers can create needs in consumers. Experts on human values would likely argue that our core needs or values exist independent of the means of satisfying them. However, marketers can create linkages between brand attributes and goals, values, or needs, as the examples above illustrate. In addition, marketing messages may, over time and repetition, link attributes of new products to novel consequences and from those to preexisting needs, values, or goals. Below is a famous example from Listerine, as discussed by Lippert (2017):

> "Edna's case was really a pathetic one," the copy reads. "Like every woman, her primary ambition was to marry.... As her birthdays crept gradually toward that tragic thirty mark, marriage seemed farther from her life than ever." Amping up the pitiful, Edna is in tears. Why, Edna, why? Halitosis, of course. And "even your closest friends won't tell you."
>
> Thus, this 1925 Listerine ad catapulted "Often a bridesmaid but never a bride" into the American consciousness as a shorthand for the-last-girl-picked-for-anything, the one who craves the spotlight but never gets it.
>
> Listerine was formulated in 1879, but it was decades later that the creator's son, Gerard Lambert, read the term "halitosis" in a medical journal and had his eureka moment.
>
> Certainly, 1920s America was primed to worry about a new social scourge, however manufactured: Immigrants had brought smells from alien foods, and

foreign germs and habits. Meanwhile, people began working and living in closer quarters. Indoor plumbing became widespread. Aided by advertisers, the American bathroom became a shrine to personal hygiene.

Bad breath became big business: According to the Listerine website, sales went from $115,000 a year in 1921 to $4 million a year by 1927. By the late 1920s, Listerine was the country's third-largest print advertiser.

Now a Johnson & Johnson product, Listerine is part of an "oral hygiene" category that has exploded into a $6 billion industry. Its most recent global campaign, begun in 2016, makes use of the line, "Bring Out the Bold." But today's ads will never have the same rocket power as the one lambasting poor Edna. Back then it was possible to believe that we could change our futures with a swish.

Warner Lambert forged a link from Listerine's antiseptic quality to the consumer consequence of eliminating bad breath and linked that consequence to the goal (value, need) of finding true love (warm relationships with others, in LOV terms). Did mouthwash marketing transform a widely accepted fact of life into a source of social fear or did it offer a welcome remedy to a social impediment that had, until then, gone unacknowledged in the public sphere? Arguably, products that make us smell and look better do not create needs, but rather answer the longstanding needs of those considered less attractive to compete with their more attractive counterparts for jobs, mates, even fairer trials.

More immediately concerning to consumer advocates, parents, and clinicians is the ubiquity of fashion and cosmetics advertising showing impossibly thin young women with flawless skin and perfectly coiffed hair. Such marketing does not show realistic enhancements of average looks, but instead presents standards that no one can meet without airbrushing and a severely restricted diet. These media images are thought to contribute cumulatively to the body dissatisfaction that is epidemic among young girls and women and to the development of eating disorders in those who are biologically predisposed. In other words, this marketing may raise the bar for what constitutes attractiveness, which is linked to self-esteem (self-respect in LOV terms). In so doing, the cosmetics and fashion industries link their brands to a promise of perfection implicit in the images so painstakingly and artistically constructed, making self-esteem unattainable for many girls and women. And the perils are not limited to low self-esteem; many cosmetic products contain potentially harmful ingredients that remain legal in the US. According to the watchdog organization Environmental Working Group (EWG):

In 2019, when the federal Food and Drug Administration – the agency that governs sunscreen safety – proposed its most recent updates to sunscreen regulations, it found that only two ingredients, zinc oxide and titanium dioxide, could be classified as safe and effective, based on the currently available information. But in the past year, numerous new studies have raised new concerns about endocrine-disrupting effects from three other ingredients: homosalate, avobenzone and oxybenzone.

Within the past year, the European Commission has published preliminary opinions on the safety of three organic UV filters, oxybenzone, homosalate and octocrylene. It found that the levels of two of them were not safe in the amounts at which they are currently used, and proposed a concentration limit of 2.2 percent for oxybenzone and 1.4 percent for homosalate. U.S. sunscreen manufacturers are legally allowed to use these two chemicals at concentrations up to 6 and 15 percent, respectively, and hundreds of sunscreens manufactured in the U.S. use them at concentrations that far exceed the European Commission's recommendations.

(Environmental Working Group, 2021a)

The Personal Care Products Safety Act, introduced to the U.S. Congress in 2019 and gathering momentum at the time of this writing (May, 2021), would give the Food and Drug Administration (FDA) "the authority to regulate personal care products and sets up a process for how this will be done, including the safety review of specific chemicals for use in cosmetic products." Currently, while the FDA has "oversight" of personal care/cosmetic products, their authority is limited to requiring ingredient listings on labels. "They do not currently regulate the chemicals in these products, or even have the authority to issue a mandatory recall if a product is harmful" (Environmental Working Group, n.d.).

On a more positive note, Apple is superb at linking innovative products to consumer needs. Steve Jobs, Apple cofounder, was a brilliant designer and marketer who, contrary to popular belief, came to advocate listening closely to consumers: "You've got to start with the customer experience and work backwards to the technology," he stated in a speech at the 1997 World Developers' Conference (Cane, 2011). Apple has enticed us to believe that we must have its beautifully designed, user-friendly iMac, iPod, iPhone, and iPad, by linking new attributes (e.g., the mouse, the touch screen) to ease of use, perhaps the most significant consequence of new technology devices. These products' user-friendly features purportedly enhance our creativity (and the pleasure that frequently accompanies creative acts) and productivity (leading to higher self-esteem in many consumers).

How Do We Weigh Brand Attributes in Our Purchase Decisions?

MEC theory explains how specific product features (attributes) lead to consequences of product use that are linked, in turn, to end-state values. Laddering interviews may reveal *why* we buy but not how we choose which brand to buy. Think about the last time you got a haircut: Was it easy to make an appointment? Could you find parking nearby or save fuel by taking public transit? Was the atmosphere pleasant, the floor swept clean, the chair comfortable? Did the barber or hairdresser cut your hair as you wanted? Was s/he personable, competent, engaged? Did you feel you got value for your money? Aside from the cut itself, what is most important to you when you go for a haircut? If you love your hairdresser and have been going to her for years, it might not matter to you all that much that she keeps you waiting from time to time. If, however, this is your first visit, your annoyance at having to wait may outweigh your liking for the hairdresser. In other words, those positive and negative emotional tags attached to our memories may vary in significance and intensity. Since very few products or service encounters are flawless, and there is always (literally) a price to pay, we must make mental tradeoffs between the good and bad aspects, and choosing to purchase the same brand or investigate a new one depending on whether our experiences are net positive or negative.

The first place a shopper typically goes in her search for product and brand information is her own memory. For an experienced, knowledgeable consumer, this "internal" search may unearth a treasure trove of information about the array of available product and brand alternatives as well as recollections of occasions when she used the product. These recollections will likely be "tagged" with positive or negative feelings, which may exert a strong influence on the ultimate decision about what to buy next.

For groceries, household supplies, and other products that do not cost much, we may retrieve from our mental shopping list the name of the brand we buy regularly and proceed straight to purchase. For more expensive or important products, an internal search may not give us all the information we need, and so we embark upon an "external" information search. The most important thing to know about external searches is that consumers trust and consult other consumers far more readily and frequently than they do marketers. We will explore this "word of mouth" in Chapter 7. Online information gathering expeditions are increasingly common, yielding an abundance of consumer ratings, reviews, and responses to one another's questions in forums, blog posts, and tweets; on Facebook walls and Pinterest bulletin boards; and in the newest consumer hangouts in cyberspace as you are reading this. Experts' product reviews are also important to many consumers, though less so than user reviews. Examples of expert review sites include *New York Times'* Wirecutter (2022), Techradar (n.d.), and Tripadvisor (which also includes user reviews) (2022).

Usually, our wallets narrow the range of alternatives we can consider purchasing, and we may limit our information search to those brands. How high an auto or mortgage loan will you be able to obtain given your salary, financial assets and liabilities, and FICO score? How much are you willing to pay for your next pair of running shoes? Which features are most important to you? Let's look at an example.

The "minimalist" movement in the running community was at its height in 2012, but it remains an important segment in 2020. Advocates advise runners wear the least amount of shoe needed to protect their feet from hazards they may tread upon. Let's observe 40-year-old Tasha, an avid runner, as she considers buying minimalist shoes. Tasha's goal is enjoyment; she loves communing with

Table 3.1 Top product ratings

	Xero Shoes Speed Force	Vibram FiveFingers KSO EVO	Xero Shoes HFS	Merrell Vapor Glove 5	Softstar Adult DASH RunAmoc
Price	USD 115	105	125	USD 90	USD 140
Overall score	76	75	73	71	70
Star rating	5	5	4.5	4	4.5
Pros	Lightweight, supple, breathable, excellent ground feel, great value	Lightweight, nimble, extremely minimal, moderate price	Versatile, durable, comfortable	Lightweight, sock-like fit, simple	Soft and supple uppers, simple design, thin sole, durable materials
Cons	Less durable, not water resistant	Permeable to water and dust, some may experience friction	Not the lightest, less casual appeal for wearing around town	Less versatile, too minimalist for untrained feet	Less secure fit for aggressive or uneven terrain
Rating (10-point scale)	Xero Shoes Speed Force	Vibram FiveFingers KSO EVO	Xero Shoes HFS	Merrell Vapor Glove 5	Softstar Adult DASH RunAmoc
Natural feel	9	9	8	7	8
Weight	7	9	6	8	7
Traction	6	6	7	7	6
Versatility	7	5	8	7	6
Durability	6	4	6	6	6
Width options	Regular, wide	Regular	Regular	Regular	Narrow, regular, wide

Data compiled from Pierotti, L. (2022, January 3). "Best barefoot shoes for woman of 2022." Outdoor Gear Lab. Retrieved from: https://www.outdoorgearlab.com/topics/shoes-and-boots/best-barefoot-shoes-womens.

nature in Portland's Forest Park and wishes to feel the grass, dirt, and even the occasional pebble under her feet. To achieve her goal, she believes a comfortable fit is the most important brand-use consequence. As she eagerly searches online for information and advice on minimalist running shoe brands, Tasha comes across a brand comparison chart from an outdoor gear review web site. Table 3.1 displays the information she finds.

The Outdoor Gear Lab experts have already tested and rated more than 20 brands on natural feel, weight, traction, versatility, and durability. The chart shows their top five picks. If Tasha is most concerned about the natural feel, she has two top brands to choose from: Xero Speed Force and Vibram Five-Fingers KSO EVO. If, however, she needs a narrow width, her only option is the Softstar Adult DASH RunAmoc. This is an example of the trade-offs we make as we choose what to buy. In our own decision processes, it is helpful to start with the goal(s) of our potential purchase and work backwards to the product-use consequences that we need to achieve the goal(s). User and expert reviews will tell us which product features are most likely to result in those consequences.

Between user and expert reviews, we have more than enough comparative brand information at our fingertips to help us make informed decisions about almost anything we purchase. Some marketing pundits contend that this unprecedented access to information may diminish the effectiveness of "emotional" branding and increase the effectiveness of building a brand based on earning trust by articulating and keeping promises to consumers – promises regarding not only product quality but also policies and practices in matters that affect society and the environment. These include choices of labor and other suppliers, treatment of employees, size of carbon footprint, animal welfare, and numerous other issues, many of which were once outside the purview of marketing and the scrutiny of consumers. According to a recent report by Francis and Hoefel (2018), these company practices and policies are especially important to Generation Z:

> [C]onsumers increasingly expect brands to "take a stand." The point is not to have a politically correct position on a broad range of topics. It is to choose the specific topics (or causes) that make sense for a brand and its consumers and to have something clear to say about those particular issues. In a transparent world, younger consumers don't distinguish between the ethics of a brand, the company that owns it, and its network of partners and suppliers. A company's actions must match its ideals, and those ideals must permeate the entire stakeholder system.

Search, Experience, and Credence Attributes

In the end, even with all the information we can obtain while shopping online or offline, there are some product features we cannot evaluate until we buy and consume a product (or experience a service), and still others that we can never judge directly. Economists who study consumer responses to information distinguish among *search, experience,* and *credence* attributes (we use the words "features" and "attributes" interchangeably). A search attribute is one we can investigate for ourselves while shopping, before we ever decide which brand to purchase. In the example of minimalist running shoes, search attributes include price, style, color, sizing, and materials (if we are in the store). Experience attributes are those that we can evaluate only after we buy and use (consume) a product; while the experts at Outdoor Gear Lab offer us their evaluation of the shoes' traction and durability, this is something the owner and wearer must determine for herself. One likely reason we seek out other consumers' reviews is that they can help us "fill in" experience attributes by imagining ourselves using the product. Credence attributes are those we cannot evaluate for ourselves because we lack either the expertise or the wherewithal to perform the tests needed; instead, we must rely on (give credence to) the words of trusted experts. In our example, the minimalist shoes' barefoot accuracy and versatility are credence attributes. Even if our runner's shoes feel good on the road but not her favorite trail, she cannot know for certain whether the cause is its lack of versatility or something about that trail. The same holds true for barefoot accuracy; regardless of how nearly "barefoot" the shoes feel to the runner, without taking the risk of running barefoot and recording the biomechanics of her running with and without the shoes, she has no way of measuring the extent to which the shoes accurately simulate barefoot running.

A wide range of products are a mix of search, experience, and credence attributes. For example, a teeth-whitening product's price and form are search attributes, its whitening efficacy and rapidity are experience attributes, and any side effects are credence attributes. For meat, the leanness, marbling, and price are search qualities, the taste and texture are experience qualities, and organic and safe (from contaminants) are credence attributes.

As we move from search to experience to credence attributes, we perceive the decision we are making as increasingly risky. The risk arises from uncertainty about being able to make the "right" decision and trepidation about what happens if we make a "wrong" one. The consequences of a bad decision range in severity from fleeting social embarrassment (e.g., when you get a bad haircut – an "experience" service), to catastrophic, as with credence attribute-laden health care choices.

Industry self-monitoring and (especially) government regulation diminish our vulnerability to many hazards associated with credence attributes. Investigative journalism and consumer watchdog organizations provide information on products both regulated and unregulated. Examples of watchdogs include ConsumerLab.com, which conducts independent lab tests on many brands of vitamins, minerals, and other supplements to check for the accuracy of their ingredient listings and for contaminants or unlisted fillers (Consumer Lab, n.d.). The EWG's Skin Deep web site and smartphone app provide information on toxicity of ingredients in a searchable database of more than 70,000 cosmetics and personal care products (Environmental Working Group, 2021b). The scientists in EWG compare brand label and web site information to more than 60 toxicity and regulatory information databases and provide safety ratings of brands and their ingredients. These kinds of resources offer us access to the information we need to make sound purchase decisions, and so reduce credence-attribute-related risks.

Further clarification is provided by web sites such as Greener Choices, which specifies the legal substantiation requirements of terms commonly found on product labels (Greener Choices, 2021). Terms that require substantiation may be considered search attributes, and those that do not are credence attributes. For some labels the legal standards are minimal: a "cage free" chicken, for example, must indeed be uncaged but may legally be kept instead in a dark, crowded space with no exit and little room even to move its limbs. Other labels, such as "Oregon Tilth – Certified Organic" engender high trust because the substantiation standards and auditing practices are stringent (Oregon Tilth, 2022). Many "green" labels require no substantiation, hence describe credence attributes. "No animal testing" and its utopian cousin "cruelty free" may also be evidence-free. "All natural" and "earth friendly" sound bucolic but may describe brands that are neither of those things. Fortunately, there are many watchdog organizations that investigate a wide range of products on the consumer's behalf.

Food safety, that is, freedom from ingredients causing foodborne illnesses, is a credence attribute that presents unique challenges to watchdog organizations because of its varied and often complex causes. The World Health Organization (WHO) reports that foodborne illnesses are common and potentially devastating to communities. They note that each year unsafe food causes 600 million cases of foodborne diseases and 420,000 deaths, and that 30% of the fatalities occur in children under five years of age. WHO further estimates that 33 million years of healthy lives are lost due to eating unsafe food globally each year, and this number is likely an underestimation (World Health Organization, 2021). WHO provides a timely overview of foodborne illnesses:

> Over 200 diseases are caused by eating food contaminated with bacteria, viruses, parasites or chemical substances such as heavy metals. This growing public health problem causes considerable socioeconomic impact though strains on health-care systems lost productivity, and harming tourism and trade. These diseases contribute significantly to the global burden of disease and mortality.
>
> Foodborne diseases are caused by contamination of food and occur at any stage of the food production, delivery and consumption chain. They can result from several forms of environmental contamination including pollution in water, soil or air, as well as unsafe food storage and processing.
>
> Foodborne diseases encompass a wide range of illnesses from diarrhoea to cancers. Most present as gastrointestinal issues, though they can also produce neurological, gynaecological and immunological symptoms. Diseases causing diarrhoea are a major problem in all countries of the world, though the burden is carried disproportionately by low- and middle-income countries and by children under 5 years of age.
>
> (World Health Organization, 2022)

Attributes and Customer Satisfaction

As we demonstrated above, the reason product and brand attributes matter to us is that we infer that they will lead to desirable consequences when we use or consume the product (brand). We expect at least one or two of the consequences to help us achieve a goal or fulfill a core value. If a brand meets our expectations, we will likely be satisfied customers. Does customer satisfaction mean we will purchase the same brand in the future? Not necessarily, but if the brand fails to meet expectations, repeat purchase is far less likely.

The minimalist shoes example shows that attributes vary in their importance to the consumer depending on her needs and goals. Does this mean that we will know all we need to if we simply ask consumers to rate or rank product attributes based on their importance, and in addition obtain their ratings of brands they are considering on those attributes? The answer is no: an attribute's importance to customer satisfaction may change if the brand in question possesses an unusually high or low level of it.

Research on determinants of customer satisfaction by Albayrak and Caber (2014) shows that attributes can relate to customer satisfaction in one of three ways:

1. Basic attributes are minimum standards a brand must possess to enter the marketplace. For a restaurant, cleanliness is a basic attribute. For a surgeon, the requisite medical training and licensures are basic; for a motor vehicle, a working engine and brakes are among the minimum requirements.

    While the presence (or acceptable level) of a basic attribute does not enhance customer satisfaction, its absence or an unacceptably low level is very likely to increase dissatisfaction.
2. Performance attributes have a linear relationship with customer satisfaction. They are typical of brands in the category. For example, satisfaction with a fitness facility has been shown to rise along with perceptions of the workout facility and the classes offered.
3. Excitement attributes are unexpected, and while their absence does not engender dissatisfaction, their presence and magnitude increase customer satisfaction. Examples may include a neck and shoulder massage by a hairdresser, a free glass of wine or cup of tea at a nail salon, and a veterinarian who responds quickly and thoroughly to client inquiries about a companion animal's dietary needs.

Innovative features may start out as excitement attributes, become performance attributes when multiple brands acquire them, and even perhaps sink to the level of basic attributes with the increasingly rapid pace of innovation. A case in point is the camera feature on mobile phones. When first introduced, it was a source of brand differentiation, unexpected and exciting. Now most mobile phones have cameras, and most of the cameras take photos that are higher quality than a rank amateur with an unsteady hand has any right to expect. The presence of a camera on a mobile phone is a basic attribute while the quality of the camera is a performance attribute: as camera quality rises, so does customer satisfaction. (See Zacarias (2020.) for further reading on this phenomenon, which is called the Kano Model.)

The Dimensions of Product Involvement

You may be shaking your head, thinking, "I don't search for all the information or even think much about the attributes of most brands I purchase. So how is this chapter relevant to my consumer behavior?" You would be correct in assuming that the extensive information searches described above do not occur for most products we buy. Your search for brand and production features, ratings, and reviews depends in large part on your level of involvement with the product or brand. And involvement is not a simple construct.

One of the richest and most meaningful methods of defining involvement is the five-dimensional one proposed by Kapferer and Laurent (1993). The authors describe these dimensions as follows:

1. The personal interest a person has in a product category, its personal meaning or importance.
2. The hedonic value of the product, its ability to provide pleasure and enjoyment.
3. The sign value of the product, the degree to which it expresses the person's self.
4. The perceived importance of the potential negative consequences associated with a poor choice of the product (risk importance).
5. The perceived probability of making such a poor choice (risk probability).

Below are the items in the surveys the authors used to measure each dimension:

Interest
   What _____ I buy is extremely important to me.
   I'm really very interested in _____.
       OR
   I couldn't care less about _____.
       OR
   _____ is something which leaves me quite cold.
Pleasure
   I really enjoy buying _____.
   Whenever I buy _____, it's like giving myself a present.
   To me, _____ is quite a pleasure.
       OR
   I quite enjoy _____.
Sign
   You can tell a lot about a person from the _____ he or she buys.
   The _____ a person buys says something about who they are.
   The _____ I buy reflects the sort of person I am.
Risk importance
   It doesn't matter too much if one makes a mistake buying _____.

It's very irritating to buy _____ which isn't right.

I would be annoyed with myself if it turned out I made the wrong choice when buying _____.

Probability of error

When I'm in front of the _____ section, I always feel rather unsure about what to pick.

When you buy _____, you can never be quite sure it was the right choice or not.

Choosing a _____ is rather difficult.

When you buy a _____, you can never be quite certain you've made the right choice.

While the dimensions of interest and pleasure are sometimes highly correlated, they are not identical. The authors, who are French, found that among their countrymen and women, champagne and chocolate gift boxes elicited moderate levels of interest and little pleasure. Both are popular ritual gifts for dinner party hosts, bosses, etc. Chocolate bars, on the other hand, evoked little interest but high levels of pleasure. In other words, our levels of interest and pleasure in a product may vary with purchase occasion and recipient, that is, as a reward or treat for oneself.

In the running shoe example above, in what sense might Tasha be highly involved in her purchase of minimalist running shoes? Her goal is enjoyment and so she expects to derive pleasure from a shoe that fits well. This author would also argue that the risk importance Tasha perceives may be higher than Kapferer and Laurent's survey items could indicate, given their phrasing. If Tasha ends up running in minimalist shoes that are wrong for her, she could injure herself even while enjoying the experience of running in them. In short, Tasha's extensive information search may be a result of her high involvement, specifically on the dimensions of pleasure (reflecting her goal) and risk importance (associated with the prospect of injury and outlay of money). If, on the days she runs with her husband, she cares about how the shoes look to him and to others, we could posit that the sign dimension of the shoes may also be prominent in her decision process.

We can relate the "probability of error" dimension of involvement to search, experience, and credence attributes. A product with mostly search attributes may be thoroughly researched prior to purchase; hence, the consumer would likely perceive a low probability of error in that instance. As for "experience" products, user reviews and stories may do much to reduce the consumer's perception of error probability. But for "credence" products and services, many of which are purchased to meet health- and finance-related goals, the perceived probability of error will likely be much higher, and the risk importance high as well. (It is much more than annoying to choose the wrong neurosurgeon.) Investor and patient ratings and reviews can give us a sense of how the service provider interacts with people, and an education and employment history may impress us (or not), but outcomes are all-important.

What do Kapferer and Laurent's dimension of involvement reveal about the myriad low-priced items we buy routinely, for example, household items, health and beauty aids, and food? While many such products may bring us pleasure (food), fun and enjoyment (cosmetics), and self-respect (household cleansers, etc.), most of us do not find them compellingly interesting. In addition, because they cost little compared to many purchases we make (e.g., motor vehicles, apparel and shoes, recreational equipment, houses), our perception of risk importance is relatively low. Most such products will not cause us harm. But there are notable exceptions, as we have seen from the increasingly frequent recalls of fresh produce, meat, and packaged goods. In short, we would expect most of our routine purchases to be relatively "low involvement," given that they would likely receive low ratings on most if not all five dimensions.

On the other hand, among consumers who have the wherewithal to research and buy organically produced food, involvement in these products may show an increase on the risk importance dimension due to the potential toxicity of pesticides commonly used in nonorganic food production. The article below weighs the benefits and costs of consuming organic versus nonorganic food:

HEALTH TIPS APRIL 05, 2019

Are organic foods really healthier? Two pediatricians [Dean Blumberg and Lena Rothstein] break it down.

What does it mean for food to be organic?

The U.S. Department of Agriculture defines organic as crops that are produced on farms that have not used most synthetic pesticides herbicides or fertilizer for three years before harvesting the food. There needs to be a significant buffer zone to decrease contamination from adjacent farm lands. Farms also have to be free from any genetic engineering, ionizing radiation or sewage sludge (yuck). And as it relates to livestock, animals must be fed organic feed, live on organic land and be raised without routine antibiotics or hormones.

Free range doesn't mean organic; it just means animals weren't kept in such small enclosures. Also, the "natural" label on food means there's no artificial flavoring or color ingredients, but that doesn't mean it's organic or free of pesticides.

Why are organic foods often so much more expensive than conventionally grown produce and meat?

On average, organic foods cost 50% more than their conventionally produced counterparts. This is largely because farmers have to pay close attention to their cultivation practices. Pests, weeds and diseases must be managed by physical, mechanical and biological controls instead of pesticides. When it comes to meat and dairy products, animals that are not raised organic are often given growth hormones that increase milk production and steroids that help promote growth, yielding more meat. Increased meat and milk production means farmers don't have to charge as much because they have more to sell.

Is organic food more nutritious than regular food?

Organic foods are not healthier, per se, in terms of nutrients. You are still getting the same benefits in conventionally grown foods as you are in organic foods.

What is organic milk? Is organic milk healthier than regular milk?

Organic milk has the same protein, mineral, lipid and vitamin content as normal milk. Nonorganic milk typically has growth hormones, which are specific to each species. So, drinking milk with bovine growth hormone, which is degraded by stomach acid, has no physiological impact on humans.

Is it safe to buy nonorganic meat?

Sex steroids like estrogen may be given to cattle to increase meat yield, making production more efficient for farmers. However, the sex steroid levels are extremely low. Treated and untreated cattle have about the same level of sex steroids. It is possible that when combined with other sex steroids, certain people can be susceptible to harm.

Antibiotics can also be used to promote growth in livestock. They are similar to those used in humans but are not meant to treat health issues. This use of antibiotics increases the development of drug-resistant bacteria, which can be transmitted to humans, making it harder to treat infections.

What effects can pesticides have on children? Can they have effects on adults?

Increased exposure to pesticides can lead to increased risk of ADHD and autism. It is also linked to reduced cognitive skills, ability to learn and memory. Exposure to pesticides may lead to the development of Parkinson's disease, fertility issues and cognitive decline later in life. There is also a potential link between cancer and pesticides. In 2015, the International Agency for Research on Cancer classified three common pesticides as carcinogenic. The primary exposure in humans was through diet.

Overall, is it better to eat organic?

Organic diets we know lead to less pesticide and antibiotic exposure, but nutritionally, they are about the same. In addition, there's no evidence of clinically relevant differences between organic and conventional milk. There isn't a concrete study that proves organic foods lead to healthier children. But eating organic is an advantage since we know pesticides can lead to neurodevelopmental issues and are strongly associated with cancer.

Should you buy all organic produce? Or are there some fruits and vegetables that are OK to buy nonorganic?

Avocados, cantaloupe, pineapple, broccoli, cabbage and corn have low levels of pesticides, so there's no real need to buy organic. In contrast, strawberries, spinach, grapes, apples, tomatoes and celery have high levels of pesticide residues. If you want to get the most bang for your buck on produce, frozen veggies can be cheaper than fresh, and they are very similar in quality.

(UC Davis Health, 2019)

Think about this decision in terms of MEC theory. The consumer's goals or values underlying food purchases may vary depending on her life stage and family composition, her beliefs regarding environmental toxins, her finances, and myriad other factors. Every purchase decision, even one that is seemingly simple and routine, is the outcome of the interplay among usage and purchase contexts, consumer traits and mindset, and the marketing of brands jostling for space in the consumer's mind and heart.

References

Albayrak, T., & Caber, M. (2014). "Symmetric and asymmetric influences of service attributes: The case of fitness clubs". *Managing Leisure, 19*(5), 307–320. https://doi.org/10.1080/13606719.2014.885711.

Cane, M. (2011, June 8). "Steve Jobs insult response" [Video]. YouTube. Retrieved from: https://youtu.be/FF-tKLISfPE.

Consumer Lab (2022). "Independent tests and reviews of vitamin, mineral, and herbal supplements". Retrieved from: www.consumerlab.com/.

Environmental Working Group (2021a). "The trouble with ingredients in sunscreens". Retrieved from: www.ewg.org/sunscreen/report/the-trouble-with-sunscreen-chemicals/.

Environmental Working Group (n.d.). "Personal care products safety act (S.1113) summary". Retrieved from: www.ewg.org/sites/default/files/u352/Personal%20Care%20Products%20Safety%20Act%20%28S.1113%29%20Summary%20.pdf?_ga=2.48994400.751733693.1621459512-867849936.1621459512.

Environmental Working Group (2021b). "EWG's skin deep". Retrieved from: https://www.ewg.org/skindeep/contents/about-page/.

Francis, T., & Hoefel, F. (2018, November 12). "'True Gen': Generation Z and its implications for companies". McKinsey & Company. Retrieved from: www.mckinsey.com/industries/consumer-packaged-goods/our-insights/true-gen-generation-z-and-its-implications-for-companies.

Greener Choices (2021). "Greener choices: Food and living safety and sustainability". Retrieved from: https://www.greenerchoices.org/.

Kahle, L. R., & Kennedy, P. (1988). "Using the list of values (LOV) to understand consumers". *Journal of Services Marketing, 2*(4), 49–56. https://doi.org/10.1108/eb024742.

Kapferer, J.-N., & Laurent, G. (1993). "Further evidence on the consumer involvement profile: Five antecedents of involvement". *Psychology and Marketing, 10*(4), 347–355. https://doi.org/10.1002/mar.4220100408.

Lippert, B. (2017, September 28). "Classic ad review: Listerine and the halitosis hallelujah." Ad Age. Retrieved from: https://adage.com/article/classic-ad-review/listerine-halitosis-hallel/310647.

Oregon Tilth (2022). "Oregon tilth: Organic certification & sustainable agriculture". Retrieved from: https://tilth.org/.

Pierotti, L. (2022, January 3). "Best barefoot shoes for woman of 2022". Outdoor Gear Lab. Retrieved from: https://www.outdoorgearlab.com/topics/shoes-and-boots/best-barefoot-shoes-womens.

Rokeach, M. (1973). *The Nature of Human Values*. , New York, NY: Free Press.

TechRadar (n.d.). "The source for tech buying advice". Retrieved from: www.techradar.com/.

Tripadvisor (2022). "Hotels: Cheap hotel deals on Tripadvisor". Retrieved from: www.tripadvisor.com/.

UC Davis Health (2019, April 5). "Are organic foods really healthier? Two pediatricians break it down". Retrieved from: https://health.ucdavis.edu/blog/good-food/are-organic-foods-really-healthier-two-pediatricians-break-it-down/2019/04.

Wirecutter (2022). "New product reviews, deals, and buying advice". Retrieved from: www.nytimes.com/wirecutter/.

World Health Organization (2021). "Estimating the burden of foodborne diseases". Retrieved from: www.who.int/activities/estimating-the-burden-of-foodborne-diseases.

World Health Organization (2022). "Foodborne diseases". Retrieved from: www.who.int/health-topics/foodborne-diseases.

Zacarias, D. (2020). "The complete guide to the Kano Model". Retrieved from: https://foldingburritos.com/blog/kano-model.

Zhou, X., Funk, D. C., Lu, L., & Kunkel, T. (2020). "Solving the athleisure myth: A means-end chain analysis of female activewear consumption". *Journal of Sport Management, 35*(1), 1–13. https://doi.org/10.1123/jsm.2019-0358.

4 The Consumer's Journey

Objectives

1. To describe and illustrate the steps consumers take on their purchase decision journeys.
2. To explore how the journey is shaped by the product and its marketing.
3. To illustrate how a marketer, consumer advocate, or the consumer herself can use knowledge about the purchase decision journey to achieve a positive outcome.

From Decision Process to Consumer Journey

The traditional model of the purchase decision process is a funnel (BMT Micro, 2016), like that shown in Figure 4.1, in which the consumer progressively narrows the number of brand alternatives down to the one she purchases. The funnel starts out wide, encompassing all the brands the consumer is aware of, usually through a combination of marketing (advertising, salespeople, etc.) and non-marketing sources (friends, coworkers, expert reviews, etc.). When the consumer recognizes that she has a need for a product (e.g., "I'm out of yogurt," "I've got to get this red wine stain out of my blouse," "I need to buy a gift for my friend's birthday") she immediately thinks of the brands she is *aware* of. If the product she needs is "low involvement," that is, an inexpensive habitual purchase like most groceries and household supplies, the next step would be a trip to the supermarket. If, on the other hand, the consumer is seeking something more expensive, interesting, or important – a new washer or dryer, another car, a dress or suit for an important occasion, a special gift – she takes steps to learn more about the most promising brands of which she is aware, *familiarizing* herself with their qualities (aka attributes, features) vis-à-vis her needs. Armed with this information, she can now eliminate any brands that do not have the features she seeks; the handful of brands left become her *consideration set*, from which she chooses and *purchases* the best alternative. If the brand performs as she expects it to, she might become a *loyal* customer, repurchasing that brand when she needs a replacement.

DOI: 10.4324/9780367426897-5

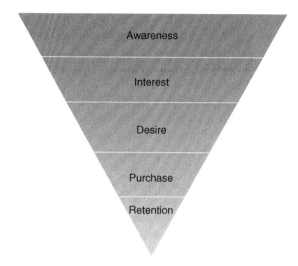

Figure 4.1 Consumer decision funnel.

The funnel is a useful metaphor for many purchases. However, consumers can now obtain all the product information they need or want anytime, anywhere with their mobile digital devices. This ability to get information "on demand" has three important implications for consumer behavior:

1. We may become aware of more – and newer – brands at any stage in the decision process, dramatically changing the shape of the funnel in unpredictable ways.
2. Many consumers routinely track products in which they have an interest even when they are not ready to make a purchase; this means that when they do decide to buy, they may already know which brand they want.
3. Access to reviews by both experts and users diminishes consumers' dependence on – and susceptibility to – marketing information sources such as ads, company or brand web sites, and salespeople.

Given the many and varied sources of product information at consumers' fingertips, it is evermore essential that marketers, consumer advocates, and consumer researchers go beyond the traditional model of the decision process to explore more deeply the consumer's entire experience with a brand, starting with her first encounter with the product or a message about it and ending with her telling friends about it or perhaps starting over with a repurchase of the same brand. A journey map documents the consumer's encounters and experiences with a brand over time. The journey may be nonlinear (e.g., jumping from brand awareness straight to purchase) and include backtracking (e.g., purchasing and returning an unsatisfactory brand). It shows the consumer's behaviors, thoughts, and feelings during every phase of the experience, and incorporates *touchpoints* – interactions with the brand.

Marketer-provided touchpoints include the product itself, one-way messages such as ads, web sites, and packaging; consumer-marketer interactions, for example, telephone conversations, live chats, or email exchanges; and contexts of brand encounters-product placements in movies or TV programs and, of course, retail settings. Non-marketer touchpoints include expert and user reviews, conversations among consumers, and contexts such as a friend's home or a consumer-created YouTube video. For example, many people make and upload videos of themselves "unboxing" new electronic product purchases.

Why go to all the trouble and expense of doing the consumer research required for creating a journey map? The answer is simple: to figure out how we can enhance the consumer's experiences with our brand. Do we need to add a how-to video to our web site? Should we add a touchpoint to reassure or check in with a consumer after purchase? Does our automated reorder system work smoothly or does it have minor glitches that drive easily frustrated consumers onto a competitor's site? Can consumers consult our web site to supplement and enrich their experience in our bricks-and-mortar store?

Consumer advocates can also learn much from mapping the consumer journey. For example, to "demarket" tobacco to teens, it would be helpful to track their cognitive, affective, and behavioral responses to events that trigger smoking during a typical day; then, those responses could be targeted for reshaping to produce healthier outcomes.

Mapping the Consumer's Journey

Here we describe two versions of the journey based on extensive consumer research in developed as well as developing economies (Hritzuk et al., 2013). One version, shown in Figure 4.2, is for "considered" high-involvement (electronics) purchases and the other, which we will discuss later, is for "habitual" low-involvement purchases (personal and home care products). We chose these journey maps because they are research-based, intuitive, and applicable to a wide range of products.

Considered Pathway

Stage 1: Open to Possibility

This mindset encompasses our awareness of available brands and our associated thoughts and feelings, many of which we may have accumulated over time. Tracking products even when we do not intend to make a purchase shows that we are in this state of mind. We are most likely to do this when we have a high

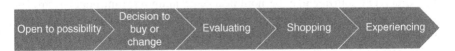

Figure 4.2 Considered pathway to purchase.

level of personal interest in the product category. (Remember our discussion of consumer involvement in Chapter 3?) While we may access company information sources, we have greater trust in non-marketing media offering expert reviews (e.g., techradar, Consumer Reports) and even more trust in user reviews. A recent series of experiments demonstrated that "positive reviews, factual reviews, and reviews appearing on social networks lead to perceptions of greater benevolence, ability, and integrity (all dimensions of trustworthiness) than negative reviews, emotional reviews, and reviews appearing on retailer sites, respectively" (Dong et al., 2019).

Stage 2: Decision to Buy or Change

Usually we can pinpoint what triggers us to switch into shopping or buying mode. The most common triggers of the decision to buy or change a considered product are the malfunctioning of the consumer's current model, a change in circumstance that necessitates an upgrade or first purchase in a product category, and learning about a new model via marketing or through *word of mouth* (other people).

While consumers may not trust marketers' product claims, they often find new product announcements intriguing enough to investigate further. Apple has repeatedly moved consumers into the decision process with its beautifully and intuitively designed innovations showcased in compelling videos.

Stage 3: Evaluating (aka Messy Middle, According to Google Researchers)

The consumer may already know which brand and model she wants based on the information she has acquired during the "open to possibility" stage of the journey. Usually, however, for complex, high-involvement purchases, she seeks more information but with greater focus on her own specific needs and wants. Interactive buying guides and expert reviews that offer detailed brand comparisons are especially useful at this stage, as are reviews by users who purchased the product for purposes similar to those of the shopper.

While this stage may require significant time and effort, many shoppers enjoy the process. Rennie and Protheroe, of Google's research team, give us an idea about the sources of the enjoyment: this stage is not merely about comparing brand features systematically and unemotionally. It also involves exploration, which many of us find enjoyable:

> In our model, between the twin poles of trigger and purchase, sits the messy middle… a space of abundant information and unlimited choice that shoppers have learned to manage using a range of cognitive shortcuts…[I]n [the messy middle], consumers loop between exploring and evaluating the options available to them until they are ready to purchase….Consumers explore their options and expand their knowledge and consideration sets, then – either sequentially or simultaneously – they evaluate the options and narrow down

their choices. For certain categories, only a brief time might be required moving between these modes, while habitual and impulse purchases may bypass the loop altogether. But other purchases, typically more complex, encourage or even oblige us to engage in lengthy exploration, generating a healthy number of options to evaluate.

(Rennie & Protheroe, 2020)

According to eMarketer reporter Cramer-Flood (2021), global retail ecommerce sales grew a whopping 27.6% in 2020. Ecommerce sales had been rising steadily for several years, but the pandemic-caused shelter-in-place orders and store closures accelerated growth. Along with greater reliance on digital media, we see that consumers' use of search has increased in range and complexity. Increasingly, we are searching for "ideas" about how to accomplish our goals rather than simply brand names or features. For example, we might search for "ideas for remodeling the kitchen" or "ideas for what to do in Jamaica." We are also more frequently asking Google to explain the "difference between" two related products, especially in the food category:

> Food – and new food trends in particular – can often be a source of confusion for consumers. So it's not surprising that we often ask Google to explain the "difference between" two products.
>
> For example, we ask for help understanding the differences between pairs of related items: cappuccino and latte, lager and beer, gelato and ice cream, baking powder and baking soda, sultanas and raisins, fromage frais and creme fraiche, whisky and bourbon, vegetarian and vegan, champagne and prosecco, cacao and cocoa, paella and risotto.
>
> (Rennie & Protheroe, 2020)

These searches reflect exploration rather than evaluation. What makes this stage the "messy middle" is that consumers often toggle repeatedly between product exploration and brand evaluation, as we "seek out inspiration, research product details, consider reviews, and compare prices" (Taniguchi, 2021).

Where do consumers search? While search engines have become the most used and useful touchpoint in purchase journey, in-store browsing, word of mouth, and brand websites/apps are also rated as highly useful, as are touchpoints that offer guidance and comparisons (e.g., salespeople, review, and comparison sites). Marketers can enhance consumer satisfaction with and enjoyment of digital searches in the following ways:

- Include on the company web site and apps ideas, knowledge, emotionally engaging content, and opportunities for people to interact with the brand and other consumers in meaningful ways. In means-end chain (MEC) terms, go beyond brand features and show consumers that your company understands and supports their overarching goals. Here are examples from companies that are masters at connecting meaningfully with consumers in the "messy middle":

Nike recently enhanced its app by adding creative services, such as foot scanning technology. This tool helps customers find the right shoe from the comfort of their home. The feature decreases potential returns, saving retailers money, and allows them to re-allocate employee time to other areas of the business.

- Show up in user-friendly ways in consumer searches.
- Bear in mind that offline (e.g., in-store, word of mouth) touchpoints remain important. Consumers seek useful ideas and information both online and offline. We are goal-driven, not media-focused or brand- or product-driven.

Stage 4: Shopping

Many consumers do all or most of their brand research and evaluation using on-line resources and visit stores only when they have narrowed their consideration set to a very few brands or decided on one. These consumers do not wish to linger or browse, but rather focus on the item(s) of interest, and once they have scrutinized and selected an alternative and completed a final price check, they seek an efficient purchase experience from a reputable retailer that offers extended warranties and full refunds for returns.

Consumers also do the opposite, treating bricks-and-mortar stores as showrooms in which to browse and learn about alternatives and completing their purchases online. To attract these consumers, bricks-and-mortar retailers should collaborate with the brands they carry to create displays that are fun, engaging, and informative, inviting consumers to explore the products tactilely and visually and providing all the facts they need in order to make a wise purchase decision. In Chapter 5, we will explore how retailers can engage and inform consumers using sensory marketing tactics.

Increasing numbers of consumers who are comfortable gathering information, evaluating brands, and shopping and purchasing online have never set foot into a store for many of their purchases. For these consumers, an efficient checkout process, free or very low-priced shipping, and the ability to return a product for a full refund are essential, as are rapid, respectfully delivered resolutions to problems or answers to questions, pre- and post-purchase.

Stage 5: Experiencing

During this stage of the journey for considered purchases, the consumer is discovering what it is like to live with the product over weeks and months or years for motor vehicles, houses, large appliances, a college education, and other important and infrequent purchases. The experience stage is, in other words, a process rather than a discrete event, and it may have many ups and downs. For example, new vehicle buyers typically feel joy at owning and using a car they have likely wanted or needed for some time, but the "new car" feeling wears off over time, to be replaced by (dis)satisfaction with the vehicle's performance and reliability.

The quality of a consumer's post purchase experience depends on her expectations about the product compared with its performance. This means that marketers should manage people's expectations. Research suggests that smartphone makers may be marketing the devices in a manner that raises consumers' expectations to unrealistic levels, thus magnifying their frustration during the experience stage (Advertising Research Foundation, 2012). The consumer's post purchase experience is now as public as she wishes it to be and exerts considerable influence over the purchase decisions of others.

Many companies seek to enhance the consumer's brand-use experience and to increase customer loyalty by offering meaningful opportunities to engage with the brand and other like-minded customers:

> Nike has multiple apps that offer different products and services to consumers, including the Nike app, the brand's ecommerce hub, Nike SNKRS, an app for Nike sneakerheads, and fitness apps Nike Run Club and Nike Training Club (NTC).
>
> (Cavill, 2021)

If our post-purchase experience is negative, we may elect to "undo" our purchase decision. We have become conditioned to expect to be able to return most products for a full refund. When consumers first started buying online, it felt risky to do so. We were basing our purchase decisions on pictures and descriptions that might prove inaccurate. Our purchases could be the wrong size or color, or have defects, or simply fall short of our expectations. Only when e-tailers instituted liberal return policies did consumers feel comfortable purchasing a wide variety of products online.

While return policies are essential to gaining customer loyalty and building reputation, they may be costly in terms of shipping and unloading inventory that may have to go to off-price channels:

> You often see that something gets delivered, and it's not what you expected, and the retailer says, "Oh, just keep it." In my case, they said, "We'll give you half off if you keep it." We said, "No, we don't want it at all. Come and take it back." Obviously, they did not want to take it back because they didn't know what they were going to do with it. This was a piece of furniture. But by the time you take it out of the crate, can you get it back in one piece? So, the return journey is difficult for retailers.
>
> (Knowledge@Wharton, 2020a)

Is the ease of returning merchandise changing the consumer journey? Wharton professor Thomas Robertson says it is:

Figure 4.3 Habitual pathway to purchase.

> [I]n this new world of returns, we're finding that the purchase decision that you think is made in-store may actually be made at home. At that point, the consumer studies the merchandise and either keeps it or returns it or exchanges it. Retailers are now recognizing that there's often this stage—at least 10% of the time—in the purchase journey. In some product categories, it's more than 10% of the time.

Robertson suggests that retailers develop better analytics to assign individual customers "risk of return" scores. If someone returns "too much," the retailer could deny them returns or cancel their accounts, as Amazon has done on occasion (Molina, 2018).

Now we turn to the consumer journey for habitual purchases, shown in Figure 4.3.

Habitual Purchases

Note that the stages for the habitual purchase pathway are fundamentally the same as those for the considered pathway, but they are ordered differently and involve different consumer activities and mindsets. According to the Microsoft research that is the basis for the purchase journeys we are presenting, the stages of the habitual path to purchase may be described as follows:

> *Open to possibility*: Unlike more considered purchase journeys, such as auto shopping, habitual journeys are typically triggered by the need to replenish a specific product or set of products. The 'Open to Possibility' moment comes later in the journey, and can 'slide in' prompted by a coupon, an ad, word-of-mouth or inspiration at the shelf.
>
> *Decision to buy or change*: For habitual purchases in developed markets, the trigger to buy or change a product happens most frequently when a consumer runs out of the existing product; however, in emerging markets, the trigger to buy or change is frequently driven by the desire for a newer item, word-of-mouth or when the consumer has seen an ad.
>
> *Evaluating*: Habitual consumers spend some time preparing for their trip at this stage; they typically make a list and select the store they will visit, but generally don't complete extensive research before getting into the store.
>
> *Shopping*: Most habitual shoppers still prefer to buy items in store. In the retail environment, their decision-making is influenced by deals, packaging

and the more tactile attributes of the product at the shelf, such as scent, product look and feel, and in-store samples. Habitual shoppers will typically complete their list and then enjoy a little browsing and 'me time' in-store. This where consumers find the most enjoyment.

Experiencing: In the final stage of the journey, habitual shoppers use their products at home, and seek to validate their choice via their own experience with the product, as well as what's fed back to them from others.

(Hritzuk et al., 2013)

Most habitual purchases are products we literally use up – food, household supplies, personal care products. We don't think about these products until we need them (remember "Got Milk?") and most of us do not gather information on them outside the store setting (or retailer web site). This means we start the pathway by using (experiencing) the product and running out of it triggers the decision to buy or change.

Many consumers make an actual or mental list of the items they need and may look for coupons before they go to the store, but they evaluate and shop for the products in the store (or on the web site) while standing in front of the physical or virtual shelf gazing at alternatives. This is when they are most likely to be open to possibility in the form of in-store samples, promotions, and displays, as well as their own recollection of a word-of-mouth recommendation (e.g., a friend mentioned she loves Bounty paper towels), an ad ("Bounty – the quicker picker-upper!"), a brand name, or a package. This means in-store marketing is essential for habitually purchased items.

The cost of trying a new or unfamiliar brand is low for habitual purchases – perhaps a few dollars and very little time evaluating and shopping – and many shoppers continue browsing after they find everything on their list. This is double-edged for marketers: on the one hand, a promotion or special display may persuade consumers to try a new brand, but on the other, earning and maintaining customers' loyalty to a brand is increasingly difficult even if the brand's performance exceeds consumers' expectations.

The COVID-19 pandemic has accelerated consumers' migration to shopping online for goods that are most likely to be habitually purchased: consumer packaged goods (CPGs) which include groceries, health and beauty products, and household supplies. Market research firm IRI reports that loyalty programs play an increasingly important role in consumers' store choices and shopping behavior:

"In 2020, we saw an economic slowdown and unprecedented shifts in consumer behavior, but there are opportunities for nimble and creative CPG retailers and manufacturers to drive loyalty in 2021," said Joan Driggs, vice president of Content and Thought Leadership, IRI. "Our Q1 2021 Consumer Connect survey focuses on loyalty programs, and we found that retailers and manufacturers that embrace and enhance loyalty programs as well as continue giving consumers multiple options for making purchases, such as online ordering or click-and-collect, can improve their chances of capturing consumers' attention and allegiance."

...Overwhelmingly, when asked their reason for obtaining a shopper loyalty card or reward membership, 74% of respondents cited free sign-up as the driving factor. Other reasons given for signing up for a shopper loyalty card or rewards membership included discounts for gas (56%), the ability to spend points (55%) and cash rewards (39%). Consumers were less moved by offerings such as access to new products (13%) or a mobile checkout capability (12%).

Benefits Influence Membership, and Membership Influences Which Stores to Shop When deciding where to shop, 51% of respondents cited shopper loyalty programs as somewhat influential, followed by 22% who said it was extremely influential. Personalization also is a key to consumer loyalty, with 85% of respondents wanting to select their own benefits and rewards, and more than 70% wanting to personalize the way they earn based on their purchases or preferences.

Successful Loyalty Program

From easy, intuitive sign-up to delivering tangible value, loyalty programs have the potential to fulfill their mission of creating and maintaining loyalty. Successful programs remain dynamic, increasing personalization while ensuring the safety and integrity of members' personal information.

(Hughes, 2021)

Customer Journeys and Opportunities for Marketers

In sum, both the considered and the habitual paths to purchase offer the following opportunities for marketers:

1. Place new products in the hands of influencers who connect emotionally with your target consumers. According to Gopi Kallayil, Chief Evangelist, Brand Marketing at Google:

   One of the traditional ways of building your brand was through celebrity endorsements—the voices and faces of Serena Williams, J Lo, and Tyra Banks. But a band of new influencers—the neofluencers as I like to call them—has emerged on the internet with unprecedented power and reach.

   In Mexico City, I was backstage at the YouTube Brandcast event, waiting for my turn to speak, when I met YuYa, a 26-year-old woman from Mexico City who creates beauty and makeup tutorials for YouTube in Spanish. YuYa has a powerful influence upon audiences in the Spanish-speaking world interested in that topic. She has 24 million subscribers and her makeup videos have been viewed more than 2 billion times. If you're a beauty brand launching a new product in the Spanish-speaking world, you have to leverage the power that neofluencers like YuYa wield. Across different categories, it's neofluencers like Marcus Brown Lee, Sofia Nysgaard, Harry Wong, and Lukas

Marques and Daniel Molo who will establish your brand in the minds of the massive audiences they can influence. Ryan ToysReview—which was just recently rebranded to Ryan's World—is a family-run channel, but the star of the show is 8-year-old Ryan Kaji, who generated $22 million in revenue in a single year.

(Knowledge@Wharton, 2020a)

2. Create compelling and cutting-edge content for the brand web site, social media, and YouTube channels, and develop product displays for bricks-and-mortar retail settings that are fun and engaging as well as informative. These will attract consumers open to the possibility to learn about the brand and to enjoy interacting with it.

3. Include on the brand web site complete and honest comparisons with competitors' brands to facilitate consumers' evaluations and to build credibility and good will. While in the store, a shopper should be able to access product and company information online – price, features, company labor practices – anything the shopper wants to know should be at her fingertips. Remember that by helping a consumer choose wisely, you are decreasing the likelihood of a return with its associated shipping and restocking expenses.

4. An app has become as essential as a web site. App customers compared to non-app customers are more loyal to the brand, spending more, buying more frequently, and buying more items (Mohsin & Abujoub, 2020).

The Google Insight Team has found that apps may be used to benefit both the company and the customer:

Traditionally, retailers relied on in-store returns, phone calls, and emails to address customer complaints. This often resulted in long queues or wait times, causing negative sentiment amongst consumers. While there has been an increase in live chats on websites, solving a customer service issue through your mobile app can be even more efficient.

Using your app to interact with customers will also allow you to aggregate customer data and spot trends more quickly. A McKinsey study shows that through machine learning and tracking of activity on an app, companies can predict which issues their clients are most likely to face, reducing the need for lengthy interactions.

(Mohsin & Abujoub, 2020)

In addition, retailers can use apps to manage order volumes more efficiently, reduce wait times, notify customers when they are next in line, and allow them to reserve a product in advance. And they can use apps in innovative ways like Nike did with its foot-scanning technology, discussed previously. Such tools help customers find the right shoe without having to leave home, and they are less likely to return the shoes they order.

Apps can also be used in-store to deliver coupons that the customer can scan on multiple purchase occasions. And they can facilitate the purchase experience with technology that enables customers to scan items as they add them to their basket, pay via the app, and leave the store without interacting with an employee if that is their preference.

5.   Make it easy for consumers to switch seamlessly between the brand's online and offline shopping and purchasing channels, ensuring that consumers have a pleasant and efficient purchase experience whether they gather information online and make the purchase in a store or learn about products by browsing in stores and make the purchase online:

From coffee shops to travel to cosmetics, brands that are forming a deep emotional connection with consumers are removing friction from the consumer journey by leveraging the latest technology. The Starbucks app, Booking. com's three-click room booking and the Sephora Virtual Artist are examples in each of these categories.

(Knowledge@Wharton, 2020b)

Wharton professor and retail strategy expert Barbara Kahn observes that China far surpasses the US in delivering a frictionless omnichannel experience to consumers:

There are a couple [of differences] that stand out. One is this notion of new retailing—and you see it with Alibaba. They've opened up these physical stores called Hema in China, and they are fully integrated omnichannel experiences. You go into that store. It's a frictionless payment process. You can pay on your phone easily. You can have a real-time customer experience there, buy fresh fish, do whatever you want. But the store also serves as a distribution center. If you buy online, you'll see automation picking out products, delivering products. Part of the store is set up for the distribution channel. When you order online, anything can be distributed within a certain radius of 30 minutes, so you can either go into the store, buy something there or order online, have it delivered, and pick it up in the store. This blurring between what's online and what's physical retail is complete. It's completely integrated, and the physical retail shows that.

The other thing that's big in China is this idea of "shoppertainment" and the importance of key opinion leaders and now even "key opinion customers," where you have these massive influencers who spend time on video blogs and live streaming, and they authentically sell out products. They have incredibly loyal consumers or followers who watch what they do on their videos, and a lot of shopping is through this live streaming event.

China is also way ahead of the U.S. on frictionless payment. There are two big payment streams there, either WeChat or Alipay, which is 90% of the transactions in China. They are completely independent universes, but these payment systems are Uber apps. It's not only that you can pay, but you can also order a car. You can access social media. You can pay attention to the shoppertainment. All of this is done in one app, and that integrates all of these processes into this seamless retailing experience. We'll start to see some of that come to the U.S.

(Knowledge@Wharton, 2021)

6. Make sure all marketer-controlled touchpoints – online and offline – communicate a consistent brand message:

Today, a brand is shaped by every digital surface it shows up on, every way it behaves and everything said about the brand on digital—often by those the brand doesn't know and hasn't authorized to speak about their product or service, let alone having carefully curated their comments. So, the consumer experience of the brand could be shaped by the brand's website or app (the only two things the brand fully controls on digital), or by a flattering review by a neofluencer or a scathing commentary by a consumer who had a bad experience with the brand and is now free not to tell just 10 of her friends but an audience of 10,000.

To succeed in this world, brands have to show up consistently across all the touch points that the consumer may access to explore or experience the brand. For example, Nike has a simple and elegant brand message—"If you have a body, you are an athlete." Put on Nike gear and "Just Do It." The company works hard to make sure that consumers experience this message consistently, whether they walk into a Nike store, visit the website or watch an inspiring video on their YouTube channel about athletes who defied failure. Nike orchestrates a consistent brand message across all its touch points.

(Knowledge@Wharton, 2020b)

7. Enhance consumers' post purchase experiences by not promising performance the brand cannot deliver in ordinary usage contexts, offering personalized (not rigidly and obviously scripted) customer support online and via telephone, providing readily accessible classes, videos, and other training on how to make the most of multifeatured products, reminding the customer when the product needs service or a tune-up if applicable, and checking in with the consumer to find out how things are going with their new purchase.

8. Respect consumers' choices:

If the brand's message is of no value, the consumer has no hesitation in swiping them into oblivion. Fortunately, there are now technology-based solutions that allow brands to talk to consumers based on their interests, passions or some self-expressed signal indicating they're interested in the brand or its category.

Similarly, consumers are increasingly vocal about privacy. They're making choices about the information brands can gather, how long it can be kept and if these brands can use that information to target them. And consumer choices on these topics are as varied as humans are. Some consumers are willing to self-declare that they're buying a new home and are open to receiving brand messages relevant to home buyers. Other are declaring that buying a new home is none of a brand's business, and when they need products and services, they'll come talk to the brand at a time and place of their choosing.

(Knowledge@Wharton, 2020b)

Moments of Truth in the Consumer's Journey

Welcome to the moment of truth…a series of four stages where customers take actions that move them toward or away from you.

(Solis, 2013a, p. 61)

We've described the purchase journey from the consumer's perspective, exploring what s/he thinks and feels as well as how s/he behaves at each stage. A marketer may view these same stages as moments of truth (MOTs), so named because they are critical junctures for a brand; amassed over many consumers' journeys, they determine whether the brand survives and if it does, how healthy it becomes. As we will see, the four MOTs roughly correspond with the five stages of the consumer's journey.

Zero Moment of Truth (ZMOT)

Originally, the ZMOT referred to "the few minutes before people buy, where impressions are formed and the path to purchase begins" (Solis, 2013a, p. 63). Before the internet, those minutes were spent either in the store, perusing packages, or with a friend or neighbor who is singing the praises – or bemoaning the inadequacies – of a brand she's used recently. The beauty of having ready access to so much brand information online, from such a variety of sources, is that it enables us to explore in depth any products and brands that especially interest us and do quick brand comparisons based not only on objective features, but also on consumers' experiences via user reviews. The search has become so essential a start to many consumers' shopping journeys, Google researchers extended ZMOT to refer to "that moment when you grab your laptop, mobile phone, or some other wired device and start learning about a product or service you're thinking of trying or buying" (Solis, 2013a, p. 63). It is Google's stance that no matter what kind of product a marketer is selling, a brand presence online is essential, even for a seemingly trivial product. The ZMOT may occur during any stage of the journey prior to purchase. In Chapter 3, Tasha's ZMOT occurred when she looked up reviews of minimalist running shoes. A consumer brand that is neither reviewed nor the focus of any business news publisher is not a credible contender for the attention of many discerning consumers.

First Moment of Truth (FMOT)

Consummate marketer Procter and Gamble, which brought us Tide detergent, Ivory soap, Pampers, and numerous additional long-lived brands, popularized the term to describe the "three to seven seconds after a shopper first encounters a product on a store shelf. It is in these precious moments that...marketers must focus efforts on converting shoppers into customers" (Nelson & Ellison, 2005). In the FMOT, we either pick up the product and put it in our shopping cart or leave it behind. This moment corresponds with the choice and purchase stage, and if indeed it is also our initial contact with a brand, FMOT may also precipitate need recognition. Picture the cereal aisle in your supermarket: Which packages stand out? Why? Does something about one of them make you want to pick it up and examine it more closely? Have you ever bought a box on impulse because it looked so good? In Chapter 6, we'll explore packaging and other aspects of sensory marketing in depth. Increasing numbers of consumers experience FMOT online, making a prominent and persuasive online presence essential, as it is the entire foundation of the decision process, choice, and purchase.

Second Moment of Truth (SMOT)

If we purchase the brand, the "Second Moment of Truth" (SMOT) comes when we use or consume the brand and decide whether we like it (experience stage). As noted previously, this evaluation hinges on our <u>expectations</u> of what the product does for us or enables us to do. Let's look at an unusual example: The first performance of Igor Stravinsky's "The Rite of Spring":

Stravinsky's dissonant masterwork violated the audience's expectations of a pleasant evening of the kind of music and dancing to which they were accustomed. Future audiences would prove far more appreciative; they knew what to expect and chose to attend, not despite any misgivings, but rather because the new piece piqued their interest.

A marketer can enhance the SMOT by communicating with the consumer after s/he has made a purchase. Like most good ecommerce sites, the pet supplies company Chewy.com sends timely emails thanking purchasers for their orders, informing them that their order has been shipped, and inviting their reviews. Chewy goes a step further than many retailers in their prompt, courteous, and responsive customer service. The consumer does not receive an automated response to a query, but rather gets to talk with a human who displays both professionalism and warmth. And the company has made significant improvements in their packing practices based on the logic of one customer's discussion with a customer representative. The humanity and transparency Chewy displays engender strong loyalty and affection from many customers.

Almost no musical work has had such a powerful influence or evoked as much controversy as Igor Stravinsky's ballet score "The Rite of Spring". The work's premiere on May 29, 1913, at the Théâtre des Champs-Elysées in Paris, was scandalous. In addition to the outrageous costumes, unusual choreography and bizarre story of pagan sacrifice, Stravinsky's musical innovations tested the patience of the audience to the fullest. ...

Harvard University professor Thomas Kelly suggests that one of the reasons that the Paris premiere of "The Rite of Spring" created such a furor was that it shattered everyone's expectations. The evening's program began innocently with a performance of "Les Sylphides." However, as the follow-up piece, "The Rite of Spring" turned out to be anything but spring-like.... When the curtain rose and the dancing began, there appeared a musical theme without a melody, only a loud, pulsating, dissonant chord with jarring, irregular accents. The audience responded to the ballet with such a din of hisses and catcalls that the performers could barely hear each other....

As Thomas Kelly states, "The pagans on-stage made pagans of the audience." Despite its inauspicious debut, Stravinsky's score for "The Rite of Spring" today stands as a magnificent musical masterpiece of the twentieth century.

(Kelly, 1999)

Ultimate Moment of Truth (UMOT)

This is the juncture at which we decide whether to share our brand experience with others – our colleagues, friends or family, our Facebook contacts, Twitter followers, blog readers, fellow forum members (Solis, 2013b). The UMOT is critically important to a brand because one consumer's advocating a brand may be another consumer's ZMOT.

In sum, while marketers have more opportunities than ever before to influence consumers' thoughts, feelings, and behaviors at every stage of the consumer journey, they also face greater consumer skepticism and more competition from other quarters including friends, experts, and social media connections. In Section 2, we'll explore further how consumers make meaning from the world around them and how marketers can participate in that process.

References

Advertising Research Foundation (2012). "Digital & social media in the purchase decision process". Retrieved from: https://thearf-org-aux-assets.s3.amazonaws.com/research/ARF_Digital_Social_Media_Purchase_Process.pdf.

BMT Micro (2016, July 22). "The consumer decision journey: The new marketing funnel". Retrieved from: https://blog.bmtmicro.com/consumer-decision-journey/.

Cavill, S. (2021, January 8). "Nike plans steady digital push in 2021 as direct-to-consumer sales grow". Retrieved from: https://web.archive.org/web/20210616205916/https://insights.digitalmediasolutions.com/articles/nike-ecommerce-dtc-digital-sales.

Cramer-Flood, E. (2021, January 13). "Global ecomerce update 2021". eMarketer. Retrieved from: www.emarketer.com/content/global-ecommerce-update-2021.

Dong, B., Li, M., & Sivakumar, K. (2019). "Online review characteristics and trust: A cross-country examination". *Decision Sciences, 50*(3), 537–566. https://doi.org/10.1111/deci.12339.

Hritzuk, N., Esquero, I., Jones, K., & Burke E. (2013). "The consumer decision journey: Retail". Retrieved from: https://vdocuments.net/the-consumer-decision-journey-retail-understanding-consumer-decision-making-along.html.

Hughes, S. (2021, March 16). "New IRI research finds pandemic continues to drive consumer attitudes in Q1 2021; Good value and strong loyalty programs fuel decision making". Retrieved from: www.iriworldwide.com/en-us/news/press-releases/new-iri-research-finds-pandemic-continues-to-drive.

Kelly, T. (1999). "Igor Stravinsky's 'The Rite of Spring'". NPR Online. Retrieved from: https://legacy.npr.org/programs/specials/milestones/991110.motm.riteofspring.html.

Knowledge@Wharton (2020a, August 10). "The high cost of returns: Should retailers re-think their policies?". Retrieved from: https://knowledge.wharton.upenn.edu/article/high-cost-of-returns-should-retailers-rethink-policies/.

Knowledge@Wharton (2020b, January 7). Five ways brands are changing their playbooks to win. Retrieved from: https://knowledge.wharton.upenn.edu/article/five-ways-brands-changing-playbooks-win/.

Knowledge@Wharton (2021, April 19). "Why some retailers succeed despite big disruptions". Retrieved from: https://knowledge.wharton.upenn.edu/article/why-some-retailers-succeed-despite-big-disruptions/.

Mohsin, T., & Abujoub, R. (2020, September). "3 ways mobile apps can help retailers drive growth". Retrieved from: www.thinkwithgoogle.com/intl/en-145/retail-app-growth-tips/.

Molina, B. (2018, May 23). "Return too much stuff to Amazon? You might get banned". *USA Today*. Retrieved from: www.usatoday.com/story/tech/talkingtech/2018/05/23/amazon-bans-customers-who-return-too-many-orders/636089002/.

Nelson, E., & Ellison, S. (2005, September 21). "In a shift, marketers beef up ad spending inside stores". *Wall Street Journal*. Retrieved from: www.wsj.com/articles/SB112725891535046751.

Rennie, A., & Protheroe, J. (2020, July). "How people decide what to buy lies in the 'messy middle' of the purchase journey". Retrieved from: www.thinkwithgoogle.com/consumer-insights/consumer-journey/navigating-purchase-behavior-and-decision-making/.

Solis, B. (2013a). *What's the Future of Business? Changing the Way Businesses Create Experiences.* Hoboken, NJ: Wiley.

Solis, B. (2013b, November 11). "The ultimate moment of truth and the art of digital engagement". Retrieved from: www.briansolis.com/2013/11/the-ultimate-moment-of-truth-and-the-art-of-engagement/.

Taniguchi, N. (2021, May). "COVID changed the consumer journey, but what's likely to stick?". Retrieved from: www.thinkwithgoogle.com/consumer-insights/consumer-journey/covid-decision-journey/.

Part 2
How Consumers Create Meaning

5 Memory and Priming

Objectives

1. To explore how memory works.
2. To examine how our unconscious, automatic mental processes shape our perceptions and behavior.
3. To investigate the skills and functions of the conscious mind and observe its interactions with the unconscious.

Introduction

The brain makes the world meaningful to us and it does most of its amazing and intricate work outside conscious awareness, using pre-wired "programs." For example, from birth, the brain "expects" to see certain very important patterns, like faces; a newborn will turn toward a face-like pattern but not a scrambled version of the same pattern. Babies treat inanimate objects differently from ones they believe to be animate (people, animals, certain toys), assuming the animate ones are in some sense autonomous, possessing internal states – for example, intentions – that the baby cannot see. All babies babble, even those who are deaf. Abundant evidence exists indicating that neural processes underlying language learning and social interactions are among the most extensively preprogrammed.

In this chapter, we will investigate how the brain makes meaning in consumer behavior contexts and explore how we call into conscious awareness the information we need in order to plan ahead, make considered decisions, and establish and achieve life goals. Since making meaning out of what our senses tell us cannot occur in the absence of any sort of memory, we begin by asking how our memories work and move on to examining the ways in which unconscious processes shape our thoughts, feelings, and behaviors. Last, we will venture into the ongoing conflicts between our conscious minds and the unconscious

DOI: 10.4324/9780367426897-7

Memory: What It Holds, How It Works

In his book *How We Learn* (2015), science journalist Benedict Carey observes:

> The brain is not like a muscle, at least not in any straightforward sense. It is something else altogether, sensitive to mood, to timing, to circadian rhythms, as well as to location, environment. It registers far more than we're conscious of and often adds previously unnoticed details when revisiting a memory or learned fact….It has a strong preference for meaning over randomness, and finds nonsense offensive. It doesn't take orders so well, either, as we all know—forgetting precious facts needed for an exam while somehow remembering entire scenes from *The Godfather* or the lineup of the 1986 Boston Red Sox.
>
> (p. xiii)

Through many decades of research, cognitive scientists have come to understand that *short-term* or *working* memory differs from *long-term* memory in important aspects. An intuitive way to think about working memory is as what you are focusing on when you perform a cognitive task like mental arithmetic, scrabble or Sudoku, or something as simple as entering your friend's new contact information into your smartphone. You remember the information you need just long enough to solve the problem, take your turn, or enter the number, and then you promptly forget it. Short-term memory can hold only very limited content. To experience its limits, try multiplying 356 times 479 without using a pencil and paper or calculator. Most of us, even those good at mental arithmetic, find this somewhat taxing, precisely because of the limits of working memory. For content in short-term memory to enter your far more capacious long-term memory, it must be processed by your hippocampus, a small structure in the brain that is essential for the formation of new long-term memories. We know about the hippocampus's role in memory formation, thanks to the handful of individuals with epileptic seizures so severe and frequent as to necessitate surgical removal of the parts of the brain implicated in the seizures. When the hippocampus is the culprit, its removal makes it impossible for these individuals to form new long-term memories after surgery, even though their working memories and presurgery long-term memories remain intact. Later, we will return to a discussion of this condition known as *anterograde amnesia*.

What does long-term memory hold and how do we go about retrieving the specific contents we want or need at any given moment? Cognitive psychology research tells us that there are three broad types of content: *semantic* or *declarative memory*, *procedural memory*, and *autobiographical memory*. Below, we explore each of these.

Semantic Memory: How Do We Know?

How do you know which foods are vegetables, what kinds of mobile devices are currently available, what menu items are typical of fast food restaurants? It seems we "just know" many things. We have at our mental fingertips a vast and complex store of knowledge about places (including branded establishments), people, animals, objects (including branded goods), and ideas – most of which we have acquired without conscious effort in the ordinary course of growing up within a particular society and culture. Cognitive scientists call this *semantic memory* as it enables us to make and verbalize meanings, to comprehend connections among concepts.

One way to think about semantic memory is as an associative network consisting of nodes – concepts, nouns – with links among them – relationship descriptors, verbs. A network of knowledge about a particular concept is called a *schema*. On the accompanying web site, you will find an example of a very simple schema for the concept of animals.

The entire network consisting of everything we know possesses several remarkable qualities:

1. It is very well-organized by degree of semantic (meaning) association, in that closely related concepts, like mammal, cow, and milk, are strongly linked, while unrelated or more weakly related ones, for example, fire and apple, are weakly linked, if at all.
2. It is highly malleable; learning is, in effect, the strengthening of some links, the weakening or destruction of others, the creation of new links between previously unlinked existing concepts, and the introduction of new concepts that become linked to existing ones.
3. It is searchable using sensory input as well as internally generated cues and more flexible in its navigability than even the most sophisticated and user-friendly web site.

Organization of Semantic Memory

The "animals" schema illustrates several aspects of how we understand semantic memory to be organized, based on many decades of cognitive science research. "Animals" is a high-level category which is subdivided into the broad categories of birds, mammals, and fish, each of which is linked to its typical characteristics (fur, wings, etc.) and instances (cow, canary, etc.). Note that this schema shows that a cow is a more typical instance of a mammal than is a bat, which displays birdlike characteristics but is not a bird. Similarly, a canary is a more typical bird than is the flightless ostrich, the largest bird in existence. What are the implications of typicality for recall? If we are given the word "bird," we will likely more rapidly retrieve the word "canary" as an instance of the category than "ostrich." But if, on a bird-watching trip, we see a canary versus an ostrich, we will likely recall the large, unusual bird more quickly if a friend were to ask about the expedition.

A fascinating property of such an associative network is the rich and complex interconnections among different concepts across a vast range of categories. For example, only five links from "animals," we encounter two fruits as well as the concept of fire! If we explore the links from fire (the "fire" schema), we will likely encounter wildfires, cooking fires, and campfires; in many cultures, the schema for cooking would eventually link back to that for animals. The concept of a canary might transport us to mining and the hazards thereof, as canaries were once used in coal mines as sentinels warning miners of the presence of carbon monoxide. The word "canary" might also lead us to the "pets" schema, which includes other instances of pets, all likely to link to the concept "not edible." The fruits at the edge of the animal schema shown above might, in turn, link to gardening – or they could link to the metaphorical meanings of fruit, for example, the fruits of one's labor, or the (religious) admonition to be fruitful and multiply. As we will discuss in Chapter 7, culture shapes important aspects of many schemata; for example, in the US, "rabbit" is in the schema for pets, hence not edible. But in Venezuela, Germany, and many other countries, rabbits are not pets and are edible.

Malleability of Semantic Memory

One way to think about learning is in terms of changes in semantic memory. According to the U.S. Department of Agriculture (2021), more than 20,000 new food and beverage products were launched in the US alone in 2020. These included new brands as well as line or variety extensions. Most were new flavors, colors, sizes, and other changes that add little if anything to consumers' product knowledge structures. When a marketer introduces such a product, consumers quickly and mostly without thinking store the concept under an existing category. But a few products are hybrids of categories formerly considered incompatible:

> There's evidence that younger drinkers are rethinking their relationships with alcohol entirely. Nearly half of regular wine drinkers, and two-thirds of millennial wine drinkers, report that they're trying to drink less, primarily for health reasons, according to Nielsen data.
>
> But few people foresaw a year-old nonalcoholic beer brand—a genre traditionally associated with low-quality O'Douls, Becks, and other grocery-store brands—becoming a breakout drink of choice for moderating millennials and weekend warriors.
>
> Tedd Kenny, owner of Top Hops Beer Shop, a craft-beer bar and bottle shop on Manhattan's Lower East Side, [commented that] Athletic Brewing has been a consistent and unexpected top seller at the popular spot....he says Athletic has "expanded the market [beyond] just former drinkers." He sees customers at his bar switching between NA Athletic beers and alcoholic craft beer in a single evening. In other words, the drinker who wants to moderate while drinking will now order an NA beer.
>
> How did Athletic create this new consumer behavior? It starts with taste. Athletic's brews stand up to other craft beers.
>
> (Peabody, 2019)

The cofounders experimented extensively different methods for removing alcohol, eventually developing a new, "all-natural" de-alcoholizing process that preserves the beer's flavor. In addition to the traditional channels of distribution for beer – bars, restaurants, and grocers – they sell direct to consumers online, a channel less readily available to brewers of beers containing alcohol because of the strict regulations imposed by the shipping companies:

> To stand out from the bigger players that are dabbling in NA and the handful of other craft nonalcoholic brewers in the space—such as California's Bravus Brewery and Missouri's Well Being Brewery—Athletic has targeted weekend warrior types who want beer but not hangovers. "It's really a very modern decision to monitor what ingredients you're consuming and be more mindful during more occasions," says Shufelt. The brand sponsors AVP Beach Volleyball tournaments, Spartan Races, and other events, including half-marathons. It also organizes group runs and has committed to donating 2% of sales to trail work in parks, which has resulted in almost $50k donated to trail and park cleanups this year. Today, Shufelt describes the Athletic consumer as "young, modern, healthy adults" and says they are "heavily barbelled in the 24 to 44 demo."
>
> (Peabody, 2019)

Notice that Athletic's success relies not only on the malleability of semantic memory, but also on the careful and wise choice of target consumers whose schemas for alcohol include the goal of moderating their consumption and who enjoy the kinds of activities the company sponsors. Their mental model for the role of alcohol in their lives makes them more open to trying a nonalcoholic craft beer, as it answers an existing need. This is an excellent example of the means-end chain at work and it shows how our product and brand schemas vary in their malleability depending on the goals, beliefs, and experiences we have incorporated into them.

If a new brand in an existing category possesses a significant advantage over current offerings, one strategy for getting consumers to pay attention to it is to design it to look just a little different from the current offerings. Dyson vacuums and Bugaboo strollers are excellent exemplars of this strategy. While readily identifiable as a vacuum cleaner, with its new technology and innovative design, the first Dyson vacuum became more than a home appliance (i.e., for women); it earned honorary status in the "power tool" schema, hence was viewed as more acceptable for men to use. Initial buyers of Dyson vacuums were so excited about their new purchase that many proudly hauled it out of the closet to show guests! Similarly, Bugaboo strollers were introduced as the exciting "all-terrain vehicle" of strollers, designed for affluent new parents worried about becoming boring people inundating their friends with baby photos and ruminating about their offspring's bodily functions. The Bugaboo is to strollers what the sport utility vehicle was to minivans – a symbol that parenthood need not mean the complete subjugation of the individual in service of the offspring. The brand, while certainly a member of the "stroller" or "baby products" schema, is also linked with social status and fun, qualities never previously associated with these categories.

New brands that launch new product categories may require more help finding a foothold in semantic memory. While Apple did not invent smartphones, its marketing of the first generation of iPhones showed consumers how this one product could enrich and transform the familiar experiences of losing oneself in music, connecting with others, finding the nearest restaurant, coffee shop, and so forth – for everything one could conceivably want or need to do, "there's an app for that!" Apple told us (APPLEFOREVER2010, 2011). The concept of this device insinuated itself into the semantic memory of an entire generation and has become a felt necessity in the lives of consumers of all ages, without those consumers pondering what they were and how to think about them.

Searchability of Semantic Memory

Recently, the author thought back to the famous department store that was a Chicago institution for decades before it was absorbed into behemoth Macy's. In her attempts to recall its name, she remembered the delicious chocolate mints that were sold only at that store, "Frango mints"; she also recalled another, more downscale department store where she shopped occasionally for shoes when she was a graduate student on a tight budget: "Carson Pirie Scott"; she could picture the lovely boutiques that graced North Michigan Avenue, known also as the "Magnificent Mile." As these closely related concepts came to mind, she felt she was circling around the store's name and it was just out of reach. "I know it starts with the letter M," she told herself, increasingly frustrated with her inability to recall the name. She finally gave up the memory search and called her friend who had lived in Chicago even longer than she had. "What's the name of that store that had the Frango mints?" she asked him. "Marshall Fields!" he replied. "You couldn't remember Marshall Fields?" he asked in wonderment at her memory lapse.

This "tip of the tongue" phenomenon is exceedingly common and well-researched. It is the conscious experience of knowing something (usually a name) but being unable to retrieve it from long-term memory. The feeling of frustration tells us there is a retrieval failure and knowing this means we can consciously marshal our cognitive resources to help reverse the failure. In the example above, the author worked on recalling aspects of Chicago that might prove relevant. When you are trying to remember a celebrity's name, you usually summon up the names of the movies in which s/he starred, a mental picture of him/her, and perhaps well-publicized acts or events in the celebrity's life. At times, this conscious search proves futile but the unconscious may continue it and wake you at 3 a.m. with the elusive name. One could hardly imagine a more ideally designed search engine, one that uses every conceivable path to find answers and perseveres regardless of what we are doing.

The moral for marketers is straightforward: For habitual purchases, do not rely on consumers' ability to recall your brand name without help. Instead, familiarize them with it through all media that will reach them, showing consistency in visual logos, sonic signatures, and messaging, and make sure the product is well-stocked wherever they shop. In other words, provide consumers multiple environmental cues to jog their memories. Even better, bank on brand recognition rather than recall. While recall requires a search of memory for a brand that is absent from the current environment – a tall order, especially for low involvement (unconsidered) purchases – recognition requires only that the brand on the supermarket shelf looks familiar to him/her.

For considered purchases, this reliance on brand recognition is not so critical, as consumers actively seek information from a variety of sources about products and brands of interest. We consumers have learned that extensively advertised brands of these kinds of products are not always the highest quality or the best choice for our circumstances.

Scripts in Semantic Memory

How do you know what steps are involved in ordering a meal at McDonald's as opposed to your favorite formal restaurant? At which establishment would you feel more comfortable eating alone? With small children? Why? How should you dress to go to each place? Could you bring your laptop and work on a paper while you're eating?

While the answers to these questions may seem obvious to you now, at one time in your life, a time you probably do not remember, they were not. You know what to expect and how to behave at restaurants and in stores, at weddings and funerals, on a first date and a first Valentine's Day with your sweetie, because you learned, mostly from watching others, largely by osmosis, without all that much conscious effort or thought. In effect, you developed "scripts" for these and many other occasions typical of your culture, your social network, and your family. Like schemas, these scripts or action sequences are a part of semantic or declarative memory. Below is an example of a very general script for grocery shopping:

Goal: Restock pantry and refrigerator
Steps:

- Make shopping list
- Drive to store
- Enter store
- Get a basket
- Pick up and peruse store circular
- Navigate as you habitually do (perimeter first, then aisle by aisle; or packaged goods first, then produce, then frozen foods; or some other path)
- Check out (at U-Scan or staffed checkout counter – there is a script for each of these processes, too; if you have never or rarely used self-checkout, your script for it may be overly simple or difficult for you to bring into working memory.
- Drive home
- Carry groceries into house
- Restock pantry and fridge

Think about how the COVID-19 pandemic has transformed this script and many others into an experience that is all or mostly online for many consumers (see, e.g., Berg, 2021; Klein, 2021).

One challenge of getting consumers to adopt new technologies is persuading them to learn new scripts for performing ordinary tasks for which they have richly developed, frequently used automated scripts. The marketer must convince potential customers that the script for using the new technology is both easy to learn and worth the effort. Walk-Morris (2021) describes the rise in contactless payments in the US during 2020, driven in part by consumers' COVID-related health concerns (making learning the new script worth the effort) and in part by retailers' increasing acceptance of mobile payments (making it easier). The US and Europe lag behind Asia in this practice. While the US has long had the infrastructure to process debit and credit cards, in China these payment forms never gained much traction. As a result, Chinese consumers leapfrogged over them and quickly adopted mobile payment practices, for which a strong infrastructure exists.

We may view our scripts as means-end chains of a sort, where we associate specific behaviors (instead of products) with consequences and ultimately goals. We construct them based on our existing beliefs and prior experiences, and those beliefs and experiences may mislead us to assume we are acting in an optimal way to reach a goal, when in reality our actions may be ineffective or even counterproductive. Consider our beliefs about individual actions we can take to slow climate change:

> Despite high concern about climate change, and high confidence that we know what to do in our own lives to combat it, misperceptions are rife, and on the specifics many often just don't know. …
>
> Looking at well-known 'green' actions, how does the public rank potential greenhouse gas savings from each? When asked to identify from a list the top three options that would most reduce the greenhouse gas emissions of an individual living in one of the world's richer markets, people around the world were most likely to choose recycling as much as possible (59%), buying energy from renewable sources (49%) and replacing a typical car with an electric or hybrid vehicle (41%).
>
> While all of these are ways of reducing personal climate change impact, none are in fact in the top three most effective measures, according to an academic review from 2017 (although buying energy from renewable sources is close in fourth place). This found that having one fewer child is the most effective way to reduce carbon emissions, followed by not having a car at all and avoiding one long distance flight. Only 1 in 10 (11%) around the world named not having a child as one of their top three measures to cut carbon emissions, 17% chose not having a car and 21% named avoiding one long-distance flight. This is even behind other, much less effective, actions such as hang-drying clothes (picked by 26%) or replacing traditional light bulbs with low energy ones (36%).

…

When asked about the warming we are already experiencing, there is little evidence that the public know that all of the last six years were among the hottest on record. When asked how many years since 2015 have been the hottest year on record, most were too unsure to answer. Those who did answer tended to underestimate. Only 4% of respondents around the world gave the correct answer of all six years.

…

According to research, going to a plant-based diet makes more of a difference to your carbon footprint than eating local, but the public guess this is the other way around. Almost 6 in 10 people around the world (57%) say eating a locally produced diet, including meat and dairy products, is a better way to reduce an individual's greenhouse gas emissions while only 20% say eating a vegetarian diet with some imported products is more effective.

(Ipsos, 2021)

Advocates of climate change reduction practices must first educate consumers about what will make the greatest difference. Then, the challenge will be to persuade people to change their behavior in significant ways.

We've discussed semantic memory, so it's time to explore autobiographical memory.

Autobiographical Memory: Do You Remember When…?

The author will never forget her first trip to Siesta Key, a small oceanfront town about an hour's drive from Tampa, Florida. The white sand, fine, soft, and yielding under her bare toes; the warm, shallow water that tasted of salt; the rough-textured grass right outside the condo she and her friend rented; the sulfurous scent of the salty sand mixing with the water from the hydrant where beachgoers cleaned their bare feet before putting their shoes back on. Also, the young man sitting cross-legged in ankle-deep water just off shore, the lapping of the waves emphasizing his meditative stillness; the red and green Christmas lights that festooned the wrought-iron fences of the mansions along Midnight Pass road – so strange to see those holiday decorations in this almost tropical landscape, warm breeze ruffling the beard of the life-sized Santa Statue in the courtyard of the condominiums adjacent to ours. And the luxurious experience of relaxing with my friend, thinking and talking about anything but work.

This account is typical of an autobiographical memory: it includes vivid recollections (or reconstructions) of multisensory experiences and it is colored by emotion (in this instance, pleasurable relaxation). It is also a partial reconstruction; as the author recounts it, more comes back to her. With effort and focus, she might even reconstruct a time line, a narrative. Also typical of autobiographical memories are the variations in the narrative each time she recalls or retells it. The depth, temperature, and wave heights of the ocean water may change as she conflates that trip with others; and where she and her friend ate will no doubt vary considerably from one retelling to the next.

Rather than an accurate moment-by-moment recording of events, an autobiographical memory is constructed and reconstructed as we recall and recount it, so that in the end it becomes a story of a story ad infinitum. To test your own childhood memories, try sharing a memory or two with your siblings or parents. Chances are very good that your versions will vary, partly because your initial experiences of the event differed and also because the memory is reshaped by each of you in different ways over time. What will be true for each of you is that your memory will be a meaningful part of your life story, which you have constructed and reshaped many times to make it coherent and perhaps pleasing.

In attempts to preserve and supplement our memories of special events, we often take photos and make videos during them. But the act of taking the photos may alter the quality of the experience itself, preventing the photographer from being in the present as s/he is documenting it for future consumption. And any posing for photos may introduce self-conscious artifice into the subject's experience. On the other hand, showing one's friends photographs or videos of special moments may enrich the documenter's memory of those occasions. In his book *Thinking Fast and Slow*, Daniel Kahneman (2013) distinguishes between what he calls the "experiencing self" and the "remembering self":

> A comment I heard from an audience member after a lecture illustrates the difficulty of distinguishing memories from experiences. He told of listening raptly to a long symphony on a disc that was scratched near the end, producing a shocking sound, and he reported that the bad ending "ruined the whole experience." But the experience itself was not actually ruined, only the memory of it. The experiencing self had had an experience that was almost entirely good, and the bad end could not undo it because it had already happened. My questioner had assigned the entire episode a failing grade because it had ended very badly, but that grade had effectively ignored 40 minutes of musical bliss. Does the actual experience count for nothing?
>
> (p. 381)

Think about which kind of vacation you would prefer: a stay at a familiar resort or a tour that takes you to several countries you have never seen before? If your goal is to relax and savor the experience, you may choose the resort; if, on the other hand, you want to return home with many photos, videos, and stories, you will likely select the tour even though it may not be as pleasant an experience initially. The travel and tourism industry serves both market segments well: resorts, spas, and many cruises are designed for consumers who give primacy to the experiencing self, and tourism ranging from country-hopping to wilderness expeditions provides rich autobiographical memories and stories to those whose remembering selves are in charge of choosing the vacation. Currently, many consumers dream of a time when they can safely travel again. The content of those dreams likely gives primacy to the experiencing self: it seems unlikely that prospective travelers are anticipating the selfies they plan to take and share. Rather, their focus is most likely on the sights, sounds, and smells of a place they are longing to visit.

Procedural Memory: How Do We Know How To...?

Procedural memories are complex motor sequences that are automated and inaccessible to consciousness:

> Riding a bike, tying your shoes...steering your car into a parking space while speaking on your cell phone are examples of [procedural memory]. You execute these actions easily, but without knowing the details of how you do it. You would be totally unable to describe the perfectly timed choreography with which your muscles contract and relax as you navigate around other people in a cafeteria while holding a tray, yet you have no trouble doing it. This is the gap between what your brain can do and what you can tap into consciously.
>
> (Eagleman, 2012, p. 56)

Scripts are, in essence, sequences of procedural memories organized by cognitively conceptualized goals. For example, each step of the grocery shopping script above may be subdivided into procedural memories of motor sequences. Making a grocery list (a cognitively conceptualized goal) usually requires writing or typing, both involving procedural memories. Driving to the store (another higher-level goal) involves all motor sequences driving entails (starting the car, driving without colliding with other vehicles, parking in a parking lot), together with a mental map of the route itself.

Perhaps one reason why many people sincerely believe that they can text while driving is that both actions rely on procedural memory, and are therefore experienced as easy to execute. Similarly, an individual who drives when drunk may experience his/her abilities as unimpaired because s/he is executing automated motor sequences not accessible to conscious awareness and assessment. This lends validity to the campaign "friends don't let friends drive drunk," encouraging sober companions to take away the impaired person's car keys.

The Unconscious

Our experience tells us we are conscious of most aspects of our environment. The author is conscious of sitting in a bookstore (pre-pandemic), reading, writing, sipping coffee, and occasionally eavesdropping on conversations at tables nearby. She is aware of the restlessness she usually feels when she must sit and write and of the temptation to buy a treat from the pastry case – surely that will help her do the hard thinking that this kind of writing necessitates! But more of her environment and mental processes escape her awareness. She does not know how many other patrons are seated at the tables around her, nor indeed how many tables and chairs there are. She cannot describe the baristas or the pictures covering the walls of the cafe. She does not know how she is thinking these thoughts or writing them in complete sentences. She does not know how she can read and have it feel so smooth and natural, and she cannot remember *not* being able to read. When she rises to take a little break, she cannot tell you how she commands her muscles to execute the motions of standing, walking, avoiding collisions with others, and then sitting again.

All the details of processes we do not typically access consciously are part of our *implicit* memory; the things we are aware of knowing make up our *explicit* memory. These two types of memories have the capacity to function separately from each other, as the following example illustrates:

> An individual with *anterograde amnesia* cannot consciously form new memories. So if you spend a day teaching him/her to play the video game Tetris, the next day s/he will have no recollection of the game – or of you, for that matter. But s/he will nonetheless show improved performance on Tetris. In other words, s/he has unconsciously learned how to play the game but that knowledge resides only in his/her implicit memory; explicit (conscious) memory contains no trace of the learning experience.
>
> (Eagleman, 2012, pp. 56–59)

Learning how to play Tetris requires the formation of a new procedural (implicit) memory, while remembering that one learned Tetris is a conscious (explicit) autobiographical memory.

Much of semantic, autobiographical, and most of all, procedural memory is implicit and we draw upon it often without being aware that we are doing so. In Chapter 6, we will describe an experiment showing that we may be affected by a logo without even being aware that we have viewed it. In brief, incidental exposure to the Apple logo makes people more creative; that particular instance of the logo was stored in implicit memory. We know this because it affected behavior following exposure to it, even though individuals were not aware that they saw it. The power of this logo to affect us even when we are not aware of having seen it is a testament to the strength of the brand meaning it evokes in implicit memory, as well as an illustration of the power of the unconscious to affect our cognitive processes and behavior.

Implicit memory can also shape our preferences and choices. Repeated exposure to a face causes us to find it more attractive even when we do not consciously remember ever having seen it. This increase in liking for the familiar is known as the *mere exposure effect*, and is one of the most robust and unsettling findings in psychological research (Zajonc, 2001). It helps explain why we so readily forgive political leaders' and celebrities' transgressions, and it underlies much of marketing. Advertisers have long known that ad repetition is critically important, especially for habitually purchased products; they just didn't know why it worked. The mere exposure effect may drive purchases of many familiar (heavily advertised) brands; when you are standing in front of the supermarket shelf or studying the assortment of brands online, at the First Moment of Truth, your mindset "open to choice," you may simply prefer (and pick up or click on) the package that looks most familiar to you, regardless of whether you can recall seeing any marketing messages for it.

It is quite common for something in the environment to cause subtle changes in our cognitions, affect, or behavior without our awareness; in effect, the environmental cue *primes* the response, much as you would prime a pump. In the example above, we would say that your brand choice may have been primed by your implicit memory of an ad for it. In other words, the mere exposure effect is a type of priming.

But there is more to priming, as the following example indicates:

> On July 4, 1997, NASA landed the Pathfinder spacecraft on the surface of Mars. This "Mission to Mars" captured media attention worldwide over the course of the following months and during this period, candy bar maker Mars Inc. also noticed a rather unusual increase in sales. Though the Mars Bar takes its name from the company's founder and not from the Earth's neighboring planet, consumers apparently responded to news about the planet Mars by purchasing more Mars Bars. This was a lucky turn of events for the candy bar company, to be sure, but what does it mean for our understanding of consumer choice?
>
> (Berger & Fitzsimons, 2008, p. 1)

It seems doubtful that consumers consciously decided to buy more Mars bars in response to the Mars landing. More likely, their temporarily increased exposure to the word "Mars" made shoppers' implicit memory of the eponymously named candy bar more accessible as they scanned choices of treats in the candy aisle. Berger and Fitzsimons (2008) support this interpretation, that is, an aspect of the environment that is perceptually (sensorially) related to a brand can increase consumers' evaluations of and preferences for that brand. In both of these studies, color in the environment caused people to think of – and prefer – the same color brands:

1. For the entire month of October, Halloween merchandise casts its orange glow over the candy and home décor aisles of supermarkets throughout the US. The day after Halloween, the portable sale bins are filled with Halloween leftovers and store shelves are stocked with brightly colored Thanksgiving and (heaven help us!) Christmas merchandise. Does exposure to all that orange in the weeks leading up to October 31 make orange versions of products more accessible in consumers' memories, that is, easier to remember? A study asking shoppers to list the first brands that came to mind when they thought of soda and candy showed that respondents asked the day before Halloween

were more likely to think of orange-packaged candy (Reese's peanut butter cups, not uniquely associated with Halloween) and orange-colored soda (Orange Crush or Sunkist) than shoppers asked a few days after Halloween. In other words, seeing a lot of orange in the environment made people more likely to remember orange versions of products.

2. Just getting people to write a little using either an orange or a green pen affected which brands they were likely to choose from a variety of products. Participants were first asked to write a few sentences about a book they liked, using either a green or an orange pen the experimenter gave them. Subsequently, they were asked to choose their preferred brands from 20 choice pairs of detergents, beverages, and candies. Some brands were green (or in green packaging), others were orange (or in orange packages), and others were neither orange nor green. More participants who had written in green ink chose green-colored brands (e.g., Sprite) compared to those who had written in orange ink, while more orange pen writers chose orange-colored brands (e.g., Fanta) compared to those who wrote with green ink.

These studies demonstrate that perceptual cues in the environment can influence our choices of brands. Chapter 5 included several illustrations of retailers (brands in their own right) intuitively using sensory cues to draw target consumers into the store and induce them to spend more money. As we learn more about how specific cues in the environment influence consumer cognitions, affect, and behavior, the sheer complexity of the retail setting will become both clearer and more manageable to consider strategically.

The priming effects we have discussed so far have been based on perceptual links between environmental cues and brands – namely common words (Mars) and colors (orange and green). Conceptual links can also prime brand recognition, evaluations, and choices, as Berger and Fitzsimons (2008) show:

1. One set of experiments investigated whether exposing people to an environmental cue conceptually related to the Puma brand of sneakers would speed up brand recognition and increase brand evaluations. Since we know from previous research that the concepts of "dog" and "cat" are closely linked in memory, we would expect people to recognize more easily the Puma sneaker brand in particular if they see dog images (conceptually linked environmental cue) just before they are shown sneaker brands. In one study, the authors showed half the participants images of dogs and half images of other things, ostensibly seeking their opinions about hues in the pictures. Afterward, the experimenters had all participants do a timed brand recognition task in which they were shown images and names of many different brands including Puma and several other sneaker brands. The participants who had been exposed to the dog images first were 30% faster to recognize Puma as a brand of sneakers. Another study found that prior exposure to dog images raised people's brand evaluations of Puma, and the more dogs they saw, the higher their ratings.

2.   The studies just described show that environmental cues with preexisting links to a brand can prime brand recognition and increase brand evaluations. The authors wondered whether they could demonstrate that a *new* conceptual link could also prime people's behavioral responses to a product. The college students in the next experiment lived on campus and ate in either of two dining halls, one with no trays and the other with cafeteria trays on which students would place their food choices.

First, in order to obtain an idea of what they ate under normal conditions, the investigators asked the students to keep journals listing what they ate each day for a week. Then, the participants were taught a slogan; half of those who ate in the dining hall that provided trays learned "Each and every dining hall tray, needs 5 fruits and veggies a day," which connects an environmental cue (the cafeteria tray) with fruit and vegetable consumption. The other half of the students who ate in that dining hall learned the slogan, "Live the healthy way, eat 5 fruits and veggies a day." The students who ate in the dining hall with no trays learned the first slogan with the word "tray" in it, which for them did not connect to the environment. All students continued to keep a food journal for another week.

The key question was whether the students who used trays and learned the first slogan, which connected the environmental cue "tray" with "fruits and vegetables" in semantic memory, would show the greatest increase in their consumption of fruits and vegetables; this would indicate that grabbing a tray had primed healthier choices because of the slogan. This turned out to be the case: the group ate 25% more fruits and vegetables than they had before learning the slogan. The other two groups showed no such increase.

Think of the implications of this finding for helping promote healthier behavior in several domains: eating well, not smoking, not texting while driving, and others. For example, many smokers light up during times of transition (e.g., while waiting for a bus) or stress (e.g., starting on a challenging project). How would you go about connecting environmental cues with encouragement not to smoke? Would you have to offer people an alternative activity?

What is most remarkable about priming is that it works behind the scenes, without our conscious minds dissecting or resisting its effects – and sometimes these effects are just what we need.

How Does Our Memory Affect Our Choices?

Take the choice of which kind of soup to buy. There's too much data here for you to grapple with: calories, price, salt content, taste, packaging, and so on. If you were a robot, you'd be stuck here all day trying to make a decision, with no obvious way to trade off which details matter more. To land on a choice, you need a summary of some sort. And that's what the feedback from your body is able to give you. Thinking about your budget might make your palms sweat, or you might salivate thinking about the last time you consumed the chicken noodle soup, or noting the excessive creaminess of the other soup might put a cramp in your intestines. You simulate your experience with one soup, and then the other. Your bodily experience helps your brain to quickly place a value on soup A, and another on soup B, allowing you to tip the balance in one direction or the other. You don't just extract the data from the soup cans, you feel the data. … each choice is marked by a bodily signature. And that helps you to decide.

Because the conscious mind has low bandwidth, you don't typically have full access to the bodily signals that tip your decisions; most of the action in your body lives far below your awareness.…

Each decision involves our past experiences (stored in the states of our body) as well as the present situation (Do I have enough money to buy X instead of Y? Is option Z available?). But there's one more part to the story of decisions: predictions about the future.…

How do I accurately simulate these futures? How can I possibly predict what it will really be like to go down these paths? The answer is that I can't: there's no way to know that my predictions will be accurate. All my simulations are only based on my past experiences and my current models of how the world works.…

Fundamentally, the brain is tuned to detect unexpected outcomes – and this sensitivity is at the heart of animals' ability to adapt and learn.

(Eagleman, 2017, pp. 110–118)

Like other animals, we are hardwired to seek rewards: Think of a reward as something that moves us closer to an ideal state. Food and water are primary rewards in that they address our biological needs. More generally, however, our behavior is guided by secondary rewards, which are things that predict primary rewards. Our choice of soups in the foregoing example requires us to integrate external and internal information.

External information includes the package label and graphics, the price, the feel of the store, app, or web site; product and brand reviews and comments from online influencers and perhaps friends and family. Examples of internal data include our schemas for soup and the brands we are choosing among, that is, our beliefs, knowledge, feelings, memories of experiences with the soups, recollections of our encounters with the brands via both marketing and non-marketing touchpoints, and perhaps our schemas representing our food budget, our nutritional goals, and the context in which we will consume the soup. Our overarching goal is to maximize the reward we want or have learned to expect.

Think about the habitual path to purchase: underlying what feels like an almost instantaneous decision is a complex, highly choreographed interplay between brain and body that results in a decision that we experience as being under our conscious control. But much of it is not subject to our conscious observation. How wise are such decisions?

[What] often gets in the way of good decision making [is that] options right in front of us tend to be valued higher than those we merely simulate. The thing that trips up good decision making about the future is the present....

This now-versus-the-future battle ... cuts across every aspect of our lives. It's why car dealers want you to get in and test-drive the cars, why clothing stores want you to try on the clothes, why merchants want you to touch the merchandise. Your mental simulations can't live up to the experience of something right here, right now.

To the brain, the future can only ever be a pale shadow of the now. The power of now explains why people make decisions that feel good in the moment but have lousy consequences in the future: people who take a drink or a drug hit even though they know they shouldn't; athletes who take anabolic steroids even though it may shave years off their lives; married partners who give in to an available affair....

(Eagleman, 2017, pp. 118–119)

So what might we do to make wiser decisions? We can take a lesson from Ulysses (aka Odysseus), a great Greek warrior immortalized in an ancient epic poem attributed to Homer. In brief, Ulysses was returning home to Greece after the fall of Troy. Like all sailors of that time, he knew that his ship would pass by an island inhabited by the Sirens, beautiful creatures who sang with such enchanting voices that many seamen had lost their lives as they ran their ships upon the rocks in their efforts to reach the Sirens' island.

Ulysses very much wanted to hear the Sirens sing, but he also wanted to live. So he hatched a plan: before his ship neared the island, he had his crew tie him securely to the mast; he also had the crew fill their ears with wax so that they became temporarily deaf. His men would be safe from the Sirens, and he would get to hear them while powerless to attempt to reach them. Thus it was that Ulysses became the only man who heard the Sirens sing and lived to tell of it. Ulysses had wisely predicted what his *future self* would do if unimpeded, and he used the insight of his *present self* to tie the hands (and feet) of that very unwise and weak future self; it would experience its great yearning but be unable to act on those self-destructive impulses.

Cognitive science research shows that this use of a "Ulysses Contract" can be very effective in helping people achieve their goals. The web site www.stickk. com, created by two economists who wished to lose weight, was the first of several to offer opportunities for people to make commitments for which they could make their future selves accountable for keeping. For example, if you want to make sure you stick to a weekly weight loss goal, the site offers you the option of choosing a charity (or an anti-charity, i.e., an organization you dislike and would never want to support) and specifying an amount to be donated each week you do not attain your goal. To keep yourself honest, you may involve a referee who confirms your weekly report.

The Ulysses contract and web site are not just for weight loss, but can work for any goal, including exercising regularly, meditating, or writing a book. This sort of contract is based on the research finding – quite well-established – that we hate to lose even more than we like to win. So rather than rewarding ourselves each time we keep our commitment, our "reward" is to avoid a financial loss.

It is our conscious mind that enables us to plan ahead, anticipating our future impulses and tying our hands (metaphorically) to prevent a behavior we know we will regret. The "considered pathway" we discussed in Chapter 4 relies on our ability to make conscious assessments of what our needs are and to carefully gather the information we need, evaluate the alternatives, and choose a brand or product that will best serve our future goals as well as our present needs.

References

APPLEFOREVER2010 (2011, December 19). "iPhone 1st gen ad" [Video]. YouTube. Retrieved from: https://youtu.be/37fMdoU8kyY.

Berg, N. (2021, January 21). "Grocery stores were already in flux. The pandemic could change them forever". Fast Company. Retrieved from: www.fastcompany.com/90596136/grocery-stores-were-already-in-flux-the-pandemic-could-change-them-forever.

Berger, J., & Fitzsimons, G. (2008). "Dogs on the street, Pumas on your feet: How cues in the environment influence product evaluation and choice". *Journal of Marketing Research, 45*(1), 1–14. https://doi.org/10.1509%2Fjmkr.45.1.001.

Carey, B. (2015). *How We Learn: The Surprising Truth about When, Where, and Why It Happens.* New York, NY: Random House Trade Paperbacks.

Eagleman, D. (2012). *Incognito: The Secret Lives of the Brain.* New York, NY: Vintage.

Eagleman, D. (2017). *The Brain: The Story of You.* New York, NY: Vintage.

Ipsos (2021, April 17). "Ipsos perils of perception: Climate change". Press release. Retrieved from: www.ipsos.com/sites/default/files/ct/news/documents/2021-04/Press%20Release.pdf.

Kahneman, D. (2013). *Thinking, Fast and Slow.* New York, NY: Farrar, Straus and Giroux.

Klein, D. (2021, February 16). "Pandemic-era restaurant habits that will outlast COVID-19". *QSR Magazine.* Retrieved from: www.qsrmagazine.com/consumer-trends/pandemic-era-restaurant-habits-will-outlast-covid-19.

Peabody, J. (2019, September 20). "Inside the nonalcoholic brewery making the year's most exciting beer". Fast Company. Retrieved from: www.fastcompany.com/90404650/inside-the-nonalcoholic-brewery-making-the-years-most-exciting-beer.

U.S. Department of Agriculture (2021). "New products". Retrieved from: www.ers.usda.gov/topics/food-markets-prices/processing-marketing/new-products.aspx.

Walk-Morris, T. (2021, March 12). "Mobile wallet industry to reach $3.5 trillion by 2023: Report". Retail Dive. Retrieved from: www.retaildive.com/news/mobile-wallet-industry-to-reach-35-trillion-by-2023-report/596621/.

Zajonc, R. B. (2001). "Mere exposure: A gateway to the subliminal". *Current Directions in Psychological Science, 10*(6), 224–228. https://doi.org/10.1111/1467-8721.00154.

6 Sensory Perception in a Consumption Context

Objectives

1. To explore how we interpret brand, product, and retailer information conveyed by each of the five senses.
2. To describe how the senses work together to influence our consumption-related thoughts, feelings, and behaviors.
3. To discuss how sensory marketing tactics may be used to help consumers develop healthier habits.

Introduction

> We experience life through our senses. When we see, hear, smell, touch, or taste, the brain takes in this objective raw data as input. Then, combining that data with our existing beliefs about the world, it creates an internal subjective model. This model isn't superficial, a framework in which you perceive new data; it stands in for perception itself. Perception really is reality.
>
> We are never consciously aware of the mental modeling process—what happens in our brains between taking in objective data and producing subjective experience. And for marketers, that lack of awareness, as much as that gap between experience and perception itself, represents opportunity.
>
> (Johnson & Ghuman, 2020, pp. 20–21)

The brain builds a narrative of your reality, based in large part on your experiences and expectations. And brands are an integral part of that reality. Through their ads, web sites, apps, emails, social media influencers, and other forms of marketing, marketers teach us what their brands can offer us, above and beyond our functional needs. Coca-Cola delivers happiness, Nike makes us better athletes, and Starbucks is all about community. These brand associations are formed gradually, over time, and outside our conscious awareness. This means that they become richly meaningful schemas that we seldom analyze rationally. Instead,

DOI: 10.4324/9780367426897-8

we may develop strong attachments to many brands, incorporating them into our narratives of our lives.

According to the Interbrand market research organization's annual brand valuation study, the top three global brands of 2020 are technology firms: Apple, Amazon, and Microsoft. On average, these brands grew 50% during the COVID-19 pandemic which accelerated demand for digital services including cloud storage, streaming, and online availability of goods previously purchased in-store.

Interbrand bases its overall valuation of a brand on its competitive and financial performance as well as the role the brand name plays in consumers' purchase decisions. To achieve status as one of the Best Global Brands, a brand must be present in Asia, Europe, North America, and emerging economies, earn at least 30% of its revenues outside its national boundaries, and be known beyond where it is marketed (Interbrand, 2020).

As the Interbrand study demonstrates, the confluence of many factors determines a brand's success. But consumers come to know brands as they do everything else in their environment – by means of their senses. A brand's identity is, in the end, what consumers think and feel about the brand based on the sum total of their sensory experiences with it. These experiences may involve any and all marketer-provided touchpoints (advertising, web sites, in-store displays, presence at sponsored events) as well as all other encounters with the brand (e.g., expert and user reviews, forums, and social media comments). This chapter focuses on sensory elements, both of the brand itself and of the environment in which it is sold.

Vision and Branding

Typically, the most prominent aspect of any object is its appearance. For a brand, this includes the logo, packaging if applicable, the product itself, and the retail contexts – offline and online – in which it is displayed and sold. We will examine how each of these elements influences consumers' cognitions, affect, and behavior.

Packaging and Logos

What's in a Logo?

How many of the logos in Pharr's (2021) logo quiz do you recognize? The answers are on the web site.

We may be exposed to hundreds of logos in a typical day, with a few we are aware of seeing – for example, the big Starbucks logo that promises us a delicious, frothy latte with the shots of espresso that get us going each morning, the Oregon Zoo logo that festoons the light rail train that is – thankfully – punctual most mornings. A vast number we do not perceive at all because we are so focused on the tasks at hand or so accustomed to these brands – the swoosh on the Nike shoes we pull on to run every evening, the "PHILIPS sonicare" emblazoned on the electric toothbrush we use for the requisite two minutes morning and evening, the Hyundai or other automaker brand emblem on the grill of the car in which we commute to work, the logos on our own and our colleagues' clothing.

Still other logos we perceive subliminally. "Subliminal" comes from the Latin words "sub," meaning "under," and "limina," which means "threshold." Subliminal perception occurs when our brains respond to a stimulus, but we are not aware that we perceive it. In other words, the stimulus is below the threshold of conscious awareness. As the following example shows, even this subliminal, so-called incidental exposure to a logo – one that appears and then disappears so quickly that we are not aware of it – can affect our cognitions, affect, and behavior. For an example of how incidental exposure to the Apple logo can makes us think and behave more creatively, see the DukeUniversityNews (2008) video on YouTube.

The Apple experiment demonstrates that familiar logos we perceive unconsciously may affect our behavior, at least in the short term. Bear in mind, though, that when we first became acquainted with the Apple logo, seeing it would have been unlikely to cause us to behave more creatively. The incidental exposure effect depends not only on a logo being familiar to us but also on how strongly we associate with it the brand or user qualities the marketer has shown us, time after time, in videos and print ads, on the brand web site, at the bricks-and-mortar stores, and through the fervent loyalty of users who would never consider switching to another brand.

A familiar logo for a brand we know well through personal use, marketing, or word of mouth embodies and serves as a reminder of our beliefs and feelings about the brand as well as our experiences with it. In other words, it is a shortcut to the consumer's version of the brand's identity. Many logos incorporate the brand name, supplementing the pictorial reminder with a verbal one. Others have had the name eliminated from the logo, arguably making the brand more meaningful globally. Starbucks did this in 2011 (Baertlein, 2011). For a brief history of its famous mermaid logo, see Klara (2014). The most significant change to the Starbucks logo occurred in 1987, when the original one, a Norse woodcut of a siren, was replaced by a more stylized version with less text. The siren is meant to evoke "the seafaring history of coffee and Seattle's strong seaport roots" (Starbucks web site). Commenting on the latest incarnation of the siren, the web site states, "For people all over the world, she is a signal of the world's finest coffee." This last remark hints at the company's desire to make the logo more globally appealing and evocative. It is a mark of a brand's strength to have its logo widely recognized even without the brand name. Notably, Starbucks was one of Interbrand's Top Global Brands in 2019.

Logos and brand names alike are changed for many reasons. The Doritos logo was redesigned in August 2019 to appeal to members of generation Z, who typically dislike overt advertising:

> PepsiCo Inc., the parent company of Frito-Lay's iconic Doritos chips, launched a new advertising campaign during the MTV Video Music Awards, an annual awards show celebrating the pulse of youth culture. The campaign,

titled "Another Level," removes all logos and names from Doritos packaging, leaving behind unmarked bags of blue and red, and the archetypal triangle snack shape.

While Doritos takes a real risk in expecting consumers to recognize a brand solely on color and shape, it is not the first brand to remove naming from it's traditional logo. Large, legacy brands like Mastercard, Nike and Starbucks have all embraced the shape-only logo trend. Doritos goes a step farther, hence, "Another Level," in removing all watermarks of brand identification.

Every brand has its reasonings for altering a known commercial presence. Mastercard introduced its modern design in early 2019 to "mark better across digital media." Starbucks wanted to expand its products outside of their own cafes and coffee. Nike was one of the first companies to jump on the de-branding trend in 1995, allowing for a less-corporate and ultimately even more recognizable brand.

But these decisions definitely do not happen without extensive consumer research.

Before a brand thinks of itself as world-renowned, it needs to take the necessary steps to determine public opinion and recognition. We can safely say that Doritos appear in most corner stores, on coffee tables during sporting events, and in lunch bags across the globe.

(Schuman, 2019)

The KFC logo evolved with the brand's dramatic transformations over the decades in response to consumer tastes and health trends. Formerly Kentucky Fried Chicken, the brand introduced chicken as a fast-food alternative to burgers, and offered its "pressure-fried" chicken coated in Colonel Sanders' special spice-enhanced batter (a secret recipe) as an alternative to the southern deep-fried chicken served in sit-down restaurants. In the 1980s, however, research emerged on the perils of fat consumption and the benefits of fitness. In short, fried food became unfashionable, a guilty pleasure. The Kentucky Fried Chicken name was shortened to KFC in 1991, in part to minimize the brand's association with the word "fried," which had come to evoke guilt, anxiety, even distaste in many consumers. It is in part KFC's responsiveness to consumer needs that has enabled the brand to meet Interbrand's valuation and earn a place among the Best Global Brands 2020. As the brand has evolved and the chain has expanded worldwide, the iconic visage of the founder Harlan Sanders (aka Colonel Sanders) portrayed on the logo has become friendlier and more welcoming. For references to more extensive readings about KFC and its founder, see Feloni (2015).

Both the Doritos and the KFC logos were redesigned yet again:

Early in 2020, Doritos went with a yellow-and-orange retro look for its taco-flavored chips, complete with a Frito-Lay logo discontinued in 1997. Starting in 2018, KFC spelled out "Kentucky Fried Chicken" in clean black-and-white text, and is now advertising buckets featuring a drawing of Colonel Sanders like the one the chain used through 1976, alongside retro-logoed Pepsi…

Branding is all about who you're trying to attract. Millennials have the least amount of wealth in the U.S., but they're adults who make up the largest part of the workforce, meaning there's a huge opportunity to court them with cheap food that is available everywhere. By reverting to logos that existed when Gen Xers and millennials were kids, brands are attempting to convey multiple meanings: comfort, quality, handmade-ness, and quite possibly an elision of all the things millennials grew up to distrust about fast food.

(Saxena, 2021)

Even very young children recognize and attach meaning to logos of brands or companies relevant to them, as a YouTube video by Ladd (2012) demonstrates. Chapter 8 will delve more deeply into the impact of marketing on children.

To be effective at evoking brand beliefs, feelings, and memories, a logo must be distinctive and easily recognized in a wide range of sizes and contexts – on products and billboards, on small smartphone screens and towering television screens, among their competitors' logos on retailer web sites packed with products, and in the lighting (or lack thereof) of the maze of merchandise displays of a bricks-and-mortar store. But most essential of all, the logo must represent a product that has earned consumers' trust and esteem by performing as promised and offering readily accessed solutions to any problem that arises.

How might we create better logos? Recent research suggests that descriptive logos, that is, those that clearly communicate the type of product or service a brand belongs to, contribute to more positive brand evaluations than do nondescriptive, more abstract ones. Examples of descriptive logos are Burger King (showing a bun), Salesforce (showing a cloud), and Doritos (displaying a triangle-shaped chip). Examples of nondescriptive logos include McDonald's, Disney, and many if not most automobile logos. Researchers' findings are summarized below:

Our studies and analyses reveal that it is easier for consumers to visually process descriptive logos and understand what a brand markets as a result. We also found that, compared with nondescriptive logos, descriptive logos:

- make brands appear more authentic in consumers' eyes
- more favorably impact consumers' evaluations of brands
- more strongly increase consumers' willingness to buy from brands
- boost brands' net sales more.

(Luffarelli et al., 2019)

These studies showed that the benefits of a descriptive logo are smaller for familiar brands. This makes sense, since our schemas for familiar brands are much richer and better established than those for unfamiliar brands.

Will the Package Lead to Purchase?

You may recall from Chapter 4 that in the consumer's habitual purchase pathway, s/he is most likely to be "open to possibility" while shopping. This gives the package a central role in persuasion, as it may represent the brand's first and last chance to convince the shopper to purchase it. In this fleeting first moment of truth, we either pick up the product and put it in our shopping cart or leave it behind. If we pick up a product, we are more likely to purchase it; this suggests that an important function of the packaging is to evoke in the consumer the desire to touch and examine it.

While packaging must be constructed to protect the product, we will limit ourselves to its sensory aspects in this chapter. The visual aspects of a package include its shape and size as well as the colors, images, and text on it.

A package must first get consumers' attention. This requires that like a logo, it must be distinctive. But most product categories have packaging norms – package formats that consumers identify with specific categories. For example, yogurt comes in a cylindrical carton and opens from the top. Most yogurt cartons gradually widen from bottom to top. Yoplait's carton is distinctive in narrowing from bottom to top, but it conforms to the normative cylindrical shape and so is readily identifiable both as yogurt and as the Yoplait brand.

The history of Pringles potato chips shows that getting attention is not sufficient to close a sale in that First Moment of Truth. Introduced by Procter and Gamble in 1973, the brand had a slow beginning. This was in part because its marketing focused on the innovative cylindrical packaging and the chips' uniform shape and resulting stackability – Madrigal (2011) includes one of the initial commercials for Pringles. While the distinctive packaging got consumers' attention, it also led them to infer that the chips were not fresh and would taste "fake." The brand languished until the 1980s, when a new flavor and marketing campaign helped it gain widespread consumer acceptance. In Madrigal (2011), the author hypothesizes that Pringles owed part of its eventual success to our acceptance of processed food as compatible with our busy lifestyle.

After the package wins the consumer's attention, it must communicate the product's identity, the brand's advantage over the competitors, and (in the US) federally mandated information about size, weight, and contents. Pepperidge Farm uses packaging to distinguish the cookie brand and to convey its premium quality. Compared to other brands, fewer cookies come in a package and instead of clear plastic that reveals the cookies within, Pepperidge Farm cookies are encased in white paper packages with graphics that are elegant in their simplicity; they include the brand name, cookie type, and a delicious-looking photo of the cookie. This distinctive packaging communicates that the cookies inside are worth the premium price.

Whether the main objective of a change in packaging is to persuade users of competitors' brands to switch, convince current brand users to buy and consume more, or get nonusers of the entire product category to try the brand, there is no substitute for testing a package with consumers in a real – or realistic – context including competitors' brands. In response to such consumer testing, Hershey introduced new packaging for its Miniatures that was both "bolder" and more sustainable. The miniatures' names were visibly enlarged, increasing their salience to consumers; not as obvious but equally compelling was Hershey's reduction of the wrapping materials to cut back on waste, a move consistent with the company's sustainability initiatives. The new packaging did not just get attention; it also increased purchase intent and rate (Candy Industry, 2014).

Another case in point is the Old Spice brand, which has shown how effectively package design can be used both to introduce a new fragrance and to nudge shoppers to recall its humorous commercials. To view a commercial from a recent campaign targeted at younger viewers, please see Old Spice (2020).

An innovative package format may communicate the prospect of a new and better consumption experience. Yoplait's very successful Go-Gurt, targeted at children, comes in squeezable tubes; kids like their sweet flavors and moms appreciate their portability. Baby and toddler food now comes in pouches – also squeezable – and brands including Happy Family, Buddy Foods, and Gogo SqueeZ have introduced flavors like cranberry and acai, which they hope will attract adults on the go. Athletes, many of whom are accustomed to high-energy snacks that they can ingest quickly, are a natural target for the conveniently packaged foods (Nassauer, 2013).

To get a better idea of what makes a package effective at the First Moment of Truth, consider Mouradian (2019). Entrants to the Dieline Awards are judged on the quality of the packaging's creativity, marketability, and innovation.

Can Packaging Mislead Consumers?

Visual elements in packaging may have unintended consequences. When Procter & Gamble introduced convenient single-load Tide Pods, the small colorful orbs in their transparent wrappings were mistaken for candy by more than 11,000 young children, who ingested them and became ill. The company subsequently encased the highly popular pods in opaque orange wrappers and placed double latches on the bowls in which they are sold in bulk (Saint Louis, 2014).

Marketers can also use packaging to mask reductions in product volume, as the following excerpt shows:

Manufacturers have become particularly adept at concealing package shrinkage, says John Gourville, a marketing professor at Harvard Business School. He says:

> If you think about how you see products, they have height, width, and depth. If you want to shrink a package without making it noticeable, you keep the height and width the same and shrink the depth. On the shelf, it looks the same as always.

Other common techniques include deepening an indent in the bottom of a beverage bottle or retaining a package's size but including less product (Dornbusch, 2014).

When ingredient prices rise, manufacturers either raise their prices, absorb all increased costs themselves, or reduce the product amount (masking it with packaging) but leave the price unchanged. As long as consumers demand the lowest possible prices, package shrinkage will persist as a response to suppliers' price hikes.

Product Appearance

Does the Product Look Like It Will Deliver?

As we saw from the Pringles example, consumers use visual cues to make inferences about the nonvisual sensory product characteristics, some of which may be experienced only after purchase. The two photos below evoke the feeling of softness, the first through the visual cues of height and colors (rather than black, which does not show softness as well), the second using the familiar and endearing image of a puppy comfortably resting his/her head on the product. Figures 6.1 and 6.2 are good examples of communicating tactile product qualities through evocative visual displays online.

We also infer weight and volume based on product, container, or package size, shape, and even graphics. All the inferences we make based on visual (and other

Figure 6.1 A stack of folded textiles – blankets and towels on the background light walls. Reprinted with permission from Alamy.com/retrieved from www.alamy.com/contributor: Olga Nikiforova / Alamy stock photo, copyright 2020, by Alamy.com.

Figure 6.2 Jack Russell puppy caught playing in toilet paper. Reprinted with permission from Alamy.com/retrieved from www.alamy.com/contributor: Antonio Gravante/Alamy stock photo, copyright 2009, by Alamy.com/reprinted.

sensory) cues constitute our expectations about the brand or product's qualities. For example, imagine yourself in a restaurant, ordering your favorite beverage. It comes either in a tall thin glass or a short wide one.

Because we give height more importance than width, we expect a tall thin glass to hold more than a short wide one. Therefore, when we drink all the juice in the tall glass, we are startled at how little we've consumed, and when we drain the short glass, we are surprised at how much we've drunk. In other words, we overestimate how much we have consumed from the tall, thin glass, and we underestimate how much we have imbibed from the short wide one. This systematic inaccuracy in our estimation of volume is known as the *consumption bias*. As you might imagine, a crafty bartender or restaurateur might use this to her advantage, altering perceived quantity with the shape of the glass.

Another example of the consumption bias is our tendency to estimate food portion by comparing it to the size of the dish containing it. Soup that fills a small bowl looks like more than the same amount of soup in a larger bowl. A fancy dessert served on one of those gigantic plates favored by expensive restaurants looks miniscule compared to a similarly sized dessert served on a saucer in a family eatery. In essence, we infer how much food is in a dish based in part on how much of the dish it occupies. This bias is so widely known that weight reduction programs encourage their members to start using smaller plates routinely and bring them to holiday feasts which are rife with tempting treats and where self-indulgence is expected (Happy Herbivore, 2017).

It seems plausible then to assume that smaller packages will curb overconsumption better than larger ones. Research finds just the opposite: we exercise more self-restraint when eating from a large package. The investigators hypothesize that we eat more from small packages because we believe that in choosing them over the large ones, we have exerted all the self-control we need to (Scott et al., 2008). See Wasnik and Chandon (2014) for more information on consumption biases and how to overcome them.

In sum, we actively interpret visual cues as meaningful information about brand and product qualities, both visible and nonvisual. Even those cues – for example, familiar logos – that we perceive but do not notice may affect our behavior in the short term.

Marketing with Music and Sound

How Does Music in a Retail Context Affect Us?

Music is highly complex structurally, varying in volume (loud or soft), tempo (fast or slow), chord (major or minor key for Western music), timbre (sound quality of instrument), and a number of other characteristics. It also varies in genre (classical or contemporary) and style (jazz, country, classical, easy listening, etc.), and most of us have marked preferences for some styles over others. In retail settings, including not only stores but also restaurants, banks, casinos, medical offices, and other places consumers frequent, music may be used to set a mood, to buttress the brand identity, to alter time perception, or to elicit some other specific consumer cognition or affect, all as a means of increasing store traffic, sales, and repeat visits.

Abercrombie and Fitch is a case in point. The retailer targets teens seeking to be sexy and cool, and does not want older consumers in the store, as they are bad for business. Loud music – almost as loud as a chainsaw – is one ploy it uses to attract target consumers and chase away the "undesirables." Many retailers employ this strategy, using music genre and volume, to signal consumers whether they are members of the target market. Passers-by may experience an instantaneous emotional reaction to the music – like or dislike, excitement or annoyance, etc. – and if they have a cognitive response to the music and to the feelings it elicits, it is likely to be something along the lines of "I'm not the person that store is trying to sell to" or "that music sounds familiar – I'm going in!" This is an example of the informative and mood-altering functions music can serve (Richards, 2012).

Music genre and style may also affect how we interact with merchandise and what we choose to purchase. To study the impact of music on consumer behavior in a wine store, researchers alternated popular music with classical pieces. When classical music was playing, customers explored more expensive wines and ultimately spent more money in the store. Another study showed that music origin may also influence wine purchase choices; in a supermarket setting, French music was associated with more purchases of French wine, German music with German wine. It may be that when we cannot directly judge product quality for ourselves, we (perhaps unconsciously) base our choices more on extraneous cues like store atmospherics – including music. This may hold true for status and experiential products in particular (e.g., wine, apparel, jewelry). Or it could be that music directs our attention to certain aspects of products (e.g., French music makes us think of – and notice – French words, brands, etc.); classical music, because of how we are socialized to regard it, reminds us of those "finer" things (Burghelea et al., 2015).

In addition to communicating target market characteristics and brand identity, setting a mood, and affecting purchase choices, music in a store setting can affect our time perception. Slow tempo music in supermarkets and restaurants may cause the consumer to slow her pace, linger longer, and consequently make more purchases. It may achieve these effects at least in part by altering time perception, causing the consumer to underestimate the amount of time spent in the establishment. Consistent with this, slow-tempo music has also been found to cause bank customers to underestimate the time spent waiting in line. (Recent research suggests that tempo may not be the only aspect of music that affects consumer behavior; see Burghelea et al. [2015] to read more about this complex and fascinating topic.)

The Sounds of Products and Brands

What Do You Hear When You Open the Package?

In 2009, Sun Chips developed a biodegradable bag – a great idea for the environment, attractive to consumers concerned about sustainability – or so it seemed. The problem was that the sound of the bag being opened was almost deafening. See CBS (2010) for an illustrative video.

Perhaps the noisy package would be more acceptable now, a decade later, when "eco-anxiety" has become all too common. But compostable packing is not good enough, according to Tony Walker, Dalhousie University biologist:

> If you want to be a better environmentalist, he suggested to reuse more items and to avoid buying "biodegradable" products. It's marketing, he said, they're mostly made of petroleum-based plastic except they're engineered to break down into infinitely smaller pieces of microplastics at a faster rate. These microplastics, which can be chipped down to the size of plankton, can get into waterways and risk being consumed by humans or marine animals.
>
> (Lum, 2020)

In other words, the environment would be better served by bulk sales of snacks that consumers scoop into their own reusable containers.

A large part of opening a package is the feeling of anticipation we experience during the process. Think of the last time you received an order from Amazon. com. Even when you know exactly what the box contains, you may still feel a tingle of anticipation as you hear – and feel – the packing tape or sticky seal ripping. The hiss of air as you break the seal of the lid on a soft drink bottle or flip the tab on a soda can, the pop of a champagne cork, the clicks you hear as you unlock your new car – all of these sounds likely elicit that feeling of anticipation because we have learned to associate those sounds with the moment of excited expectation we experience at the threshold of consumption.

How Does the Product Sound?

Like visual aspects of products, the sounds they make give us information about their identity, performance, and other qualities. An expensive, sleek sports car's motor sounds different from that of a spacious, comfortable family minivan. But electric vehicles (EVs), which have motors with few moving parts, are, according to *Time* magazine contributor Alejandro de la Garza:

> shockingly quiet. That might sound like a blessing for city dwellers and others sick of traffic noise, but it can create added risk for drivers (who rely on engine noise to get a sense of their speed) and pedestrians (who listen for oncoming traffic). For automakers, it also compromises decades of marketing based on the alluring rumble of a revving engine, especially in sports cars and trucks.
>
> (De La Garza, 2021)

The sounds of appliances, like refrigerators, dishwashers, and coffeemakers, as well as "power tools" like vacuum cleaners and lawn mowers, inform us about their performance and stage of processing. The clatter of the refrigerator ice maker reassures us that it is functioning as it should, the smooth roar of the lawn mower (gas or electric) tells us the machine will safely and effectively cut the grass, and the beeping of the oven communicates that it has reached a target temperature. Some product sounds are inevitable consequences of use, while others are designed into the product because consumers want or need them. The beeps and buzzes indicating stage of processing are designed to increase the product's user-friendliness.

The distinctive sounds many foods make when we bite into them are also meaningful to us. We infer degree of freshness based on the "crunch" of foods ranging from apples and celery to cookies and potato chips, and that crunch is an integral part of the consumption experience, enhancing our enjoyment (Twilley, 2015).

What Does the Brand Say?

In addition to shaping and informing our shopping and product usage experiences, music and sounds may be designed to identify specific brands, a process known as *sonic branding* (Coffee, 2013). After you read this section, you are strongly urged to explore the work of Audiobrain, a global leader in sonic branding and interactive audio. Audiobrain (2021) describes sonic branding and its roles in marketing as follows:

Sonic Branding is the **art** and **science** surrounding the strategic development and deployment of the **consistent, authentic** sound experience of a brand. It can range from a **Brand Theme** & **Sonic Logo** to a fully comprehensive **Sonic Identity** across all brand touchpoints. A brand's sonic identity provides the **strategic** and **creative** alignment of this experience to develop a narrative that delivers **unified, memorable**, and **unique** communications. A well-developed sonic identity **increases brand awareness** and **differentiation** while saving costs over time by providing a **clear** and **consistent** audio framework that is easily revised, repurposed, and expanded as a brand's needs change.

In De La Garza (2021), the author points out that the quiet of an EV provides an opportunity for marketers to create unique soundscapes for these vehicles:

> "We shouldn't be trying to communicate that there are moving pistons in this thing," says Danni Venne, lead producer and director of innovation at Made Music Studio, an audio branding agency that designed the engine sound for a recent iteration of the Nissan LEAF. "We're somewhere else now technologically." The LEAF sound, Venne says, has "a little bit of a singing quality to it." GM also took a step in the musical direction, creating EV sounds using sampled guitar, piano and didgeridoo. "We want it to sound organic, yet futuristic," says GM sound engineer Jigar Kapadia.
>
> Then there's whatever BMW is doing with its i4 electric-sedan concept. At low speeds, the i4 sounds like an electrified orchestra warming up for a performance. But as it accelerates, the tone becomes deeper and lower. Then comes a high-pitched skittering effect, as if some kind of reality-bending reaction were taking place under the hood. "We conceived a sound to celebrate the car, intended as a highly complex performative art installation," says BMW sound designer Renzo Vitale.

Most consumers can reproduce, in their minds or aloud, Intel's four-note signature sound. But most have neither seen nor comprehend the workings of Intel's main product – a computer chip. We do not buy chips, but rather computers. But the Intel brand is nonetheless a highly regarded consumer brand because the company has marketed it directly to consumers, and the sonic signature punctuates all of its commercials. As a result of years of very effective marketing campaigns, we seek out "Intel-inside" computers; that brand's microchip has become an essential component, engendering consumer trust in a product most of us do not understand. Much like a visual logo, the sound of the Intel brand reminds us of all we believe, feel, and have experienced that is brand related. Little wonder that Intel is in the top 20 of Interbrand's Best Global Brands of 2020.

There are more opportunities than ever before for marketers to employ music, sound, and interactive audio to enhance and enrich consumers' brand experiences and, ultimately, their brand schemas. David Ciccarelli, founder and CEO of

Voices.com (2022), the largest marketplace for audio and voiceover products and services in the world, recommends the following:

How Retailers Can Hone Their Sound

As retailers begin to explore sonic branding, they should start by conducting a thorough analysis of all the auditory channels through which customers experience their brands. This could include platforms like YouTube, SoundCloud, Spotify and iTunes; voice-activated devices like Google Home and Amazon Alexa; marketing channels such as television, radio and podcasts; and toll-free phone numbers that customers might dial to receive assistance. Social media also presents a unique opportunity for retail businesses to sonically connect with customers.

As retailers assess each channel, they should focus on these four attributes:

1. **Accessibility**: Retailers will want to make sure their audio messaging is multilingual, especially if their audiences are global. Where applicable, retailers should use subtitles to ensure that audiences who can't hear their messages can still receive them via text.
2. **Artistic quality**: If retailers are relying on spoken messages, professional voice talent is essential. Likewise, music and other sound effects will reflect brands' attitudes and personalities. Retailers should professionally craft these elements and align them with brand elements used elsewhere.
3. **Technical requirements**: All audio should be normalized to broadcast standards of −3 decibels with a noise floor below −60 decibels. Room tone should be minimized, and equalization should cover the full spectrum of frequencies.
4. **Documentation**: Retailers' brand standards should ideally be documented in a style or brand voice guide. If existing documentation doesn't cover auditory channels, they should update it as they begin to implement sonic branding.

When retailers have a distinct brand voice, it's possible to achieve a strong emotional connection with audiences. But first, they need to know what kind of emotional relationship they want to create. Do they want to inspire feelings of health and sustainability? Do they want to convey toughness? Or could it be that they want to build a reputation for being fun and lighthearted? Whatever retailers' branding goals may be, sound—with its incredible ability to evoke an emotional response—can help as they meet customers online.

The Significance of Scent

Smell is the most primitive of the senses. Its role in finding food and warning of danger is vital for survival. The organization of the olfactory system is somewhat primitive too: receptors are dendrites of neurons that go directly to the brain. Within two or three synapses, the brain can recognize an odor (Marin, 2015).

Olfaction is perhaps the most powerfully evocative of all of the senses. Though the human nose is far less acute than a dog's, we can still distinguish among millions of odors. Olfaction differs from vision and audition, in that our olfactory receptors are nerve cells with relatively short and direct access to the limbic system, which governs emotional responses, some forms of memory, and appetite. Our responses to smells are immediate and a fragrance alone can call forth a vivid, emotionally charged autobiographical memory (Hackländer et al., 2019).

The following article illustrates how consumers' responses to the scent of a product may help detect illness – if we pay attention!

Coffee is Being Widely Used as a COVID-19 Diagnostic Tool

Long cherished for its life-affirming, neuron-boosting aroma, coffee is now being held up all over the globe as an at-home diagnostic tool to help curb the ongoing COVID-19 pandemic.

A DCN review of scientific literature and anecdotal advice from scholars of taste and smell shows dozens of examples of coffee being used as the barometer for a kind of sniff-test for COVID-19, in part for its distinct smell and also for its availability in homes throughout the world.

The CDC now lists the loss of smell, known as anosmia, as one of the most common symptoms of COVID-19, with most recent studies indicating that about 50% to as much as 80% of people testing positive for the virus have suffered from anosmia.

The apparent good news—especially for coffee professionals who rely on olfactory observations for critical job functions—is that that most people suffering from COVID-19-induced anosmia do ultimately have their senses of taste and smell fully restored, according to preliminary research. ...

Given the prevalence of anosmia among COVID-19 carriers, the high percentage of asymptomatic carriers of the virus and the widespread availability of coffee, doctors everywhere are urging people to mask up and smell the coffee.

"One of the things that can be done pretty easily, pretty objectively by someone at home would be to take some ground coffee and see how far away you can hold it and still smell it," Tufts University School of Medicine Professor James Schwob recently told the University's news service....1

Researchers are applying these methods on a more rigorous scale, using coffee in olfactory test strips, while a recent article in the British medical journal BMJ encourages medical practitioners to employ coffee as a diagnostic tool....

Of course, smelling coffee is not a perfect science and it should not be confused for a legitimate medical test.

(Daily Coffee News Staff, 2020)

Logoscents

Marketing with scent is an old idea; a 1934 Forbes article, titled "'Sell by Smell' may be the next big slogan in marketing," enthusiastically encourages owners of indoor commercial spaces – stores, hotels, casinos – to use scent to give these spaces an "olfactory character" – to create logoscents that would serve the same purpose as a visual or sonic logo, instantly identifying the brand and vividly reminding consumers of their brand experiences. Gilbert (2008) writes:

> Most major international hotel chains—including Sofitel, Le Meridién and The Ritz-Carlton—already diffuse their unique aromas throughout their properties, but smaller brands have started focusing on fragrance as well. In fact, many have taken scent branding a step further and begun selling a hotel's fragrance in sprays, sticks and candles for you to purchase. …Hoteliers hope that whiffs of these scents will make you link their property with positive memories and emotions, as well as establish and market their brand…
>
> Famed hotelier Ian Schrager commissioned New York City-based bespoke fragrance creator Le Labo to concoct the Gramercy Park Hotel's scent. Le Labo founder Fabrice Penot and his partner visited the hotel to begin research and development when construction was still under way. The duo realized the fireplace was a central fixture in the lobby and formulated a scent that combined the smell of wood and hints of leather in a candle called Cade 26. Starting at $90, the candle is available for purchase through the Gramercy Park Hotel.…

Ambient Scent and Behavior

Much like music, ambient scent may affect purchase behavior. A field study in a men's and women's apparel store found that when a vanilla scent (perceived as more feminine) was diffused throughout the entire establishment, sales of women's apparel increased, while the spicy, floral scent rose maroc (considered more masculine) was associated with greater sales of men's clothing. Overall, gender-appropriate aromas (vanilla for women's apparel, rose maroc for men's) yielded an average sale of 1.7 items for USD 55.14 per customer, while gender-inappropriate scents led to an average per person sale of only 0.9 items for USD 23.01, about half as much. This increase in sales may be the result of shoppers' more positive impressions of the store and higher evaluations of the merchandise quality, selection, and styles when aromas were gender-congruent (Spangenberg and Sprott, 2006).

As increasing numbers of consumers shop online, what happens to the role of scent in marketing? Aradhna Krishna, a leading scholar of sensory marketing, comments:

> For the last 10 months during the pandemic of Covid-19, we have tried to keep safe by shopping online. We no longer go to the farmers' market and

feel the tomatoes before buying them. We no longer smell the colognes in Sephora, or do free tastings at Whole Foods Market and Trader Joes. But, we cannot use our olfactory, gustatory or haptic senses while making our online purchases; we need to rely on vision and audition—that is, on our sight and our hearing. How can the lack of these senses impact buyers? Obviously, they no longer get the full sensory pleasure of shopping in a physical market. But there is much more to how each sense can affect the buying process.

For example, my research published in the Journal of Consumer Research, shows that people can "smellize" food. That is, people can imagine food smells, and this imagination can make people salivate for the food and desire it, just as real smells do. This communication is possible even in an online context.

(Wood, 2020)

In other words, marketers should not underestimate the evocative power of our memories of scents. These memories can enrich our online shopping experiences – if marketers will start including smell imagery in their communications.

Music and Scent

Just as music positively affects sales if it reflects the visual identity of retailer or merchandise, ambient scent works best when it "matches" the music. Both scent and music can affect our arousal levels, for example, slow tempo music and lavender tend to relax and calm us, while fast-tempo music and citrus scents tend to energize us. A field study in a gift store showed that music and scent matching in arousal level, whether high (grapefruit and fast tempo music) or low (lavender and slow tempo music) resulted in higher sales than did mismatches (fast music and lavender, slow music and grapefruit) (Burghelea et al., 2015).

What Touch Tells Us

Touch, aka haptic sense, has not received nearly the scrutiny accorded to vision and audition in consumer research. Nonetheless, it is for many consumers an essential aspect of the shopping experience. It serves an instrumental function, providing information about tactile as well as non-tactile product and brand qualities, and it also offers hedonic benefits (pleasant, enjoyable), serving an autotelic function (an end in itself).

What Do We Learn by Touching the Merchandise?

Touch communicates the tactile properties of texture, temperature, and weight; from these we infer non-tactile qualities that are more difficult to evaluate directly, such as craftsmanship and durability. The importance of touch in shopping for apparel and linens is self-evident to many consumers; less readily apparent is the relevance of tactile information in choosing electronic devices such as smartphones, tablets, and laptops. Expert electronics reviewers frequently comment on the "feel" of a new device, using words like "cheap," "plasticky," "bulky," or "solid," "well-designed," "comfortable." While the experts can and do assess non-tactile properties directly, the brand's feel remains an important consideration, perhaps because our interactions with these devices have a significant tactile component.

Research pre-COVID-19 showed that consumers vary in their "need for touch" (NFT) in shopping and consumption contexts. High NFT shoppers are much less satisfied with online shopping experiences (Krishna and Schwarz, 2014). Even low NFT consumers may have been hesitant to purchase apparel online as the "fit" could be unpredictable from the dimensions provided. Many apparel sites began permitting fully refundable returns to reduce the perceived risk of purchasing clothing without first trying it on. During the pandemic, the few apparel retailers still open for business did not allow shoppers to try on clothing. The acceleration of digital commerce coupled with consumers' concerns about hygiene have created an opportunity for forward-thinking marketers. Though not yet widely available, technology exists enabling consumers who need hard-to-find sizes or simply prefer to shop online, to get a perfect fit by "trying on" clothing virtually (Wiggers, 2020).

Taste

We have saved taste for last because it is inherently multisensory (Krishna & Schwarz, 2014). When you pick up a potato chip to eat, you see it and develop expectations about how it will taste; does it look wholesome and homemade or is it so perfectly shaped that it must surely be factory-produced? Is it the right color or perhaps rather orange-tinted because spices were added? Does it smell fresh and authentically "potato-like" or like a chemical with an unpronounceable name? You taste the chip's saltiness and other flavors, all made possible by your sense of smell; you feel the rough texture of the ridges with your fingers and mouth, and you hear yourself crunching down on the chip. Research shows that the crunch sound is essential to consumers' enjoyment of chips; when the sound is masked by headphones, consumer satisfaction and pleasure are much diminished (Moss, 2014). And smell and vision are so essential in setting taste expectations that without them, we cannot distinguish a potato from an apple or red wine from coffee.

Visual cues alone may shape our taste expectations. For example, when we are asked to discriminate among flavors of fruit juice, color trumps taste. When we see cookies in the bread aisle, we may conclude they are healthier, hence not as tasty. Seeing the brand name can alter our taste experience (Krishna & Schwarz, 2014). When you pick up a potato chip to eat, you see it and develop expectations about how it will taste. Advertisers, who know the importance of vision in setting taste expectations, hire food stylists, whose sole purpose is to make the food look as appetizing as humanly possible. This may involve laboriously trimming the uneven edges of a hamburger bun, going through hundreds of boxes of corn flakes to find those with the best shape, painting a raw turkey to give that succulent just-baked look, and other such adjustments. For large markers, the return on investment in this level of attention to detail makes it worthwhile.

How Might Sensory Marketing Help Consumers Become Healthier?

Visual cues can be our allies or enemies as we strive to improve our health-related behaviors, both because they are prominent in the environment and because their impact on us often dominates the effects of our other senses. As discussed above, a simple change like eating from smaller dishes may help us eat less, as does removing the food from view. Similarly for cigarettes: showing them in advertisements meant to help people stop smoking may actually trigger the urge to smoke. The other senses may be brought into play: for example, music helps us exercise more vigorously (Patania et al., 2020). More links to research on this important topic are provided in the discussion questions for this chapter.

Conclusion

As demonstrated above, our senses mediate our marketplace and post-purchase consumption experiences in powerful ways that we can also harness in service of our well-being. Research on how the senses interact to shape experience becomes considerably more complicated going from one to two senses; including all five senses in a properly designed study is exponentially more complex, but that is precisely the field research we need in order to understand more completely how to use sensory marketing tactics strategically and how to respond to them in ways that serve us best as consumers.

References

Audiobrain (2021). "Sonic branding project". Retrieved from: www.audiobrain.com/work examples.

Baertlein, L. (2011, January 5). "Starbucks cuts name and 'coffee' from logo". Retrieved from: www.reuters.com/article/us-starbucks/starbucks-cuts-name-and-coffee-from-logo-idUSTRE7045YF20110106#targetText=The%20new%20green%20logo%20is, led%20sailors%20to%20their%20deaths.&targetText=The%20company%2C%20based%20in%20Seattle, it%20went%20public%20in%201992.

Burghelea, M. R., Plaias, I., & El-Murad, J. (2015). "The effects of music as an atmospheric variable on consumer behaviour in the context of retailing and service environments". *International Conference on Marketing and Business Development Journal, 1*(1), 377–392. www.mbd.ase.ro/RePEc/aes/icmbdj/2015/ICMBDJ_V1_2015_150.pdf.

Candy Industry (2014, April 23). "Hershey debuts new Hershey miniatures package". Retrieved from: www.candyindustry.com/articles/86207-hershey-debuts-new-hershey-miniatures-package.

CBS (2010, October 5). "Sun chips ditches compostable bag" [Video]. YouTube. https://youtu.be/cuhWtnujroQ.

Coffee, P. (2013, January 17). "What is 'sonic branding'?". *Adweek*. Retrieved from: www.adweek.com/performance-marketing/what-is-sonic-branding/.

Daily Coffee News Staff (2020, December 14). "Coffee is being widely used as a Covid-19 diagnostic tool". *Daily Coffee News*. Retrieved from: https://dailycoffeenews.com/2020/12/14/coffee-is-being-widely-used-as-a-covid-19-diagnostic-tool/.

Deighton, K. (2019, January 7). "Mastercard removes name from circles logo in an act of digital 'simplicity'". *The Drum*. Retrieved from: www.thedrum.com/news/2019/01/07/mastercard-removes-name-circles-logo-act-digital-simplicity.

De La Garza, A. (2021, April 6). "Electric cars can sound like anything. That's a huge opportunity to craft the soundscape of the future". *Time*. Retrieved from: https://time.com/5951773/electric-car-sound-future/.

Dornbusch, J. (2014, February 11). "Increasing food prices spark trend of package downsizing". *Boston Globe*. Retrieved from: www.bostonglobe.com/lifestyle/food-dining/2014/02/11/the-incredible-shrinking-package/Ti6VwQCCcg0whLdr8bHnyJ/story.html.

DukeUniversityNews (2008, April 24). "Apple really does make you 'think different'" [Video]. YouTube. Retrieved from: https://youtu.be/yHzUFZcLamQ.

Feloni, R. (2015, June 25). "KFC founder Colonel Sanders didn't achieve his remarkable rise to success until his 60s". *Business Insider*. Retrieved from: www.businessinsider.com/how-kfc-founder-colonel-sanders-achieved-success-in-his-60s-2015-6.

Gilbert, A. (2008). *What the Nose Knows: The Science of Scent in Everyday Life*. New York, NY: Crown.

Hackländer, R. P. M., Janssen, S. M. J., & Bermeitinger, C. (2019). "An in-depth review of the methods, findings, and theories associated with odor-evoked autobiographical memory". *Psychonomic Bulletin & Review, 26*, 401–429. https://doi.org/10.3758/s13423-018-1545-3.

Happy Herbivore (2017). "The crazy world of food psychology". Retrieved from: https://happyherbivore.com/podcast/how-to-eat-less-feel-satisfied-plate-color-food/.

Interbrand (2020, October 20). "Zoom and Tesla enter the ranks of Interbrand's 2020 best global brands report". Retrieved from: https://interbrand.com/newsroom/interbrand-reveals-2020-best-global-brands-report/.

Johnson, M., & Ghuman, P. (2020). *Blindsight: The (Mostly) Hidden Ways Marketing Reshapes our Brains*. Dallas, TX: BenBalla Books.

Klara, R. (2014, September 29). "How a topless mermaid made the Starbucks cup an icon". Retrieved from: www.adweek.com/brand-marketing/how-topless-mermaid-made-starbucks-cup-icon-160396/.

Krishna, A., & Schwarz, N. (2014). "Sensory marketing, embodiment, and grounded cognition: A review and introduction". *Journal of Consumer Psychology, 24*(2), 159–168. https://doi.org/10.1016/j.jcps.2013.12.006.

Ladd, A. (2012, January 29). "Fresh impressions on brandmarks (from my 5-year-old)" [Video]. YouTube. Retrieved from: https://youtu.be/N4t3-__3MA0.

Luffarelli, J., Mukesh, M., & Mahmood, A. (2019, September 12). "A study of 597 logos shows which kind is most effective". *Harvard Business Review*. Retrieved from: https://hbr.org/2019/09/a-study-of-597-logos-shows-which-kind-is-most-effective.

Lum, Z.-A. (2020, January 20). "SunChips' failed noisy compostable packaging gets the last laugh". *HuffPost*. Retrieved from: www.huffpost.com/archive/ca/entry/sun-chips-compostable-bag_ca_5e1f1e8fc5b674e44b90b2a8.

Madrigal, A. C. (2011, April 6). "The Pringle as technology". *The Atlantic*. Retrieved from: www.theatlantic.com/technology/archive/2011/04/the-pringle-as-technology/236903/.

Marin, A. (2015, January 27). "Making sense of scents: Smell and the brain". *BrainFacts.* Retrieved from: www.brainfacts.org/thinking-sensing-and-behaving/smell/2015/making-sense-of-scents-smell-and-the-brain.

Moss, M. (2014). *Salt Sugar Fat: How the Food Giants Hooked Us.* London: Random House Trade Paperbacks.

Mouradian, N. (2019, May 8). "Announcing Dieline Awards 2019 first place winners". Retrieved from: https://thedieline.com/blog/2019/5/8/announcing-dieline-awards-2019-first-place-winners.

Nassauer, S. (2013, February 12). "The push for grown-up 'squeezies'". *Wall Street Journal.* Retrieved from: www.wsj.com/articles/SB10001424127887324196204578300280004277610.

Old Spice (2020, January 22). "Time out | Old spice" [Video]. YouTube. Retrieved from: https://youtu.be/UoiFt6Hr0cE.

Patania, V. M., Padulo, J., Iuliano, E., Ardigò, L. P., Čular, D., Miletić, A., & De Giorgio, A. (2020). "The psychophysiological effects of different tempo music on endurance versus high-intensity performances". *Frontiers in Psychology, 11.* https://doi.org/10.3389/fpsyg.2020.00074.

Pharr, D. (2021, April 20). "Can you name the cars (or car companies) from their logos?". Retrieved from: www.sporcle.com/games/g/carlogos.

Richards, C. (2012, December 21). "Retailers pump up the volume to help drive up sales". *Washington Post.* Retrieved from: www.washingtonpost.com/lifestyle/style/retailers-pump-up-the-volume-to-help-drive-up-sales/2012/12/21/993bd196-4ae9-11e2-a6a6-aabac85e8036_story.html.

Saint Louis, C. (2014, November 10). "Detergent pods pose risk to children, study finds". *New York Times.* Retrieved from: www.nytimes.com/2014/11/10/health/detergent-pods-pose-risk-to-children-study-finds.html.

Saxena, J. (2021, March 25). "Fast food's retro glow-up". *Eater.* Retrieved from: www.eater.com/22338642/fast-food-chains-design-retro-minimalist-sans-serif.

Schuman, N. (2019, August 28). "How Doritos scrapped its logo to engage Gen Z". *PRNEWS.* Retrieved from: www.prnewsonline.com/Doritos-Scraps-Logo-to-Engage-Generation-Z.

Scott, M. L., Nowlis, S. M., Mandel, N., & Morales, A. C. (2008). "The effects of reduced food size and package size on the consumption behavior of restrained and unrestrained eaters". *Journal of Consumer Research, 35*(3), 391–405. https://doi.org/10.1086/591103.

Spangenberg, E. R., & Sprott, D. E. (2006). "Gender-congruent ambient scent influences on approach and avoidance behaviors in a retail store". *Journal of Business Research, 59*(12), 1281–1287. https://doi.org/10.1016/j.jbusres.2006.08.006.

Twilley, N. (2015, October 26). "Accounting for taste: How packaging can make food more flavorful". *New Yorker.* Retrieved from: www.newyorker.com/magazine/2015/11/02/accounting-for-taste.

Voices (2022). "The world's #1 voice marketplace". Retrieved from: www.voices.com/.

Wasnik, B., & Chandon, P. (2014). "Slim by design: Redirecting the accidental drivers of mindless overeating". Insead. Retrieved from: https://sites.insead.edu/facultyresearch/research/doc.cfm?did=53579.

Wiggers, K. (2020, June 5). "Amazon's new AI technique lets users virtually try on outfits". Retrieved from: https://venturebeat.com/2020/06/05/amazons-new-ai-technique-lets-users-virtually-try-on-outfits/.

Wood, S. (2020, December 26). "Sensory marketing during Covid?". *Journal of Consumer Research.* https://consumerresearcher.com/sensory-marketing-in-covid-lockdown.

7 Sociocultural and Interpersonal Influences on Consumer Behavior

Objectives

1. To explore how our cultures and social identities influence our consumer behavior.
2. To investigate how and why people share product and brand information and experiences.
3. To describe how marketers and consumer advocates can include interpersonal influence tactics in their messaging.

Introduction

Up to this point we've explored how the consumer's mind works to shape thoughts and feelings and guide purchase decisions. But the social forces at work behind our consumption practices are equally important to understand in order to obtain a full and rich vision of consumer behavior. In this chapter we'll begin with a discussion of cultural influences on consumers, then examine how subcultures and broad social groupings affect our consumer behavior, and move on to investigate the more immediate and pervasive impact of the people we know best and trust most: family and friends.

How Does Culture Influence Our Consumer Behavior?

First, what do we mean by "culture"? This definition captures its complexity:

> Culture consists of shared elements that provide the standards for perceiving, believing, evaluating, communicating, and acting among those who share a language, a historical period, and a geographic location. As a psychological construct, culture can be studied in multiple ways—across nations, across ethnic groups within nations, across individuals within nations (focusing on cultural orientation), and even within individuals through the priming of cultural values.
>
> (Shavitt et al., 2008)

DOI: 10.4324/9780367426897-9

Note the reference to "standards": culture tells us how to think, feel, and behave; while we may internalize it as a "psychological construct," we do not always follow its tenets, either individually or collectively.

Dimensions of Culture

In his quest to understand how employees behave in large organizations, social psychologist Geert Hofstede conducted pioneering research in which he surveyed more than 100,000 IBM employees from over 70 national subsidiaries. He found systematic differences in responses across but not within national borders, which led him to posit that national cultures vary widely in identifiable ways, which he characterized as dimensions The Hofstede dimensions represent "independent preferences for one state of affairs over another that distinguish countries (rather than individuals) from each other. The dimensions were developed inductively from data covering many countries." The dimensions are as follows:

- *Power Distance Index* captures how people in a culture view some as having more power, others less. High power distance societies are more hierarchical and the unequal distribution of power is accepted as normal. In low power distance cultures, power inequality is a source of discomfort and attempts are made to correct or camouflage it.
- *Individualism versus Collectivism* contrasts loosely knit societies, in which people look after themselves and their immediate families, with tightly knit social structures that place the group's interests above those of its individual members. Both extremes involve trade-offs. The individualist gets to put her own interests first, but she may not have anyone to turn to if things go wrong. The collectivist society with its subjugation of individual wishes to group interests, may at times feel claustrophobic, but in hard times people can rely on one another for help and support.
- *Masculinity versus Femininity* reflects the extent to which a society values achievement, assertiveness, and competition as opposed to cooperation and quality of life.
- *Uncertainty Avoidance Index* refers to the extent to which people in a society are comfortable with the uncertainty and ambiguity of not knowing the future. In their need to control the future, cultures with high uncertainty avoidance may have rigid beliefs and behavioral norms and a low tolerance for nonconformity. Cultures with low uncertainty avoidance have a more laissez faire approach to daily life and concomitantly a higher tolerance for diverse beliefs and behaviors.
- *Long-Term Orientation versus Short-Term Normative Orientation*: A society with a long-term orientation values its history and traditions more than the future and resists change. A culture with a short-term normative orientation espouses a pragmatic perspective that emphasizes shaping a better future, for example, through educational advancement.

- *Indulgence versus Restraint*: An indulgent culture encourages members to seek pleasure by gratifying basic human wants and needs, while a society that values restraint imposes strict standards of behavior instead.

An important caveat about these dimensions is that they are meant to be used to compare national cultures; the author never intended them to provide a nuanced understanding of a specific culture. They would argue that while this approach to the study of cultural differences provides a useful overview of a group's espoused values, it does not enlighten us about how individuals actually think, feel, and behave. Below is a brief description of each dimension:

In a provocative study that illustrates an appropriate application of the dimensions to better understand why obesity is more prevalent in some countries than in others, Wallace et al. (2019) quantified associations between these six dimensions and mean population body mass index (BMI; a measure of obesity) in more than 60 countries over a 25-year period from 1990 to 2014. After removing the effects of variations in income inequality, national income, education, and proportion of the population living in urban versus rural areas, the authors found that obesity is indeed related to high or low values of several of the dimensions, and offer the following explanations:

- **Individualism (vs. Collectivism)**: Individualism is very highly correlated with national wealth. Individualistic societies tend to view obesity as an issue of personal responsibility whereby people are responsible for their own lifestyle choices of diet and exercise. Interventions for obesity, which stem from this worldview, are based on consumer ethics, including education and social marketing, to help individuals to navigate the obesogenic environment. In contrast, collectivist societies may be more sympathetic to more effective public health policies, which change the environment. Other aspects of collectivist societies, such as communal eating patterns and sharing resources, could also mediate a potential protective influence of this worldview.
- **Uncertainty avoidance (vs. Uncertainty tolerance)**: Characteristics of higher uncertainty avoiding cultures, which may predispose to obesity, include high levels of nervousness, stress, and anxiety; viewing obesity as something that they did not cause and cannot be prevented; relying on health experts to treat obesity rather than public health strategies to prevent it; a tendency to ignore diet and exercise recommendations; and a belief that there are many barriers to physical activity. These barriers to physical activity may be due to real environmental and safety barriers, as higher uncertainty-avoiding societies tend to also have higher levels of crime and corruption.
- **Indulgence (vs. Restraint)**: More restrained societies tend to value more self-control and restraint from natural human impulses, particularly hunger cues. In comparison, indulgent societies are associated with emotional and uncontrolled eating habits. Parental indulgence increases overindulgence that ultimately prevents children from creating self-efficacy and controlling their

natural desires and impulses on their own and creates stress and affects overall health later in life. Further, overindulged children tend to overeat, have higher spending, and have difficulty making their own decisions.

- **Long-term orientation (vs. Short-term orientation)**: These societies focus on long-term goals and use a more pragmatic approach in preparation for future outcomes. In an increasingly obesogenic environment, a culture that heavily discounts the more distant future in favor of the near future may be at greater risk of obesity because the longer-term consequences of obesity, such as getting diabetes or suffering social bias, are not given as much weighting as would happen in a culture with a longer-term orientation.
- **Power distance**: High Power distance societies are accepting of inequalities and power hierarchies more than other societies. Power distance influences, for example, the relationship between doctors and patients (doctors being power holders). High Power distance societies may be less prone to obesity as they are more likely to follow the advice of an authority, such as a doctor or a health institution.
- **Masculinity (vs. Femininity)**: Members of these societies are assertive and status oriented, and gaining results are of great importance. Masculinity stands for a society in which emotional gender roles are clearly distinct: Men are supposed to be assertive, tough, and focused on material success; women are supposed to be more modest, tender, and concerned with the quality of life. Its opposite, femininity, stands for a society in which emotional gender roles overlap: Both men and women are supposed to be modest, tender, and concerned with the quality of life. Smaller gender differences in BMI could be hypothesized in more feminine societies.

While it is acknowledged that culture does change over time (e.g., due to secular changes, migration, and changing demographics), it was considered to be only slowly changing compared with the changes in population BMI. Studies have shown that while the culture of countries does change, the relative position of countries remains largely the same (Wallace et al., 2019).

Cultural influences on an individual's consumer behavior may be best represented in the schemas and scripts that s/he has internalized over years of unconscious absorption punctuated by the occasional question. Mostly, we remain unaware of the extent to which our culture shapes our cognitions, affect, and behavior. Only when we encounter different cultural dictates and norms are we able to see that our own culture is just one of many. Below are two examples of such encounters.

Debra Samuels, food and travel writer, cookbook author, and teacher, tells this story:

> When we lived in Japan, my son went to a Japanese elementary school. I needed to send him to school with lunch. On his first day, he went with a peanut butter and jelly sandwich, carrot sticks and a cookie, just like any good American mom would send.
>
> (Figure 7.1: Photo of Japanese children (lunchboxes), 2016, iStock photo)

Figure 7.1 Japanese schoolchildren bento (lunchboxes). Reprinted with permission from iStock.com/usako123, 2016.
Source: iStock.com. Copyright 2016 by iStock.com/usako123.

> He came home crying, "My lunch isn't cute." The lunch had to be cute. I didn't know. What's cute?
>
> At which point I needed to learn how to make lunch Japanese style, obento. I went out and bought a book called *100 Ways To Make Obento*. My son Brad and I worked our way through the book for the entire year.
>
> Moms every day make their children lunches. It's not considered an onerous task, it's considered part of their job. The job of the mother is to make a nutritious lunch that looks attractive, and the child's job is to eat it all up.....

Samuels internalized the values of which she spoke. Her initial motive was to ensure that her son would feel a sense of belonging among his schoolmates, but she came to see the social and emotional significance of the box preparation:

> I took on the values that were transmitted in this box. I kind of look at it as Japanese culture in a box. I learned that aesthetics were important, I learned about balance, and I learned about the give and take from the receiver and the giver. It's a cooperative relationship.
>
> I used to think Japanese women were crazy for spending the amount of time that they did on lunch boxes and creating these things, but the children eat it all up and they remember. Any Japanese adult, they remember their mother's bento boxes with a lot of fondness.

(Kasper, 2011)

A post in response to this story conveys a different perspective on the intersection between "cute" and "edible":

> My kids would freak at the idea of eating a cute smiley creature   the giraffes, Snoopy, cows, and the smiley tomatoes would all return home and I would be asked to "save" them. They would probably give them names. So Thermos hot leftovers it is! But I can cut hearts and cars out of cheese.
>
> (Olga O.)

Our second example illustrates that some customs, however sound scientifically, do not travel well:

> Growing up in South Korea, Jamie Cho knew from childhood that if she got sick, she had to put a face mask on, even if it was just a common cold.
>
> "My parents told me it was to keep myself and others safe," she told HuffPost. "I would see others wear masks as well, especially during the winter seasons."
>
> The masks weren't just a medical accessory, she said. For many, they served an aesthetic purpose: something a woman might put on to cover a makeup-less face while running errands or a K-Pop star might slip on to avoid being spotted by fans in an airport.
>
> Cho distinctly remembers that when her family moved to New York, her mom told her that she had to stop wearing masks in public because people would think she was ill or would look at her funny.
>
> "She was scared of me seeming more foreign than I already was at the time as a young immigrant," the college student said. "Because of that, I've never worn a mask in a Western country prior to COVID."
>
> (Wong, 2020)

Why did many westerners find wearing a mask during the COVID pandemic so unpalatable, even abhorrent? An MIT study offers insight into this conundrum:

> Around the world and within the U.S., the percentage of people wearing masks during the Covid-19 pandemic has varied enormously. What explains this? A new study co-authored by an MIT faculty member finds that a public sense of "collectivism" clearly predicts mask usage, adding a cultural and psychological perspective to the issue....
>
> "Our data both within the United States and across the world shows that collectivism is a strong and important predictor of whether people in a region wear masks or not," says Jackson G. Lu, an assistant professor at the MIT Sloan School of Management and co-author of a new paper detailing the results....
>
> "In collectivistic cultures, people consider wearing masks not only a responsibility or duty, but also, a symbol of solidarity—that we're standing together and fighting this pandemic together," Lu says.

In analyzing the results, the researchers controlled for a large set of other factors that might influence mask wearing, including the severity of Covid-19 outbreaks in states, government policies, political affiliations across the public, education levels, population density, per-capita income, age, and gender.

They found that a U.S. state's collectivism rating is a strong and consistent predictor of mask usage no matter what. For example, Hawaii, has the highest collectivism rating in the U.S., and the second-highest level of mask usage (slightly behind Rhode Island). On the other end of the spectrum, a handful of states from the Great Plains and Mountain West have both low collectivism scores and low levels of mask wearing, including Wyoming, South Dakota, Montana, and Kansas....

In countries around the world, as in the U.S., the results were the same: Collectivism scores again predict which countries tended to have high levels of mask wearing.

(Dizikes, 2021)

This study illustrates the intra-cultural as well as intercultural variation in attitudes and behavior around mask-wearing. It also shows that long-practiced cultural norms help shape our responses to changes imposed by external circumstances. And finally, it demonstrates that up-to-date consumer research is essential for marketing success. We should never assume that our existing experienced-based perspectives on a culture are correct. All of us are subject to biases, many unconscious. Consumer research serves to counter our biases and to reveal a timely and accurate portrayal of current and potential customers (Bump, 2020).

The impact of national culture on consumer behavior is pervasive. In the next section we turn our attention to reference groups, which influence consumers differently depending on the individual's sense of self.

What Are Reference Groups and How Do They Influence Our Consumer Behavior?

As social beings, we seek to feel a sense of belonging to groups beyond immediate family; this drive to belong may be satisfied by a few close friends, a religious, or cause-related affiliation; a professional organization; shared loyalty to a sports team, band, or brand; a community coalescing around a passion for running, knitting, neuroscience, or any of a million other activities; or people who come together to grapple with a shared challenge, for example, addiction or chronic illness, parenting an autistic child or caring for an elder with Alzheimer's.

Any or all of these may function as a *reference group*, to which we turn for information, advice, or guidance; as such, the group influences how we think, feel, and behave in a specific area of our lives. The fact that we care what others think of us not only goes a long way toward the maintenance of a strong social fabric, it also accounts for trends in product choices and for new product successes.

There are three main types of reference groups: membership, aspirational, and dissociative. We may be members of the reference groups important to us, although many such groups have no formal membership and may not even meet formally. Some important reference groups may also be aspirational for us, that is, we seek to emulate the other members, though we may not have close ties to them. Finally, dissociative reference groups are those we do not want to join or emulate; indeed, we do not ever want to be mistaken for a member of a group we define as dissociative. Note that a membership group for one person may be an aspirational one for another and a dissociative one for yet a third. Note also that reference group influence is, more often than not, context-specific. In the foregoing examples of cultural influences on consumer behavior, Japanese moms were an aspirational reference group for Debra Samuels in the context of preparing food for one's children. The second and third examples illustrate the importance of the distinction between individualist and collectivist groups in the context of adherence to mask-wearing strictures. For Jamie Cho, a normative behavior in her culture of origin (South Korea) became a potential liability in New York, where a mask might set her apart as belonging to a dissociative reference group, that is, a very sick individual. And in the MIT study, wearing a mask identified individuals as either socially concerned rational decision-makers who base their behavior on scientific evidence or as socialist radicals who seek to prevent others from exercising their individual freedoms. This is a clear illustration of how one person's membership group may be a dissociative one for others.

From the shoes we wear to the logo-laden cups we carry, our consumer choices define and delimit us as one sort of person and not another. Many of the students at a university near Nike headquarters and in the same region as the original Starbucks wear (carry) these brands' logos with conscious allegiance, declaring themselves as aspirants to athletic excellence and consumers who care about socially sustainable practices like fair trade and ethical treatment of laborers. These consumers likely dissociate themselves from Styrofoam-using Hummer drivers, many of whom reciprocate the animosity.

Reference groups and referent others help shape our self-concept, which may be viewed as a self-schema. Who am I? What kind of person am I? We come to know ourselves in relation to important others. And as our world and our roles in society increase in complexity, so also do our reference groups multiply and our self-schemas become richer. All of us have, at a minimum, a gender identity (I am female), a national identity (I am British), a cultural identity (I am Asian), and a sexual orientation identity (I am a heterosexual). These are membership reference groups. Many of us also have a professional identity (I am a professor), a family identity (I am single), and other identities shaped by our interests and experiences (I am a cat mom, I have a sustainable lifestyle). We incorporate these identities into our self-schema, and they profoundly affect our consumer behavior. Our gender identification affects our choices of clothing and cosmetics. Our national identity, even if we are not the least bit patriotic, determines which products and brands are available to us and the behavioral norms we are expected to adhere to, our cultural identity likely influences some kinds of purchases (e.g., food) more than others, and our family identity affects the quantity and perhaps quality of the groceries we buy regularly. And each of these identities may be fine-tuned by our attitudes, beliefs, and experiences: "I am a mom who does not allow my child to have processed food"; "I am a dog mom who is training my puppy using only positive reinforcement."

Our reference groups exert more influence on our consumer choices if those choices are visible and meaningful to group members. What we wear, drive/ride, eat, if (and how) we stay physically fit – all of these are highly visible in many contexts and identify us as belonging to this group and not that one. Thompson's (2021) annual survey from the American College of Sports Medicine (ACSM) *Health and Fitness Journal* illustrates how professionals in the health fitness industry serve as aspirational *reference groups*, in a unique position to lead the way in fitness and to observe fitness trends as they gather momentum and display staying power. The following top five trends for 2021 are based on more than 4,000 responses from industry practitioners in all four industry sectors (community, corporate, commercial, and clinical):

1. **Online training**. The COVID-19 pandemic resulted in the temporary closure of clubs around the world, forcing innovations in fitness class delivery. Many clubs developed online training programs for groups and individuals. Classes or one-on-one training may occur live via Zoom or a similar videoconferencing platform; or they may be prerecorded and available at the client's convenience.

2. **Wearable technology**. These devices range from simple pedometers to watch-sized computers with biosensors tracking heart rate, body temperature, calories, sitting time, sleep time, and much more. They are more accurate than ever and may be very helpful to those aspiring to increase their activity levels. Many are associated with apps that offer opportunities to compete with oneself or other active individuals (membership groups) and to view inspiring stories of people who have overcome significant challenges to achieve fitness (aspirational group).

3. **Body-weight training** requires minimal equipment because the body itself is used to provide resistance. The elbow plank is an excellent example.

4. **Outdoor activities** became more popular during the COVID-19 pandemic, as socializing outdoors proved safer than indoor gatherings. Small groups convene to take walks, go on bike rides, or go hiking. The activities may be relatively brief and easy to schedule around work and family obligations or longer for those so inclined, even extending to planned weeklong excursions. Participants may meet in a local park, hiking area, or on a bike trail typically with a designated leader. For many, these membership groups serve as a great source of motivation to become and remain active, and they also provide an opportunity for face-to-face social interaction, which was especially needed during the COVID pandemic.

5. **High-intensity interval training**. These exercise programs, typically involving short bursts of high-intensity bouts of exercise followed by a short period of rest, have been found to be especially effective at increasing aerobic and other aspects of fitness when done in moderation.

What happens when we do not measure up to reference group norms we have internalized? Our self-schema demand some sort of consistency between our beliefs and behaviors, and the complexity of our social roles helps us find a way to resolve the anxiety we may feel when we experience internal inconsistencies between the two:

> Take for example a consumer feeling "unathletic" after skipping a workout. She may compensate for this discrepancy symbolically by purchasing athletic apparel, or directly with a longer workout on her next gym visit. Both of these behaviors would help reinforce a positive association between the self and the identity. Rather than approaching a positive self-association, the consumer may also respond by reinforcing a negative self-association with the identity. For example, if feeling unathletic, the consumer may respond by disidentifying with the athlete identity by avoiding athlete-congruent behavior below baseline. This effect may be more prominent for consumers lower in collective self-esteem and also when approaching the identity seems less feasible. Rather than positive or negative reinforcement of a given association, the consumer may seek a different, "neutral" route. For example, the consumer may engage in escapism, where they intentionally focus on domains that are irrelevant to the discrepancy. Alternatively, the consumer may instead reinforce a different, unrelated identity. This type of fluid compensation may manifest as the consumer reinforcing her Asian identity after feeling "unathletic."
>
> (Saint Clair, 2018)

While marketers do not determine our reference group membership or aspirations, they can increase the likelihood of our sharing brand-related content. Next, we discuss how and why consumers share, whether by means of reviews and recommendations or by sharing marketing content.

What Is Word of Mouth and Why Is It Important?

Word of Mouth (WOM) "consists of informal communications directed at other consumers about the ownership, usage or characteristics of particular goods and services and/or their sellers" (Westbrook, 1987).

Since we listen best to people whose opinions we trust and care about, WOM from reference group members – friends, colleagues, family – is especially effective at persuading us to purchase or avoid specific brands. Marketing research firm Keller Fay recently found that WOM about British supermarkets is strongly correlated with sales. Aldi, which received the most positive WOM, showed the highest sales growth, and Tesco showed among the lowest sales growth and the least positive WOM (Morgan, 2015).

Online word of mouth (eWOM) is "any positive or negative statement made by customers – potential, real or former – about a product or company, which is made available to other people via the Internet" (Thorsten et al., 2004). For purposes of this discussion, we are also considering consumer sharing of content (retweets, videos, etc.) as a form of eWOM. WOM (eWOM) is considered the Holy Grail of marketing, because in general we believe that other consumers are not motivated by financial self-interest, hence more trustworthy than marketers. Below, we discuss what motivates people to talk about brands and products, which kinds of brands are most likely to generate WOM, and what sorts of information are most likely to be shared. Then, we will explore the impact of WOM on consumer cognitions, affect, and behavior.

Motives for Engaging in WOM and eWOM

What motivates a consumer to blog or talk about a product or to share branded content? Studies show that people who engage in WOM (eWOM) typically have social, emotional, and/or functional motives for doing so.

Social motives for talking about brands include *self-enhancement*, that is, enhancing others' perceptions of one's product expertise or social status; *uniqueness*, the desire to be viewed as different and special in some aspect; *altruism*, the drive to help others by recommending excellent products; and the simple human *desire to converse*.

If the motive for WOM is enhancement of perceived expertise, positive comments about high-quality or premium brands would best serve the speaker's purpose. If the motive is to appear unique among peers, talking about unique, that is, highly differentiated, brands would be most effective. The Bugaboo stroller and Dyson vacuum, discussed in Chapter 6, are examples of brands that are both premium and highly differentiated. One could make the case that a person motivated by altruism could equally well share positive information about high-performing brands and negative WOM warning others away from inferior brands. Finally, the individual who just wants to converse might succeed best by focusing on brands that are relevant to a variety of listeners; in the US, the iPhone, with its considerably greater market share, should generate more conversation than an android smartphone.

Emotional motives, both positive and negative, often underlie WOM. For complex or expensive purchases, for example, a new car or house, excitement and anxiety may coexist in equal measure; WOM may serve to maintain or increase the feeling of excitement while diminishing the concomitant anxiety. Hence the lengthy conversations we have offline and online about these major purchases and the delight in showing them to appreciative others.

Marketing messages can elicit the emotions most likely to drive WOM. Nike, a brand marketed from its beginning as our ally in the struggle to achieve worthy goals, to exceed our personal best, to compete continually with ourselves and others, has brilliantly generated positive WOM by inspiring us with commercials featuring both "normal" people and celebrities, and providing opportunities for aspiring athletes of all kinds to engage in conversation (NikeTalk, 2022).

Some products, for example, health-related ones, may be both anxiety-provoking and avoided in consumer conversation. Arguably, direct-to-consumer advertising of prescription pharmaceuticals may encourage WOM by vividly portraying the brands' emotional benefits that result from ameliorating physical ailments, thus putting a positive spin on products that were traditionally unsought and mostly unwanted. An example is Viagra, the advertising of which destigmatized erectile dysfunction and transformed its treatment from a shameful secret into a positive and exciting lifestyle choice – in large part, by encouraging WOM in mainstream media.

An innovative study by marketing professor Jonah Berger and Daniel McDuff of Microsoft Research investigated the emotional "triggers" that motivate people to share advertising content. Several thousand participants in five countries were asked to watch a random set of commercials on their home computers while their webcams recorded their facial expressions. Their emotional responses were coded (labeled) based on their facial expressions using algorithms built for that purpose. Why not just ask people how they feel? Because we are not very proficient at labeling our emotions and our desire to please the researcher may bias our responses. Facial expressions may be quite revealing, in part because they are often involuntary.

The investigators found that two aspects of an emotion – its positive or negative valence and the physiological arousal associated with it – help explain our choice to share content that evokes that feeling. The positive emotions of awe, excitement, and humor lead to sharing content, while contentment (much less arousing, hence not as motivating) does not. Similarly, the negative emotions of anger, anxiety, and disgust motivate viewers to share content, while the much less arousing feeling of sadness does not.

The marketing implications of this research are first that simply making people feel good does not motivate them to share. Rather, the content must "fire them up." Second, content that evokes negative emotions is not only permissible, but may also be desirable in some cases. And third, the authors caution, increased sharing does not always lead to increased sales (Knowledge@Wharton, 2021).

Functional motive: A final motive for engaging in WOM is to provide brand information for which there is especially high demand, for example, for brands that are new and/or those types of products for which the information available is difficult for nonexperts to comprehend. (Note that altruism or the desire for reciprocity [e.g., information exchange] may often underlie this motive.)

Cultural Differences in eWOM

Emerging research on cultural differences in eWOM suggests that the individualism-collectivism dimension may shape the content of the reviews that consumers write. For example, research scholars Poompak Kusawat and Surat Teer-akapibal conducted a sentiment analysis of a dataset containing reviews by 233,446 customers from 6,611 Airbnb accommodations, and found that "consumers from individualistic (vs. collectivistic) cultures express more negative review sentiments when they experience a negative discrepancy between the description on the Air-bnb website and the actual performance," and that "review sentiment is attenuated when the cultural distance [i.e., dissimilarities in background between hosts and guests] is high" (Kusawat & Teerakapibal, 2021).

Why Do Persuasion Attempts Work?

Certainly we are social beings who are hardwired to pay attention to others' responses to us. But what are the psychological principles that explain why some persuasion attempts (through WOM or reference groups) work and others do not? Robert Cialdini, who conducted the pioneering studies investigating this question, evolved six principles of social influence, described briefly in *Psychology Today* (Kenrick, 2012):

> In brief, we are inclined to go along with someone's suggestion if we think that person is a credible expert (*authority*), if we regard him or her as a trusted friend (*likeability*), if we feel we owe them one (*reciprocity*), or if doing so will be consistent with our beliefs or prior commitments (*consistency*). We are also inclined to make choices that we think are popular (*consensus*), and that will net us a scarce commodity (*scarcity*). We follow these general rules because they **usually** work to lead us to make the right choice. But because we often use them unthinkingly they are commonly exploited by compliance professionals and con artists, many of them wearing nice business suits, religious robes, or reassuringly friendly smiles.

Principles of Social Influence

Authority: We tend to trust and comply with the advice of people we recognize as expert in the domain in question. For almost any product or service, low involvement or high involvement, inexpensive or costly, online comparative brand ratings and reviews by purported experts abound. Chapter 4 provides numerous examples of such sites.

Why does authority work so well? It reduces perceived risk of making the wrong choice and the effort we expend traversing the (often unfamiliar) vast terrain of the evaluation part of the purchase journey.

Likeability: We are more likely to follow someone's advice or comply with their request if we find that person likeable. Along with an air of authority, this is a trait most if not all highly successful salespeople possess. We especially like people who resemble us in key ways but are slightly "better." The salespeople at Abercrombie and Fitch are not only young and attractive, but also possess poise many teens lack and covet. The middle-aged saleswomen at Chico's project an aura of mature self-confidence and in addition show expertise using clothing and accessories to accentuate their attractive features while minimizing their flaws.

Reciprocity: When someone gives us something or does a favor for us, most of us feel a distinct discomfort until we reciprocate with a gift or favor approximately equal in magnitude. The salesperson who spends a significant amount of time providing us great service makes us more inclined to feel we must buy something. The charity that sends us greeting cards may elicit higher donations. The free samples at Costco and other grocery retailers nudge many of us to put the product into our baskets to please the smiling woman or man who has just offered us a toothpick holding a morsel of the newest something. If, however, we look closely at any of these market transactions, we may find ourselves resisting the urge to reciprocate, as we realize that the marketer is trying to elicit that very action. In other words, when market norms apply and we see that it's "just business," our discomfort upon receiving the "free gift" may dissipate.

Consistency: We view ourselves as having stable preferences and ways of behaving, and it is this perceived stability that shapes our sense of who we are. I am a busy urban person who buys coffee at Starbucks; I am frugal and make coffee at home; I recognize and enjoy fine wine; I am a professional and look the part. What does this have to do with social influence? Simply, if you can persuade a potential buyer to take even a small step toward purchase, you make it all the more likely that s/he will take the next step and the next.

At LA Fitness and many other fitness facilities, personal training is the "extra" that brings in the real money. Thus, all new members get one free training session, the first step toward committing to a regimen of a number of sessions for a fixed price. The free trial subscriptions to antivirus programs, audible book providers, and other such services also encourage us to take the first step toward commitment.

Consensus: The power of user reviews is well-documented. Consensus in the form of conformity is perhaps even more powerfully persuasive. All those white cords denoting Apple devices will make the black Android cord that much more prominent. The dedicated yoga practitioners around you may make you feel doubly embarrassed as you fall over clumsily when you attempt that headstand everyone else is maintaining gracefully, quietly, and seemingly without effort. Perhaps it's time you too started attending class more often.

Scarcity: Ah, the persuasive power of "only one left…" Airline ticket vendors use scarcity to invoke a feeling of urgency: "only one seat left at this price." Amazon does it too, with products ranging from books to jewelry to cat food: "only 1 in stock…" Even National Geographic's artisan sellers' site includes such messages. (Of course, the artisans' products, handmade, already possess an aura of uniqueness, if not scarcity.)

Why does scarcity entice us even when we do not need the product in question? The evolutionary answer is, of course, survival. But is there another answer more relevant to the prosperous world in which so many of us now comfortably reside?

Responding by clicking the "checkout" button effectively ends our purchase journey, freeing us to move on to a new activity; and the implication that supplies are depleted because so many people have already purchased the product takes us back to the principle of consensus.

Now that we've laid the foundations of consumer behavior, we are ready to explore the consumer experiences of marginalized people, many of whom are impeded in their attempts to access the information, products, and services that should be available to all consumers.

References

Bump, P. (2020, April 13). "8 social media platforms that weren't founded in the US". Hub Spot. Retrieved from: https://blog.hubspot.com/marketing/social-media-platforms-that-werent-founded-in-the-us.

Dizikes, P. (2021, May 20). "Study: Culture influences mask wearing". *MIT News*. Retrieved from: https://news.mit.edu/2021/masks-collectivism-covid-culture-0520.

iStock (2016). Photo of Japanese children bento (lunchboxes). Retrieved from: http://www.istockphoto.com/.

Kasper, L. R. (2011, October 1). "The celebrity chef (No. 492)" [Audio podcast episode]. *The Splendid Table*. American Public Media. Retrieved from: www.splendidtable.org/episode/2011/10/01/the-celebrity-chef.

Kenrick, D. T. (2012, December 8). "The 6 principles of persuasion: Tips from the leading expert on social influence". *Psychology Today*. Retrieved from: www.psychologytoday.com/us/blog/sex-murder-and-the-meaning-life/201212/the-6-principles-persuasion.

Knowledge@Wharton (2021, February 2). "What makes some ads more shareable than others?". Retrieved from: https://knowledge.wharton.upenn.edu/article/makes-commercials-shareable/.

Kusawat, P., & Teerakapibal, S. (2021). "The roles of culture in online user reviews: An empirical investigation'. *Journal of Global Marketing, 34*(3), 189–204. https://doi.org/10.1080/08911762.2021.1903641.

Morgan, B. (2015, September 24). "Lidl and Aldi lead on word of mouth". *Research Live*. Retrieved from: www.research-live.com/article/ews/lidl-and-aldi-lead-on-word-of-mouth/id/4013918.

NikeTalk (2022). "NikeTalk". Retrieved from: https://niketalk.com/.

Saint Clair, J. K. (2018). "A beautiful MIN(D): The multiple-identity network as a framework for integrating identity-based consumer behavior". *Advances in Consumer Research, 46*, 386–391. Retrieved from: www.acrwebsite.org/volumes/2412351/volumes/v46/NA-46.

Shavitt, S., Lee, A. Y., & Johnston, T. P. (2008). "Cross-cultural consumer psychology". In C. Haugtvedt, P. Herr, & F. Kardes (Eds.), *Handbook of Consumer Psychology* (pp. 1103–1131). New York: Taylor & Francis.

Thompson, W. R. (2021). "Worldwide survey of fitness trends for 2021". *ACSM's Health & Fitness Journal, 25*(1), 10–19. https://doi.org/10.1249/FIT.0000000000000631.

Thorsten, H.-T., Gwinner, K. P., Walsh, G., & Gremler, D. D. (2004). "Electronic word-of-mouth via consumer-opinion platforms: What motivates consumers to articulate themselves on the Internet? *Journal of Interactive Marketing, 18*(1), 38–52. https://doi.org/10.1002/dir.10073.

Wallace, C., Vandevijvere, S., Lee, A., Jaacks, L. M., Schachner, M., & Swinburn, B. (2019). "Dimensions of national culture associated with different trajectories of male and female mean body mass index in countries over 25 years". *Obesity Reviews, 20*(S2), 20–29. https://doi.org/10.1111/obr.12884.

Westbrook, R. A. (1987). 'Product/consumption-based affective responses and postpurchase processes". *Journal of Marketing Research, 24*(3), 258–270. https://doi.org/10.2307/3151636.

Wong, B. (2020, September 18). "Why East Asians were wearing masks long before COVID-19". *HuffPost*. Retrieved from: https://www.huffpost.com/entry/east-asian-countries-face-masks-before-covid_l_5f63a43fc5b61845586837f4.

Part 3
Consumer Welfare

8 Marginalized Consumers

Objectives

1. To describe the barriers to marketplace access marginalized consumers encounter.
2. To explore how marginalized consumers use products to deal with unfair treatment in and beyond the marketplace.
3. To provide examples of best practices that include marginalized consumers in the marketplace.

What Is Marginalization and How Is It Related to Marketing and Consumer Behavior?

What does it mean to be marginalized? The website Oxford Reference.com (2022) defines marginalization as a "spatial metaphor for a process of social exclusion in which individuals or groups are relegated to the fringes of a society, being denied economic, political, and/or symbolic power and pushed towards being 'outsiders.'"

From a global perspective, marginalized groups may include both indigenous people and immigrants, people of color (POC), LGBTQ consumers, girls and women, financially disadvantaged consumers, and people whose physical, cognitive, and/or emotional characteristics or challenges diverge from existing concepts of "normal." There are overlaps among these groups; for example, women, POC, LGBTQ, and consumers with disabilities are all at increased risk of joblessness and homelessness when compared to their "mainstream" counterparts. This list is by no means exhaustive. At various times in different cultures, the elderly, military veterans, felons, and many others have been and may continue to be marginalized. As psychologist Willie Garrett points out, marginalized individuals are all around us, and each of us will experience marginalization at some point:

DOI: 10.4324/9780367426897-11

Those of us who feel a sense of personal empowerment in our lives may see the marginalized as being somewhere or someplace else, and not within our living circle. The marginalized are very skilled in keeping a low profile. They have been repeatedly hurt, and [are] aware of the stereotypes applied to their group. They are all around us, right in our community, on the job, or residing in our own homes. They are our children, siblings, relatives, co-workers, neighbors, and partners. Everyone I know has a marginalized person within their network. We are all guaranteed that over our lifespan we will all have physical, mental, and emotional issues that will make us a marginalized person as well. None of us are immune from injury, disease, mental illness, and changes due to aging.

(Garrett, 2016)

Marginalization occurs in a variety of contexts, most notably economic, social, and political. People who are economically marginalized experience barriers to amassing wealth or becoming employed, often due to negative stereotypes. POC, women, and people with physical or mental disabilities frequently encounter stereotyping that characterizes them as incompetent in general or incapable of performing specific tasks.

Political marginalization occurs when specific communities are targeted by practices that make it difficult if not impossible for them to vote and otherwise have a voice in the political process. In the US, such practices have recently included gerrymandering (restructuring voting districts in order to isolate racial minorities), requiring voter ID, and limiting access to polling facilities.

Social marginalization occurs when specific groups or individuals face obstacles that prevent them from participating in leisure activities readily accessible to others. One common example is denial of access to clubs or organizations, and another is failure to welcome members of racial minorities or to accommodate people with disabilities in retail environments.

These types of marginalization frequently co-occur. Marginalized individuals are more likely to lack access to adequate education and health care, to experience poverty, to be unemployed or underemployed, and to be isolated socially. Marginalization in the marketplace results in lack of access to adequate information, to reasonably good quality products at an affordable price, and to customer services needed to obtain information, to complete a transaction, or to solve a problem after purchase. Globally, people with disabilities regularly face barriers to access. Nationally, ethnic groups are routinely denied access to information, products, and services readily available to mainstream consumers. In the US, for example, African Americans have been singled out for poor treatment by many retailers.

This chapter first explores barriers to access encountered by consumers who are marginalized based on individual characteristics. Then, we describe how marginalized consumers use products and services to respond to unfair treatment in society and in the marketplace. We conclude with a discussion of best practices for including marginalized consumers in marketplace activities.

How Are Marginalized Consumers Treated in the Marketplace?

The aim of this section is to document and illustrate three marketplace barriers a wide range of marginalized consumers face: barriers to internet access, to adequate customer service, and to obtaining products designed with their needs in mind. No attempt has been made to cover challenges each marginalized group experiences, as that is beyond the scope of this book.

Access to the Internet: The Digital Divide

We have access to an unprecedented amount of information about products, companies, and services we need or want with the click of a mouse or the tap of a finger. But many consumers still lack such access. Almost half the world's population lacks internet access altogether. According to a new joint report from UNICEF and the International Telecommunication Union, more than six in ten of the world's school-age children and young adults lack internet access in their homes. People living in poverty and those in rural areas are far less likely to have internet access than are their wealthier urban counterparts. Henrietta Fore, UNICEF Executive Director, speaks of the magnitude and gravity of this lack of access:

> That so many children and young people have no internet at home is more than a digital gap – it is a digital canyon. Lack of connectivity doesn't just limit children and young people's ability to connect online. It prevents them from competing in the modern economy. It isolates them from the world. And in the event of school closures, such as those currently experienced by millions due to COVID-19, it causes them to lose out on education. Put bluntly: Lack of internet access is costing the next generation their futures.
>
> (UNICEF, 2020)

The UN estimates that nearly three billion people, 37% of the global population, have never used the internet. More than nine in ten of these people live in developing countries, according to the UN's International Telecommunication Union (ITU). The agency reported that while COVID significantly increased the number of people online, many struggle with slow connection speeds and the necessity of sharing these connections among family members.

The ITU added that those most likely to be online are younger people, men, and urban dwellers. Older adults, women, and those in rural areas are less likely to use the internet. Those excluded from the digital world often face poverty, illiteracy, and limited access to electricity, the ITU added (Agence France-Presse, 2021).

Access to the internet is not the whole story, however. In many urban areas in the US, people residing in low-income communities may, in fact, have internet service, but it is likely to be so slow and expensive that it is difficult if not impossible for residents to access online education and other services needed to function and thrive in a world that is increasingly reliant on digital media.

Affluent communities are predominately white, while low-income neighborhood tends to be Black or Hispanic. For this reason, the refusal of large internet service providers to provide adequate broadband services in poorer communities is called "digital redlining." Redlining practices are denials of services based on race and are examples of systemic racism, that is, racial discrimination that is an integral part of accepted practices and processes in business, government, and other institutions. Most such practices are now illegal, but digital redlining is still legal.

How many people in the US are, in effect, digitally excluded? According to Microsoft, which tracks how quickly people download its software and security updates, an estimated 120.4 million people, more than a third of the U.S. population, cannot access the internet at broadband speeds. The pandemic made home broadband essential for attending classes, working from home, virtual doctor visits, and scheduling appointments for COVID-19 vaccinations.

A joint study from the Alliance for Excellent Education, National Indian Education Association, National Urban League, and UnidosUS found that 34% of American Indian/Alaska Native families and about 31% each of Black and Latino families have no access to high-speed home internet compared with 21% of white families. Lack of high-speed home internet access during the pandemic caused many children in low-income households to fall behind in school, and it will be a challenge for them to catch up to their more affluent peers, even as schools are reopening.

Consistent with their free-market status in the US, ISPs build networks where they will reap the largest financial gains. If internet access were instead considered a utility like electricity, gas, and landline phone service, ISPs would face regulations, including price caps and coverage requirements, resulting in speedy service for almost all households regardless of income (Tibken, 2021).

Barriers to Internet Content Access by People with Disabilities

The World Health Organization (WHO) estimates that more than one billion people (15% of the earth's population) live with some type of disability, and observes that the number is rising as life expectancy increases and medical advances enable more people to survive trauma and disease (WHO, 2021). While many forms of mobility impairment are visible, most disabilities, including sensory and cognitive impairments, are not immediately obvious. Our colleagues, friends, and family are likely to include people with some form of disability, whether it is a mental illness, neurodivergence, a sensory impairment, or mobility-related.

People with disabilities routinely encounter barriers to internet and web site access. Commonly encountered problems include video and audio content without closed captioning, images lacking verbal descriptions for screen reading software, web sites that are difficult to navigate, and content that cannot be navigated using a keyboard instead of a mouse.

The Americans with Disabilities Act mandates that companies make their retail establishments and marketing messages (including web sites) accessible to people with visual impairments. This mandate has led many businesses to search for readily available low-cost software that purportedly makes the subscriber's web site accessible, thus helping organizations avoid lawsuits. These solutions are problematic in two ways: typically automated products do not resolve all accessibility shortcomings of a web site, and the prominence of the software seller's claim about avoiding lawsuits implies that placating litigious blind people is the most important reason to make one's web site accessible. This is hardly an inclusive marketing orientation. Recent studies find that most ecommerce, news and information web sites contain accessibility problems.

Moreover, the Americans with Disabilities Act was signed in 1990, well before the internet had become a vehicle for commerce and consumer information. Businesses and trade associations maintain that making their websites usable by all is a costly and complex undertaking. The resulting number of lawsuits filed over companies' inaccessible websites is growing, and as the U.S. populace ages and many more individuals encounter visual problems, the issue will become more pressing (Jimenez, 2019).

Shopping While Disabled or Black

Seema Flower likes to go shopping. She enjoys the social interaction that comes from visiting the high street, as well as touching clothes before she tries them on.

Flower has retinitis pigmentosa – a genetic eye condition that causes gradual loss of vision. She has been registered as blind since she was 12 and, when she does go shopping, she uses a white cane and goes with a support worker. Loud, pumping music, disorientating lighting and poorly placed fittings can all make Flower's shopping experience more difficult.

"I have a passion for retail and I'm a very tactile person," she tells Drapers. "I like to feel clothes to get an idea of what they're like. The social aspect of going out to visit shops is also important, because having a disability can be very isolating."

"Shopping should not be a daunting experience for anyone – it should be stress-free and enjoyable, whoever you are."

"I need staff to approach me, not stand in front of me without saying anything. It's also about little things, like handing me the card machine and telling me how much my items cost, rather than relying on body language and visual communication." It is clear that more training is needed to ensure store staff are confident and comfortable when interacting with shoppers with disabilities. Whether a result of inexperience, or a lack of confidence, training or interest, at times Flower [is often] left feeling unwelcome and excluded. Poor examples of service included staff wandering off mid-interaction, holding up products without describing them or pointing to items and having to be reminded that Flower is blind.

(Sutherland, 2019)

The fashion industry has repeatedly been taken to task for not including people with disabilities in its advertising and on runways, and this exclusion extends to brick and mortar retail. Journalist Frances Ryan, who writes about marginalized populations, asked her Twitter followers what would make clothes shopping more accessible for them. Suggestions included making fitting rooms comfortable for two people so that companions can help or critique in private, and including seats for mobility-impaired consumers. Other followers tweeted that it would be helpful to see mannequins with disabilities. An individual with an auditory processing disorder commented that loud music is distracting and unpleasant and that aisles should be wide enough to accommodate people with mobility aids (De Elizabeth, 2018).

While many individuals with disabilities encounter indifferent, avoidant, or patronizing salespeople, POC often experience outright hostility from retail employees. In her study, "Shopping while Black," sociology professor Cassi Pittman (2017) describes African-Americans' experiences with retailer staff, many of whom are less than welcoming. Pittman observes, "Money is portrayed as a great equalizer. This research contests that idea. The privileges and entitlements that come with economic resources are often not afforded to African-American shoppers."

From her interviews with 55 middle-class African-American shoppers in the New York City area, Pittman learned that most reported experiencing "racial stigma and stereotypes when shopping" and more than half reported being perceived as a shoplifter, receiving poor or no service, and being perceived as poor. Study participants reported that they were commonly followed around the store, directed to the sale section unprompted; ignored, made to wait, and skipped over for nonminority customers; and told the price of expensive clothing items before asking or trying them on. These behaviors, which were typical of staff in high-end apparel stores, were especially challenging for professionals shopping for work clothes in such establishments. Such treatment extends well beyond pricey clothing stores to include grocery stores, drugstores, boutiques, and big-box outlets.

Pittman noted that "[T]hese findings are especially useful for people who don't believe these things happen, and provide evidence for people who go through this and feel they aren't allowed to talk about it."

While U.S. law prohibits stores from refusing to sell to a customer based on race, there are no laws requiring that they provide the same level of service to everyone. And retailers are not specifically included in civil rights laws that protect a right to service in restaurants, hotels, and movie theaters.

The marginalization many POC experience when shopping extends to buying or selling a home. Through extensive fieldwork and interviews of participants in each of the four major stages of the homebuying process, Professor Elizabeth Korver-Glenn found that both individual and institutional practices had a hand in shaping the disparate outcomes from finding a real estate agent to applying for a loan and assessing home value. And the impacts, given the established research on the effects of neighborhood-level inequalities, are far-reaching (Binkovitz, 2018).

The study showed that to navigate the first stage, establishing a real estate agent-client relationship, agents typically turn to their personal networks for new client referrals and frequently rely on "tacitly legal behaviors that code or signal racial stereotypes but assuage their ethical or legal concerns" (Binkovitz, 2018):

> One white agent, the study notes, had a home seller who didn't want to sell to a Middle Eastern client "because he did not want to 'support terrorists.'" Other white agents said white sellers often didn't want to sell to black buyers because they assumed it would affect home values for their white neighbors. These agents only "rarely" reminded clients that they could not discuss race and never refused to work with someone who expressed explicitly discriminatory preferences, the study notes.
>
> (Binkovitz, 2018)

The study found that in the second stage, marketing a house, racially discriminatory practices result in "spatialized hierarchy of race." These practices include housing listing databases with neighborhood boundaries that prioritize "specialization for majority-white areas" and agents' racially based assessments of clients' potential risks.

In the third stage, evaluation of mortgage loan applications, the study found that racially driven risk assessments continue:

> One loan officer recounted a story from a colleague at another mortgage company of a black couple that got "scrutinized to death" and ultimately declined despite being well-qualified for the loan. Other investigations have also documented how mortgage discrimination is a persistent problem for people of color.
>
> (Binkovitz, 2018)

The fourth stage, which occurs only if the loan application is approved, involves assessment of the house itself. This too is a subjective process presenting

> ...yet another opportunity for stereotypes to enter the process with significant material outcomes. The study also found that agents and lenders often tried to sway the outcome. By this time in the housing exchange process, the study concludes, the minority buyer—if not at some point categorically excluded—has been repeatedly subjected to widely shared racial beliefs about

their ability to care for homes, financial instability, potential for danger, and desirability as a neighbor.

(Binkovitz, 2018)

While racially based discrimination is prohibited under U.S. law, the study concludes that "existing policy is not being enforced" (Binkovitz, 2018).

For the original study, see Korver-Glenn (2018).

Cultural Bias in Product and Service Design

Many products and services are designed for consumers regarded as "normal" or "mainstream," and even when they are adapted for consumers who differ from society's perception of what is normal, the adaptation itself may stigmatize the purchaser. In the apparel industry, for example, women's clothing is typically a good fit only for those who are not overweight or especially tall or short. In the US, clothing for heavier women is termed "plus-sized." While two-thirds of American women wear plus sizes, they are buying fashion at a lower rate than their "straight-sized" counterparts. This is because retailers and manufacturers are not measuring up to these consumers' expectations. Common grievances include poor fit, frumpy style, cheap fabric, and reduced availability and visibility of plus-sized clothing, which may be "online only" or hidden in the back of a store. And many women argue that the name itself "otherizes" them. Many so-called plus-sized models have hourglass figures, but clothing made for that shape does not work for the millions of female consumers with an apple shape (Magner, 2019).

In addition to subpar products, marginalized consumers routinely encounter service providers who have not been trained to serve customers with a range of needs not taught in traditional programs. The U.S. hair salon industry suffers from systemic racism:

> Last month, activist, speaker, and public academic Rachel Cargle shared the feedback she offered a salon owner after a profoundly horrible—and illuminating—experience she'd had at one of their salons.
>
> "I encourage you to take into deep consideration that your Black employees are working twice as hard (PERFECTING how to do Black hair as well as white hair) and your Black clients are getting half the service—sitting in your chairs worried that their stylist may not be equipped and then, in some instances like mine, we are walking out feeling completely exhausted regarding why we have to have such an irregular experience doing something so simple as getting our hair washed and blown out," Cargle wrote. "Unless you are having each stylist prove competency in textured hair, unless your Black employees express that they feel safe and protected against white aggressions from customers and colleagues, unless a Black client can walk in feeling they have as much of a chance to feel beautiful when they leave as a white woman would...unless these are all truths than yes, Black

people are indeed simply second hand customers because nothing about your salons proves otherwise."

(Valenti, 2020)

Hairstylists must complete a course of training, but neither their curriculum nor their apprenticeships include working with textured hair. Indeed the goal of many stylists who encounter textured hair, including "waves, coils, or curls," is to straighten it. Adding insult to injury is the paucity and high price of ethnic hair care products available at retailers (Schiffer, 2020) – and the fact that until quite recently, Walmart, CVS, and Walgreens locked the displays of brands targeted at African Americans (Dwyer, 2020).

We conclude this section with an example that illustrates how cultural bias in product design may be life-threatening:

> Today, if a woman in the United States gets into the driver's seat of most cars, she is 73 percent more likely than a male driver to be severely injured if the car crashes. She is also 17 percent more likely to die. Fatality and injury risks are also higher for older adults, heavier adults and children than it is for young to middle-aged men who weigh around 170 pounds.
>
> (*New York Times*, 2021)

How can this be true? In the US, automakers are required by law to perform crash tests on their vehicles and to use many years of accumulated crash data to incorporate safety features like airbags into their designs. But automakers are still using crash test dummies designed based on the average-sized man several decades ago. Crash test dummies representing women are only placed in the passenger seat, based on a 1950s mindset about traditional gender roles. And dummies representing obese adults are nonexistent despite decades of data documenting consumers' steadily increasing BMIs (body mass indexes). Safety advocates suggest that this neglect of a significant proportion of consumers is likely to change only with new dummies, technology designed for virtual testing, and more stringent regulations.

How Do Marginalized Consumers Use Products and Services to Counteract Effects of Marginalization?

How do marginalized consumers gain access to information, goods, and services denied them? Many use self-presentation to counteract negative stereotypes and thus gain greater acceptance in the marketplace, while others employ technology to gain access to goods and services needed.

Self-Presentation Enhancements Using Dress

A recent Ipsos survey of affluent Americans reveals how affluent African Americans use personal presentation to combat the racial stereotyping they face (Davis,

2020). The survey findings highlight clear and significant differences between affluent white Americans and their African American counterparts in attitudes and behaviors regarding presentation and outward appearance. Affluent African Americans are twice as likely as whites to definitely agree with the statements: "I have an excellent sense of style," "My fashion represents who I am as a person," and "Being well-dressed is important to me." This difference holds across gender and age cohorts. The investigators explain these results and offer guidance to marketers, for who these differences represent an opportunity:

> Clothes are a readily processed indicator of class outweighing race. The point of the purchase takes on a value beyond the clothes themselves. The clothes provide a means to get the respect that is only provisionally granted by white society. Anderson [2014] points out that Affluent African Americans perceive dressing casually as a liability. Doing so increases their likelihood of being challenged in restaurants, in retail stores, in their buildings, in banks and other financial institutions, or while jogging in one's own neighborhood. This performance strategy is not fool proof, as there still exist multiple instances of being stopped for engaging in any activity "while black", or of backlash for "flaunting" indicators beyond one's perceived station, but it does increase the odds of acceptance.
>
> The search for respect manifests itself in other attitudinal statements related to customer service. Affluent African Americans, across both gender and age, place more importance on personalised and superior service at levels higher than their white counterparts. Across the entire battery of luxury and style statements in the Affluent Survey, African Americans consistently over-index against whites...
>
> Brands and marketers should understand that wearing and owning designer and luxury brands is one of many strategies affluent African Americans employ to build respect and status in the white world. Prioritising and building strong customer service models will be a valuable tool for building customer loyalty and respect among black consumers, recognizing the symbolic meaning of any purchase that involves display. That these strategies, which are essentially defensive and conservative, align with a fashion-forward sensibility make the affluent African American consumer unique. By recognizing this dichotomy and empathizing with the strategies African Americans employ luxury brands can create a deeper relationship with a group that is more passionate, and already outspends it [*sic*] white counterparts in the category.
>
> (Davis, 2020)

Achieving Agency through Technology

Internet access is no longer a luxury to be enjoyed only by those who can afford to spend money on electronics; it provides access to social services, job opportunities, and housing prospects that are otherwise out of reach of those who need these services most urgently:

On a sweltering day several months ago, 35-year-old Terry Phillips got his first cell phone. He was sitting on the side of a freeway off-ramp in Sacramento with a cardboard sign, when a car pulled up and the driver held a brown paper bag out the window. Despite his stiff knees and unrelenting cough, Terry stood to receive the bag. Inside, he found several granola bars, a bottle of water, and—to his surprise—an old iPhone and a charger inside....

Terry's iPhone is a lifeline beyond a meal or a warm bed. It places the power to find work and social services in the palm of his hand: At the click of a button, he is able to communicate with friends and loved ones. Terry is connected as never before, and he says he now has "friends to see and a reason to wake up every morning." In this sense, his phone has offered him something charity frequently fails to: It has given him agency, opportunity, and community.

(Hackett, 2019)

The agency smartphones offer extends beyond access to services and community. Many marginalized consumers use smartphones to document and disseminate video evidence of "marketplace harassment, false accusations, or worse," according to research conducted by Assistant Professor Akon Ekpo, PhD. "They have become the 'voice' of those often not heard and ignored" (Ekpo, 2022).

Ekpo observes that ecommerce is another example of differences in use of technology:

When we thought about ecommerce, we thought about how it was convenient to have something delivered to your door. Juxtapose that to the marginalized person who worries about and anticipates that when they go into a retail space, they will be followed by security personnel, detained or falsely accused of criminal activity, or just ignored by sales personnel. The idea of e-commerce not only changed the way people shop, but it also allowed marginalized consumers to continue to participate in the market without the worry of going into a physical retail space.

(Ekpo, 2022)

For the Unhoused, Possessions May Symbolize Hope and Connection

A common misconception about people who are unhoused is that the few possessions they are able to carry with them must be utilitarian in nature because surely there is no physical or mental "place" for symbolic possessions. True, utilitarian objects are needed to survive. But possessions with no utilitarian value but rich symbolic meaning are essential for survival of the spirit, as Ron Hill's extensive research has amply demonstrated (Hill, 1991; Hill & Stamey, 1990), and as the following excerpt from the *LA Times* eloquently illustrates:

When you live on the streets, things show up and then leave. Things get stolen. Things get lost. Things get swept up by city cleaning crews.

One day you might have a soft blanket. The next day it's nowhere to be found. Things come in and go out like the tides.

Sometimes what disappears—IDs, medicine—is essential. But for people regularly treated as if they don't belong, even the loss of nonessential belongings—a stuffed animal, a shiny ring—can wipe out desperately needed solace and hope.

The other day, I met Jason Antoine Logan in the West Valley, in an alley between office buildings off a little street wedged between the 101 Freeway and Ventura Boulevard. ...

[H]e said it felt good to be asked about himself. So when I suggested it, he gladly showed me all his most important possessions, which he carries in a backpack that he is never without. There wasn't room for much.

A cellphone, to communicate with his street family and his family by blood—which is local but, he says, does not want to help him.... A flashlight, which he called "the homeless person's key to the city." A butane torch for heating and cooking food and for lighting cigarettes even in the wind. Basic toiletries. A little saw (whose blade he had covered in duct tape for safety) to dig with or cut things like branches. A solar charger, "the latest homeless attraction." A small mirror to make sure he looks vaguely presentable.

When I asked him his favorite possession, he first pointed to a couple of simple bracelets around his wrist. On one he'd attached two keys he happened to find. He said he didn't know what they opened but they opened something, which made him feel "classy, like I'm getting something accomplished."

Then he dug back into the backpack to show me a few items he'd recently scavenged from another homeless person's encampment, after she'd been ordered to vacate her spot in front of a bank. A jumble of cuff links in a small cardboard jewelry box, a glittering costume tiara.

"It's like a metaphor for me," he said of the tiara, which took up a lot of space in the backpack. "Like I could be moving on one day to another phase. Like it's all going to be all right, we're going to be all right."

Viewing consumer behavior through the eyes of marginalized individuals shows how resourceful and resilient humans are and also lays bare the profound impact of marginalization on the human spirit.

Best Practices for Marketing to Marginalized Consumers

To communicate effectively with any consumer, marginalized or not, it is essential to learn to view the world – and your brand or retail establishment – from their perspective. There is no roadmap for this, but below are best practices for including marginalized consumers in marketplace activities, with accompanying examples from companies that are leaders in this area:

Best Practice 1: Include Marginalized Individuals in Your Market Research

The wants and needs of prosperous "mainstream" consumers are privileged in market research as they are in the marketplace as a whole. As societies become increasingly diverse in ethnicity, gender identity, and sensory, physical, and cognitive-emotional challenges, market researchers must also become more inclusive.

Example 1: Tommy Hilfiger, Marks & Spencer

While it is still rare for marketers to consult consumers with disabilities as a part of their product and communications research, firms like Tommy Hilfiger and Marks & Spencer (M&S) are leading the way (Hammett, 2019).

In 2018, these companies as well as smaller ones including River Island and Asos became more inclusive in marketing practices ranging from advertising to marketing research and product design. M&S and Tommy Hilfiger both launched clothing designed for adults and children with physical and mental disabilities based on research involving people in the disabled community. Tommy Hilfiger's adaptive clothing includes features like one-handed zippers, wider openings, adjustable waists, and magnetic closures. All of their adaptive offerings remain true to the style of the brand.

Similarly, M&S conceived, designed, and developed their Easy Dressing kids wear line in a two-year collaboration with customers. They started the process with a survey of 300 parents and, like Tommy Hilfiger, maintained the brand style:

> "Parents passionately told us that disabilities don't define their children, so the adaptations shouldn't define their clothes, it's why all the products are inclusively designed and modelled closely on our main collection," explains Rebecca Garner, M&S's kidswear designer.
>
> Offering great value was a key consideration throughout the development, so our Easy Dressing products are priced in line with the rest of our kidswear range. One thing we're very proud of on this range is the imagery we've used online, it was absolutely vital for us that the range was inclusively modelled.
>
> (Hammett, 2019)

According to research firm Coherent Market Insights, the global market for clothing designed for children and adults with disabilities is predicted to reach to reach USD 400 billion (GBP 308 billion) by 2026 (Sutherland, 2019).

Example 2: Avon

Avon, global beauty and personal care brand that revitalized the brand after foundering in the early 2000s, conducted a global survey of 8,000 women to understand what concerns troubled them most during the pandemic. In other words, Avon went beyond surface issues of beauty and skin care in an effort to gain a deeper understanding of woman consumers as individuals, many of whom are marginalized. Based on the survey finding that more than four in ten lost confidence during the pandemic, the company partnered with a diverse group of models varying in race, ethnicity, and ability to build awareness on its "My Story Matters" platform, "a space to give women a chance to share their authentic, un-edited stories" (Fieldgate, 2021).

Best Practice 2: Include Marginalized People in Your Advertising and Other Marketing Communications

Consumer marginalization is important to explore in a broader context of social justice, and as the population becomes more diverse in race and ethnicity, sexual orientation, and identified range of disabilities and processing differences, it is essential that brands reflect this diversity in their messaging if they wish to establish authentic connections with younger customers in particular. Deloitte's 2021 Global Marketing Trends Executive Survey of 11,500 global consumers found the youngest respondents (from 18 to 25 years old) gave greater weight to inclusive advertising when making purchase decisions (Brodzik et al., 2021).

Example 1: Maltesers Disability Campaign

In 2016, British confectionary company Maltesers launched its most successful advertising campaign in a decade, featuring disabled cast members openly making reference to their disabilities.

> "New boyfriend" launched in September 2016 during Channel 4's Paralympic Games coverage. It opens with a familiar scene that could be lifted from an episode of US comedy *Girls* – a young woman tells two friends about having sex with her new boyfriend. Yet a couple of details are less familiar. The woman speaking is in an electric wheelchair and the awkward experience with her boyfriend that she describes was caused by a spasm, a symptom of her cerebral palsy. To illustrate her point, she spills a bag of Maltesers on to the table and the three women burst into laughter.
>
> (Oakes, 2017)

Michele Oliver, vice president of marketing at Mars UK, said the ad campaign led to a sales uplift that exceeded expectations, and YouTube views and brand affinity were double the company's targets.

Example 2: Doritos Mexico's LGBTQ-Related Campaign

November 1, *Día de Muertos* (Day of the Dead), is a time to remember and honor loved ones who have passed away and to celebrate love and acceptance as a community. Doritos Mexico launched a 2021 *Día de Muertos*-related campaign with a short film titled "Nunca Es Tarde Para Ser Quien Eres" ("It's never late to be who you are"):

> The ad shows a family celebrating Día de Muertos as the eldest presumed matriarch remembers her late brother. As his spirit enters the living world, he introduces an accompanying spirit to the rest of the family: his male partner. As the family welcomes the couple with tear-inducing acceptance, the snack brand leaves consumers with a message about culture and the importance of embracing identity.
>
> The heartfelt ad is a continuation of the company's #PrideAllYear effort, which expands queer-friendly messaging beyond Pride and into other major holidays, such as Christmas and Mother's Day. The platform stems back to 2016 with the international brand's first edition of Doritos Rainbow in Mexico, which has been geared towards breaking down the existing stigma in Mexican culture.
>
> The ad campaign garnered over four million views on YouTube, and responses have been "overwhelmingly positive," with many consumers praising the Doritos brand for "bridging the Mexican culture and the LGBTQ+ community together—a feat that is not often seen in advertising."
>
> (Venegas, 2021)

Best Practice 3: Design Your Physical Retail Establishments and Entertainment Venues to Ensure That All Facilities and Merchandise Are Readily Accessible to People with Varying Physical and Cognitive Differences

Retailers are slowly making progress in this area. In the US, while the Americans with Disabilities Act mandates that public spaces be made accessible to people with disabilities, widespread enforcement is difficult if not impossible, given that there are more than a million retail establishments according to the U.S. Bureau of Labor Statistics. Larger chains have made significant advances in their adherence to the ADA, especially with accommodations for people with mobility aids. These accommodations, which include ramps, wider aisles, and larger fitting rooms, are also welcomed and appreciated by parents shopping with babies or toddlers and their strollers in tow.

Example: Accommodating Hidden Disabilities

How can retailers identify and accommodate shoppers with disabilities that are not immediately obvious? Below are a few ingenious strategies that show that retailers, large and small, can find solutions:

> Following a trial, Sainsbury's made lanyards for shoppers with hidden disabilities available in all its stores nationwide last month. The lanyards, which are decorated with sunflowers, are a sign for store colleagues that the shopper has a hidden disability – such as autism, dementia or visual impairment – and may require extra help.
>
> This week, shopping centre owner Intu announced it would be introducing sunflower lanyards at all its locations. After a successful trial at its Metrocentre and Eldon Square centres, it also loans out sensory backpacks for autistic people. They include items such as ear defenders, sunglasses, fidget toys and visual symbols to help with communication. In addition, it has rolled out autism training to staff.
>
> Becoming more accessible is not the preserve of retail giants such as Debenhams and Sainsbury's. There are also steps smaller retailers can take to better welcome shoppers with disabilities.
>
> Irish menswear independent Galvin Tullamore, winner of Best Customer Experience at this year's Drapers Independents Awards, introduced weekly "Autism Quiet Evenings", last year. These allow customers with autism to shop in a calmer environment with lower lighting, no music, and reduced till sounds, and it offers additional assistance if required. Judges said the quiet evenings were an "amazing and thoughtful touch". Intu also hosts regular "quiet hours" at its centres.
>
> Rose Martin, owner of Glasgow womenswear independent Nelly McCabe, stresses that you do not need a vast budget to make meaningful changes: "I first became aware of the need to make retail more accessible in 2011, when my mum started using a wheelchair. The shopping experiences we had were awful. You can't navigate the aisles, the person in the wheelchair is totally ignored, staff are completely unaware. We used to dread going shopping.
>
> At our store, we've made adjustments that don't cost a lot of money, like making sure the aisles are wide enough for people with walking aids, and having a mobile card machine that someone in a wheelchair could use on their lap. You don't need to be a big hitter to create a more inclusive environment."
>
> (Sutherland, 2019)

Best Practice 4: Design Websites, Apps, and All Other Digital Media to Be Accessible to People with Disabilities

The Web Content Accessibility Guidelines (WCAG), developed by the Worldwide Web Consortium, address problems encountered by people with sensory, physical, cognitive, and other disabilities, as well as neurodivergent ways of processing information. WCAG state that content must be POUR: Perceivable, Operable, Understandable, and Robust (W3C WAI, 2019):

Information and user interface components must be presented to users in ways they can *perceive*. This means that users must be able to comprehend the information being depicted: It can't be invisible to all their senses.

User interface components and navigation must be *operable*: The interface cannot require interaction that a user cannot perform.

Information and the operation of a user interface must be *understandable*: Users must be able to understand the information as well as the operation of the user interface.

Content must be *robust* enough that it can be interpreted reliably by a wide variety of user agents, including assistive technologies: As technologies and user agents evolve, the content should remain accessible.

(Bureau of Internet Accessibility, 2019)

Best Practice 5: Incorporate Human Diversity and Universal Design Principles into Your Products and Services, Ensuring That They Are Accessible and Inclusive

Example 1: Herbal Essences' Accessibility

In January 2020, Herbal Essences became the first mass hair care brand in North America to add tactile markings to its bottles designed to help consumers with visual impairments distinguish between shampoo and conditioner, with raised stripes on shampoo and circles on conditioner.

Herbal Essences has taken steps beyond the shower with technology that makes it easier for low-vision shoppers to search for the perfect product and shop independently. The brand has introduced an Alexa skill and the By My Eyes app, which answers consumers' questions about Herbal Essences ingredients and makes recommendations based on information gathered from the shopper. The consumer enables the Alexa skill by saying "Alexa Open Herbal Essences":

Then, you can ask questions such as "Alexa, what Herbal Essences shampoo is good for curly hair?" The Be My Eyes app is a free service that connects blind and low vision people with sighted volunteers through a live video call. Herbal Essences' has gone a step beyond with a specialized help feature that directly connects blind users with in-house experts to get assistance as they shop in-store, get ready at home or have hair care questions throughout the day.

(Businesswire, 2019)

Many sighted consumers may also appreciate not having to read a label to identify their shampoo, and may welcome hair care advice from the Be My Eyes app.

Example 2: Legos' Inclusiveness

> Danish company Lego recently launched "Everyone is Awesome", "a 346-
> piece set of 11 monochrome mini-figurines in the colours of the Progress
> Pride Flag. Brown and black figures represent ethnic diversity; pale blue,
> white and pink reflect the transgender banner. Each comes with an individual
> hairstyle but no defined gender (except for the beehive bewigged purple drag
> queen)."
>
> (*The Economist*, 2021)

Lego launched its new product line with a five-minute video on its website of
product designer Matthew Ashton telling the story of his own struggles as a gay
teenager growing up in the 1980s, at the height of the aids epidemic.

Best Practice 6: Take Opportunities to Serve Underserved Communities

Example: In the US, low-cost internet providers are finding ways to bring internet access to underserved communities. For example, in Los Angeles and Denver,
budget ISPs are building networks to provide affordable internet service in public
housing. In East Cleveland, nonprofit PCs for People is partnering with the state,
Microsoft, and other businesses to offer inexpensive internet plans (Tibken, 2021).

Best Practice 7: Make DEI Efforts a Core Priority at All Levels of the Organization

Based on extensive consumer and executive research, Burns et al. (2021) recommend the following strategies:

- Invest in creating a diversity and inclusion strategy throughout the organization. H&M provides an example with its "Layers" program. Ezinne Kwubiri,
  North America Head of Inclusion and Diversity, describes the program as:

  an interactive learning workshop where the teams come together, and we talk
  about a bunch of different biases and identifying gaps amongst their teams or
  even them as an individual that may be hindering a business decision. What I
  love about it is that it goes a step further than just regular unconscious bias training…asking them 'when was the last time you [sought] an opinion outside of
  your general team? How do you go about getting focus groups? Where is a time
  you felt isolated about a decision and how did it make you feel?' The concept of

it is…peeling the layers. For people to have more of a reflective experience as to what their contribution may be to fostering diversity and inclusion.

Research supports the efficacy of such reflective training (Assare, 2020):

- Hold organizational leaders accountable by creating a team that tracks their progress on diversity and inclusion initiatives. For example, Nike tracks progress and shares it publicly.
- Provide momentum to diversity and inclusion efforts by compensating leaders based on their progress implementing DEI initiatives. The big box retailer Target tied achievement of diversity and inclusion goals to the compensation of their top 300 leaders (Glenn Taylor, "Moving toward inclusion: More retailers appoint C-level diversity officers," Retail Touchpoints, September 26, 2019, retailtouchpoints.com). Among Target's diversity and inclusion goals were increasing the number of multi-cultural products on shelves (for example, greater diversity in doll assortment) and ensuring recruitment, hiring, and retention of top diverse talent.
- Regularly ask customers for their comments and suggestions, and act on suggestions that are aligned with the organization's strategy.

In sum, as consumers themselves become ever more diverse, most will expect businesses to reflect this diversity. Gone are the days when racist, homophobic, and disability-related slurs and behaviors were tolerated. Younger consumers especially are choosing brands that stand behind social justice, equity, and inclusiveness. It is these companies that are attracting brand loyalty and experiencing high growth rates. Companies must act as they speak, embracing and listening to consumers traditionally marginalized.

References

Agence France-Presse (2021, November 30). "More than a third of world's population have never used internet, says UN". Retrieved from: www.theguardian.com/technology/2021/nov/30/more-than-a-third-of-worlds-population-has-never-used-the-internet-says-un.

Anderson, E. (2014). "The White space". *Sociology of Race and Ethnicity, 1*(1), 10–21.

Assare, J. G. (2020, March 18). "How H&M has completely revamped their diversity and inclusion training". Retrieved from: www.forbes.com/sites/janicegassam/2020/03/18/how-hm-has-completely-revamped-their-diversity-and-inclusion-training/?sh=595115fb5df0.

Binkovitz, L. (2018, July 12). "Study: When looking for and buying a house, racial inequality and discrimination compound". Retrieved from https://kinder.rice.edu/2018/07/11/study-when-looking-and-buying-house-racial-inequality-and-discrimination-compound.

Brodzik, C., Cuthill, S., Drake, N., & Young, N. (2021, October 19). "Authentically inclusive marketing: Winning future customers with diversity, equity, and inclusion". Retrieved from: www2.deloitte.com/us/en/insights/topics/marketing-and-sales-operations/global-marketing-trends/2022/diversity-and-inclusion-in-marketing.html.

Bureau of Internet Accessibility (2019, September 13). "What are the four major categories of accessibility?". Retrieved from: www.boia.org/blog/what-are-the-four-major-categories-of-accessibility.

Burns, T., Ellsworth, D., Field, E., & Harris, T. (2021, January 13). "The diversity imperative in retail". Retrieved from: www.mckinsey.com/industries/retail/our-insights/the-diversity-imperative-in-retail.

Businesswire (2019, October 9). "Herbal essences continuing commitment to inclusive design and accessibility for all". Retrieved from: www.businesswire.com/news/home/2019100 9005512/en/Herbal-Essences-Continuing-Commitment-Inclusive-Design-Accessibility #:~:text=Herbal%20Essences'%20has%20gone%20a, care%20questions%20throughout%20 the%20day.

Davis, K. (2020, June 30). "Affluent African American consumers in context: Buying while Black". Retrieved from: www.ipsos.com/en/affluent-african-american-consumers-context-buying-while-black.

De Elizabeth (2018, June 30). "People with disabilities share how shopping can be more accessible". Retrieved from: www.teenvogue.com/story/people-disabilities-share-shopping-more-accessible.

Dwyer, C. (2020, June 12). "Walmart, CVS, Walgreens to end practice of locking up Black beauty products". Retrieved from: www.npr.org/sections/live-updates-protests-for-racial-justice/2020/06/12/875903192/walmart-cvs-walgreens-to-end-practice-of-locking-up-black-beauty-products.

Ekpo, A. (2022). "Marketing research needs to be driven by social justice". Retrieved from: www.luc.edu/quinlan/about/newsandevents/archive/marketing-research-and-social-justice.shtml.

Fieldgate, J. (2021). "'We landed on two inspirational women who were perfect' – Behind the Campaign, Avon My Story Matters". Retrieved from: www.prweek.com/article/1721391/ we-landed-two-inspirational-women-perfect-behind-campaign-avon-story-matters.

Garrett, W. (2016, April 1). "Marginalized populations". Minnesota Psychological Association. Retrieved from: www.mnpsych.org/index.php?option=com_dailyplanetblog&view= entry&category=division%20news&id=71:marginalized-populations.

Hackett, T. (2019, April 2). "Smartphones are changing how homeless people survive". Retrieved from: https://psmag.com/ideas/smartphones-are-changing-how-homeless-people-survive.

Hammett, E. (2019, February 6). "What brands are doing to be more inclusive for people with disabilities". Retrieved from: www.marketingweek.com/how-brands-are-being-more-inclusive-for-people-with-disabilities/.

Hill, R. P. (1991, December). "Homeless women, special possessions, and the meaning of "home": An ethnographic case study". *Journal of Consumer Research*. https://doi.org/10.1086/209261.

Hill, R. P., & Stamey, M. (1990, December). "The homeless in America: An examination of possessions and consumption behaviors", *Journal of Consumer Research*. https://doi.org/10.1086/208559.

Jimenez, A. (2019, December 20). "Special software can help the blind access the internet but not every website supports it. A wave of lawsuits is pushing to change that". Retrieved from: www.chicagotribune.com/business/ct-biz-lawsuits-over-website-accessibility-20191220-ix72527ky5bvxaykh7aeixwyhe-story.html.

Korver-Glenn, E. (2018). "Compounding inequalities: How racial stereotypes and discrimination accumulate across the stages of housing exchange". *American Sociological Review*. Retrieved from https://search-ebscohost-com.uportland.idm.oclc.org/login.aspx?, https:// doi.org/10.1177/0003122418781774.

Magner, E. (2019, February 4). "We asked you for your biggest issues with size-inclusive fashion– here are the top 3". Retrieved from: www.wellandgood.com/plus-size-fashion-problems/.

New York Times (2021, December 27). "Crash test dummies made cars safer (for average-size men)". Retrieved from: www.nytimes.com/2021/12/27/business/car-safety-women.html.

Oakes, O. (2017, May 18). "Maltesers disability campaign 'most successful' in decade". Retrieved from: www.campaignlive.co.uk/article/maltesers-disability-campaign-most-successful-decade/1433980.

Oxford Reference.com (2022). "Marginalization". Retrieved from: www.oxfordreference.com/view/10.1093/oi/authority.20110803100133827.

Pittman, C. (2017). "'Shopping while Black': Black consumers' management of racial stigma and racial profiling in retail settings". *Journal of Consumer Culture*. https://doi.org/10.1177/1469540517717777.

Schiffer, J. (2020, November 6). "Lagging in diversity, haircare targets Black customers". Retrieved from: www.voguebusiness.com/beauty/lagging-in-diversity-haircare-targets-black-customers.

Sutherland, E. (2019, November 7). "Are you discriminating against shoppers with disabilities?". Retrieved from: www.drapersonline.com/insight/analysis/are-you-discriminating-against-shoppers-with-disabilities.

The Economist (2021, June 5). "LEGO unveils its first LGBTQ set". Retrieved from: www.economist.com/business/2021/06/05/lego-unveils-its-first-lgbtq-set.

Tibken, S. (2021, June 28). "The broadband gap's dirty secret: Redlining still exists in digital form". Retrieved from: www.cnet.com/home/internet/features/the-broadband-gaps-dirty-secret-redlining-still-exists-in-digital-form/.

Unicef (2020, December 1). "Two thirds of the world's school-age children have no internet access at home, new UNICEF–ITU report says". Press release. Retrieved from: www.unicef.org/press-releases/two-thirds-worlds-school-age-children-have-no-internet-access-home-new-unicef-itu.

Valenti, L. (2020, July 8). "The hairstyling industry has a racism problem, and it starts with beauty school". Retrieved from: www.vogue.com/article/hairstyling-industry-racism-bias-beauty-cosmetology-school-salons-red-carpet.

Venegas, N. (2021, October 29). "Doritos' viral Día de Muertos ad gorgeously celebrates LGBTQ+ communities". Retrieved from: www.adweek.com/brand-marketing/doritos-viral-dia-de-muertos-ad-gorgeously-celebrates-lgbtq-communities/.

W3C Web accessibility Initiative (WAI) (2019, May 10). "Accessibility principles". Retrieved from: www.w3.org/WAI/fundamentals/accessibility-principles/.

World Health Organization (2021, November 24). "Disability and health". Retrieved from: www.who.int/news-room/fact-sheets/detail/disability-and-health.

9 Children and Adolescents as Consumers

Objectives

1. To explain why children and adolescents are more vulnerable to common marketing tactics than are adults.
2. To identify products and describe marketing aimed at children and adolescents.
3. To explore the consumer socialization of children and adolescents and discuss how we can guide them in becoming wise consumers.

What Makes Children and Adolescents Especially Vulnerable to Marketing Appeals?

The human brain takes a very long time to develop fully. Even in late adolescence, the frontal cortex, which helps us control our impulses, is still developing. This means that compared to adults, children and adolescents are more likely to respond uncritically and positively to marketing appeals that emphasize fun, excitement, and – most of all – immediate gratification. What is it that makes adults better at resisting these persuasion attempts? The answer: Our brains have developed "executive functions":

> Being able to focus, hold, and work with information in mind, filter distractions, and switch gears is like having an air traffic control system at a busy airport to manage the arrivals and departures of dozens of planes on multiple runways. In the brain, this air traffic control mechanism is called executive functioning, a group of skills that helps us to focus on multiple streams of information at the same time, and revise plans as necessary.
>
> (Center on the Developing Child, n.d.)

There are three executive functions that enable us to navigate the world successfully:

- **Working memory** is our ability to hold and use multiple information "chunks" (e.g., scripts and schemas) for brief periods. It enables us to juggle different tasks, for example, to interrupt grocery shopping to change the baby,

DOI: 10.4324/9780367426897-12

recall where the shopping cart is, and resume shopping without backtracking. It is working memory that guides us through the multistep scripts for tasks like preparing a meal, running weekly errands, taking care of the dog, and participating in social activities, for example, games like checkers where the players have to remember whose turn it is and what the rules are.

- **Inhibitory control** enables us to filter out distractions from an important task, resist temptations like sugary snacks, control emotions like frustration and anger, and think before speaking. In a consumer behavior context, inhibitory control clears the path to successful resolution of product problems, empowers us to save up for significant purchases, to moderate our ingestion of "junk food" and "trash TV," and to turn off all our screens at bedtime.

- **Cognitive flexibility** enables us to switch scripts or schemas when the situation changes. This executive function helps ensure that we behave appropriately in different social settings – at work versus home, with close friends versus distant family members, on a first versus 15th date. This capacity also enables us to change our plans on the fly when circumstances dictate and to view problems from different perspectives. Consumer contexts that require flexibility in our choices of scripts include casual versus formal dining, shopping at bargain versus high-end retailers, choosing gifts for family, friends, or colleagues, adapting to the quickly changing communication norms and modalities that accompany technological advances, and troubleshooting minor performance problems inevitable in innovative products like smartphones, smart TVs, wearable technology devices, and so forth.

These executive functions typically develop in children who have proper adult guidance. The authors aptly observe that "Contrary to popular belief, learning to control impulses, pay attention, and retain information actively in one's memory does not happen automatically as children mature, and young children who have problems with these skills will not necessarily outgrow them" (Table 9.1).

Development of executive functions. Adapted from Center on the Developing Child at Harvard University (2011).

Given that children do not automatically develop executive functions, the following observations of research analysts at the Annie E. Casey Foundation are especially concerning:

> Uncertainty and instability were already a daily reality for millions of families before the pandemic hit. Since March 2020, a growing tide of lost income and jobs have destabilized millions more families.
>
> Absent action to prevent an eviction and foreclosure crisis, the data indicate a looming housing catastrophe for communities of color. Food insecurity—already a problem for more than one in 10 households before the pandemic—has also increased. At the same time, the pandemic has dramatically disrupted childcare throughout the nation, with centers forced to close and many parents left scrambling for alternatives.
>
> (Annie E. Casey Foundation, 2020)

Table 9.1 Development of executive functions. Adapted from Center on the Developing
Child at Harvard University (2011)

Working Memory	Inhibitory Control	Cognitive Flexibility
ADULT: Can remember multiple tasks, rules, and strategies that may vary by situation	ADULT: Consistent self-control; situationally appropriate responses	ADULT: Able to revise actions and plans in response to changing circumstances
5–16 YEARS: Develops ability to search varying locations, remember where something was found, then explore other locations	10–18 YEARS: Continues to develop self-control, such as flexibly switching between a central focus and peripheral stimuli 7 YEARS: Children perform at adult levels on learning to ignore irrelevant, peripheral stimuli	13–18 YEARS: Continues to show improvement in accuracy when switching focus and adapting to changing rules 10–12 YEARS: Can follow changing rules, even along multiple dimensions
4–5 YEARS: Comprehends that appearance does not always equal reality 3 YEARS: Can remember and apply two rules simultaneously	4–5 YEARS: Reductions in perseveration, can delay eating a treat, can remember and follow an arbitrary rule	2–5 YEARS: Can shift actions according to changing rules

Children in low-income households are at greater risk of unintentional injuries
due to household hazards; less likely to receive all the nutrition needed for normal
cognitive and physiological development; and at increased risk of suffering the
negative effects of chronic stress on the formation of healthy neural networks.
These conditions hold true for increasing numbers of young children in the US
and elsewhere in the world. When we talk about marketing to children, it is
important to bear in mind that a large percentage of them have little chance of
achieving the prosperous lifestyles of their peers portrayed in advertising messages.

Products and Marketing Tactics Aimed at Children and Adolescents

Leading child experts from around the world joined efforts on a WHO-UNICEF-
Lancet Commission to produce a "landmark report on child health and well-being,
entitled 'A future for the world's children?'" Among the report's observations is
the following:

> The rapid rise in childhood obesity is one of the most serious public health
> challenges of the 21st century, with the number of children and adolescents
> affected by obesity increasing more than ten times from 11 million in 1975 to
> 124 million in 2016.

Children are frequently exposed to harmful commercial marketing, typically seeing tens of thousands of advertisements a year for addictive substances and unhealthy commodities including fast food and sugar-sweetened beverages which contribute to obesity and chronic diseases, as well as online gambling services, which can harm their relationships, school achievement, and mental health.

The marketing and inappropriate use of breastmilk substitutes (formula milk)—a US$ 70 billion industry—is associated with lowered intelligence, obesity, increased risk of diabetes and other non-communicable diseases, accounting for an estimated loss to society of US$ 302 billion.

- Evidence suggests that children in some countries see as many as 30 000 advertisements on television alone in a single year, many for harmful products.
- A review of 23 studies in Latin America reported that advertising exposure was associated with a preference for and purchase of unhealthy foods by families and children who are overweight and obese.
- In a sample of five- and six-year-olds in Brazil, China, India, Nigeria, and Pakistan, 68% could identify at least one cigarette brand logo; 50% could do so in Russia and 86% in China.
- In a study of 11- to 14-year-olds from Los Angeles, United States, African-American youth were exposed to an average of four to one alcohol advertisements per day.
- In Iran, food advertising during children's programs is dominated by food items that are potentially harmful to oral health, as are almost two thirds of food adverts during children's television in the United Kingdom.

(Clark et al., 2020)

As the foregoing summary shows, many children are exposed to a high volume of advertising, much of which is for harmful products, and this continued exposure may have a cumulative negative impact on their preferences and habits. The research discussed below takes a deeper dive into the tactics brands employ in their advertising aimed at children.

Researchers in Spain who analyzed the content of breakfast food commercials targeted at children versus adults found that the breakfast foods advertised to children contained, on average, more than three times the amount of sugar in brands targeting adults. These unhealthy brands typically appeal to their young target consumers using a hedonistic approach. Because they lack the ability to control their impulses toward immediate gratification, children are especially susceptible to appeals that promise that a product will bring them enjoyment, even happiness. A consequence of such advertising campaigns is that children repeatedly and insistently ask their parents to buy the advertised brands. This "pester power" effect results in the purchase of more processed foods that the whole family may end up consuming.

Study coauthor, Open University of Catalonia Professor Mireia Montaña, recommends that Spain and by extension, other countries in the EU develop more stringent regulations, along with several other actions focused on reducing childhood obesity. These include effective education on nutrition for parents and children alike and increasing the tax on certain products, as Spain has done with soft drinks (Open University of Catalonia, 2021).

A multicountry review of marketing tactics promoting food to children via TV commercials corroborated and extended the findings from the study described above. The authors found that the most common appeals in children's advertisings are premium offers, promotional characters, nutritional claims, taste, and fun (Jenkin et al., 2014). Premiums are free gifts, vouchers, or rebates either included in the food package purchased or available in exchange for mail-in proof of purchase. Promotional characters include those identified with the food brand (e.g., Tony the Tiger and Ronald McDonald); licensed characters such as Sponge Bob Square Pants and Spiderman; and celebrities familiar to children and their parents (e.g., sports figures) or popular people parents would likely find persuasive (scientists, health professionals).

Health and nutrition claims, more persuasive to parents than to children, ranged from vague statements about well-being, strength, or growth to assertions that the advertised food contains a specific health- or growth-enhancing nutrient. Taste and fun, especially appealing to children, are often emphasized through nonverbal cues showing the consumer's experience of the food itself as well as the consumption context.

Increasingly, children and adolescents are targeted via apps. A recent review of 135 commonly downloaded apps aimed at children aged five and under revealed that 95% of them contain advertising. Formats include distracting and often misleading banner ads, pop-up videos, and familiar commercial characters encouraging purchases to make the game more fun. All free apps reviewed contained advertising compared to 88% of purchased apps. Author Jenny Radesky, MD, expressed concern that children from lower-income households are more likely to use free apps, which contain "more distracting and persuasive ads" (Radesky, 2018).

Consumer Socialization

What do we know about how children learn about brands, marketing, and consumer behavior more generally? We term this acquisition of knowledge and skills "consumer socialization," and note that it involves cognitive as well as social development. The cognitive part of consumer socialization relies in part on the acquisition of executive functions, discussed above, and in part on children learning to categorize objects and reason abstractly. Their schemas and scripts (categorizations of knowledge) are initially based on simple perceptual cues like shape, size, and color. Eventually, children learn to categorize objects based on abstract qualities that define core concepts in a category. For example, they may first classify all beverages clear in color as water and later develop schemas at multiple taxonomic levels. These might include a schema for beverages, sub-schemas for water and soft drinks, and under soft drinks are colas and clear beverages (John & Chaplin, 2022).

Young children's understanding of brands is typically based on their personal experiences. For example, a video of a five-year-old child asked to identify a series of brand logos (Ladd, 2012) identifies unfamiliar ones based on their shapes and colors and familiar ones in terms of her experiences (e.g., she identified the GE logo as "where my grandpa works" and the Xbox logo as "that's what we use to play games at Ryan's house"). And their acquisition of common consumer scripts like shopping begins as concrete steps they observe parents making as they navigate a specific retail establishment. Only later do these scripts become generalized to other environments. Think about the prominent role of working memory in shopping and other consumer scripts, and how essential cognitive flexibility is to the development of scripts that are both abstract and general and finely tuned to context (John & Chaplin, 2022).

Given their rudimentary understanding of products and brands, how do young children make decisions in consumer contexts? Research shows that, not unexpectedly, they choose based on perceptual attributes and their choices are often inconsistent with their initial preferences for specific attributes. Older children and adolescents, who typically have greater cognitive flexibility, investigate more relevant attributes and use a variety of decision strategies (John & Chaplin, 2022).

How do children respond to advertising? Young children (below age eight) typically distinguish between television programming and commercials based on perceptual cues (commercials are shorter) rather than selling intent. Older children come to understand the selling intent of commercials, but it still affects their brand choices, at least in the short term. Young adolescents comprehend that advertisers may employ deception to their quest for sales. To a degree, this knowledge of advertising tactics serves as a cognitive defense against misleading persuasive attempts, but because inhibitory control does not fully develop until the mid-20s, promises of fun, happiness, and social acceptance remain compelling to adolescents (John & Chaplin, 2022).

As noted above, increasingly advertisers blur the line between marketing and entertainment by promoting their brands to children and adolescents using interactive apps and games. Even older children and adolescents do not readily identify the selling intent of those in which brands are embedded. For example, a survey of 5,200 Canadian youth in grades four through 11 found that three quarters of them identified brand-centered games as "just games" and not "mainly advertisements" (An et al., 2014). The brands appearing in such games are more likely to garner uncritical acceptance if the player enjoys the game and does not consciously employ cognitive defenses against the implicit persuasion attempts.

As for the social components of consumer socialization, family exerts the earliest and most significant influence on concepts of money, spending and saving, and product purchase and usage. Research on how parents help shape children as consumers found that parental styles impact the degree to which children are permitted or encouraged to practice making consumer decisions. Authoritarian parents foster dependence by placing high value on conformity and discouraging expressions of independent thought. Their children learn primarily by observing parental behavior and absorbing parental dictates about how to handle money and which products and brands are best. Permissive parents, in contrast, are more nurturing and place a lower value on conformity. Their children are likely to be allowed to make consumer decisions starting in childhood, but may not be given much guidance in developing wise fiscal and other consumption-related practices. Authoritative parents combine nurturing with strict discipline and are most likely to devote conscious effort to socializing their children to become wise and responsible consumers by actively engaging them in discussions of marketing and media from an early age (John & Chaplin, 2022).

One important aspect of children's socialization is development of gender identity. When parents and other adults interact with girl and boy babies in stereotypical ways, the children learn quickly that little girls are more passive, preferring quiet play with cuddly dolls and plush toys in pastels, while little boys are more active, gravitating toward trucks and cars, tools, and more, and developing their visuospatial skills in their play activities. Research has found evidence of such stereotyping even among adults who do not consciously embrace traditional gender roles. For example, in one study (Glass, 2017), boy and girl babies were dressed as the opposite gender and adult male and female subjects were observed interacting with them in a playroom setting. When subjects thought they were playing with a little girl, many showed the child the dolls and plush toys provided and did not encourage physical activity. Little boys, on the other hand, were shown toy cars and trucks and encouraged to try out a riding toy. From infancy, humans are sensitive to social cues from their adult caregivers, whether such cues are conscious and intentional or merely remnants of implicit learning the caregivers carry unconsciously from their own childhood.

As children mature, their peers and the media are increasingly influential. An increasingly popular form of "advertainment" is YouTube videos hosted by child influencers. These YouTube stars, who excitedly unwrap presents, play with and review toys and simulate shopping expeditions, garner millions of views, and earn billions in revenue from the brands featured in their videos. About 90% of the items featured are unhealthy foods like burgers, fries, milkshakes, sugary snacks and beverages, and other junk food. Endorsements and product placements feature food from McDonald's, Taco Bell, Carl's Jr., Chuck E. Cheese, and Hershey's. This is concerning, given that four in five parents with children under 11 report that they permit them to watch YouTube and that childhood obesity rates are skyrocketing:

> "The way these branded products are integrated in everyday life in these videos is pretty creative and unbelievable," said Marie Bragg, an author of the study and an assistant professor of public health and nutrition at the New York

University School of Global Public Health. "It's a stealthy and powerful way of getting these unhealthy products in front of kids' eyeballs."

(*The New York Times*, 2020)

Children aspire to be like these influencers, who appear to be prosperous, self-assured, and arbiters of taste in toys and food. Research shows that by middle childhood, children begin to stereotype people based on their possessions. These inferences, initially absorbed from adults, become more consistent and adult-like as children get older. While adolescents may know at a cognitive level that they do not need to emulate their peers and social media influencers to become high-functioning adults, their emotional drive to belong, to "fit in," remains strong. This drive, along with the adolescent's propensity to engage in risky behaviors (Pechman et al., 2020), has led to widespread use of alcohol, e-cigarettes and vaping, cigarettes, marijuana (Kann et al., 2018), and fast food. Nine of ten adult smokers start before age 18, and seeing friends use tobacco, alcohol, and other harmful products increases the likelihood of consumption (Centers for Disease Control and Prevention, 2022).

No discussion of child and adolescent consumer socialization would be complete without addressing the impact of technology devices on development. These consumer products have changed the lives of adults and may be altering cognitive and social development (Orlando, 2020):

> Even before they can say the words, "Hey, Siri," kids are awash in smartphones, tablets and a torrent of interactive content. The average child younger than 2 spends around 40 minutes a day looking at screens—and that daily dose only increases as the years go by. One survey estimates that almost half of all American teenagers say they're online nearly constantly.
>
> The proliferation of screens—and their potential impact—has sparked concerns. The American Academy of Pediatrics has recommended that kids under 18 months avoid screens altogether, apart from the occasional video chat. The group's 2016 report on media use for children cites risks ranging from poor sleep to stunted language skills. Many Silicon Valley parents, including tech titans like Mark Zuckerberg, restrict their children's screen time.
>
> (Orlando, 2020)

The question of how all this screen time affects cognitive and social development is the focus of much current research, but we do not yet have definitive answers. Here's what we know so far:

• Video deficit: While screens are at least as attention-getting for infants and toddlers as they are for us adults, the little ones don't learn nearly as much from screens as they do from in-person interactions. This is true for cognitive tasks like language learning as well as for integrative knowledge about how things and beings work in the world. In brief, they do not initially understand that screen content is meant to represent three-dimensional objects.

- Rewiring the brain: MRI scans of preschoolers' brain show that higher levels of screen time are associated with lower amounts of white matter in the brain. White matter is fibrous tissue that connects different parts of the brain and supports development of complex skills, including language acquisition. Though troubling, these are preliminary findings that did not measure parents' screen time. Lead author John Hutton, a pediatrician and researcher at Cincinnati Children's Hospital, comments, "That's one thing we didn't measure in the study that I wish we had. Because kids that grow up with a lot of screen time tend to have parents using a lot of screens." Screen time has a high opportunity cost: Every moment spent on a screen is one less moment spent interacting with one's child.

- Benefits of video action games: Multiple studies indicate that playing fast-paced videogames, including many involving shooting targets, improves depth perception, visual memory, spatial awareness, and the ability to switch between tasks. Remember the executive function of working memory? It appears that in addition to improving visual short-term memory, these games help many older children develop the ability to filter out distractions and focus on a task (comment by C. Shawn Green, a psychologist at the University of Wisconsin-Madison who specializes in cognitive neuroscience).

- Drawbacks of videogames: Do violent games increase aggression and desensitize players to violence? This is a hotly debated question. There is no definitive evidence that playing such games increases violent tendencies. On the other hand, time spent gaming is time not spent on social interactions or physical activities that benefit the whole body.

Teens with smartphones: Research on how smartphone use impacts cognitive, emotional, and social functioning is largely correlational in nature and the findings are mixed. The widespread concern that excessive smartphone use causes a variety of ills including attention deficit disorder, anxiety, and loneliness, causal evidence is scant. As longitudinal data accumulates, we will be able to determine the legitimacy of these concerns.

(Wilmer et al., 2017)

Smartphones offer many benefits including connecting and coordinating with family and friends, immediate access to numerous legitimate sources of information, news, and entertainment, ready access to help in unsafe situations, and ability to document violence perpetrated on others. Downsides include the ready access it provides to content that is deceptive or destructive to well-being and the many and varied distractions it offers us when the task at hand is tedious or onerous. Remember the executive function of inhibitory control? It can be challenging even for adults (who should have good impulse control) to resist checking frequently for emails and texts.

The following guidelines to screen time may help parents of young children. What parents of adolescents need to remember is that the child's resemblance to an adult is only apparent. The teen's brain is not yet fully developed, and the neural connections supporting inhibitory control in particular are not complete. Teens still need rules about when and where smartphone use is acceptable and interactive discussions about how to assess content. Parental controls, provided by Google, Apple, and other major tech companies helps curtail use of harmful content but it is not a panacea, and there is no substitute for parents' guidance.

A Pediatrician's Guide to Screen Time:

> When you hand a child an iPad, says John Hutton, a pediatrician and researcher at Cincinnati Children's Hospital, you're not just giving them a toy. "It's a really powerful tool," he says. "It's more powerful than the computers that sent rockets to space 30 years ago." And despite how quickly children might seem to adjust to new tech, that doesn't mean they know how—or when—to use it.

Here are a few tips from Hutton on helping kids navigate our increasingly wired world:

> Remember toddlers are not small grown-ups. At different ages, children's needs change along with their brains and emotional development. And while children under the age of 2 might be drawn in by flashing screens, they're still not learning much from them at that age.
>
> Go slow. For preschoolers, gradually introduce different types of media that are slower-paced and encourage learning. (Think shows like Sesame Street, says Hutton.) From there, work your way up to more challenging—yet still age-appropriate—content.
>
> Help children choose their own content. While it's important to limit your child's choices, give them some control over what they're watching. For example, ask them if they'd rather watch Cinderella or Cars rather than letting them go hog wild.
>
> Keep devices in a central location. You should be able to monitor how they're being used. In other words, don't let them disappear from view. "I would never let it go into a child's bedroom," says Hutton.
>
> Don't lose sight of real-world experiences. Whether it's going outside, playing with blocks or drawing a picture, be mindful of the things that screens might be replacing. "It's not all about 'restricting' screen time," says Hutton. "It's being open to all of the other things out there that are healthy for kids."
>
> (Orlando, 2020)

How Can We Teach Children to Be Wise Consumers?

Given the ubiquity of in-app and online branded games and the rise of social media influencers, it may be that our wisest course of action is to ensure that children become media literate, if not at home, then in school programs. Media literacy is an essential skill for all of us in this world of information overabundance; to be well-informed citizens, productive workers, and creative beings, we need ever more sophisticated strategies for filtering out the noise and focusing quickly on the nutritious food for thought. Where better to begin than in the classroom?

As you may recall from Chapter 5, the brain is wired for two types of processing and memory: explicit, conscious knowledge and implicit thoughts, feelings, and behavioral impulses that exert their influence outside the scope of our conscious awareness. Young children sometimes appear to be chaotic beings driven by unfettered, unlabeled, and uncontrolled impulses. Part of helping a child develop and strengthen executive functions is drawing their attention to the need to modify their behavior to suit the context. Eventually, of course, this explicit learning becomes automated and implicit, which is why few adults must be reminded to use their "inside voice" or to refrain from wresting a coveted object away from its owner.

Helping children become smart consumers involves teaching them to modify their responses in two contexts at least, viewing ads and shopping. As we saw earlier, young children start out not knowing that ads are created by marketers for the express purpose of selling products and therefore must be viewed with skepticism. But skepticism alone will not keep a child from purchasing, or urging a parent to purchase, the advertised product. Self-control at the point of purchase is needed as well.

Researchers give the following example:

> ...imagine a child being given a choice between two brands of chocolate. The explicit system might provide the child with the information that he or she has consumed the chocolate before, or that he or she has seen an ad about the chocolate. In contrast, the implicit system provides behavioural impulses, but does not allow insights into the bases of the impulses. Imagine that the child was exposed to some ads for one of the chocolate brands, and the implicit system formed associations of this brand with eating and taste. Later, the child might not be aware of the prior exposures, but follows the automatic impulse towards the brand, which has its origin in the prior exposure.
>
> (Büttner et al., 2014)

Given that the child's impulse to purchase and consume is likely implicit (automated and not susceptible to analysis), Büttner et al. argue, we should ideally teach children self-control techniques that work at an implicit unconscious, automatic level. These authors recommend the three techniques of setting goals, learning through imitation, and forming implementation intentions.

Self-control goals start out as explicit instructions of the child's caregiver; they might be "When we're in the supermarket, don't take anything off the shelf." An alternative goal may work even better, as its activation may inhibit the tempting impulse and redirect the child's attention to a constructive, prosocial activity:

"Would you please help me find the milk?" or "Today we're looking for healthy food to buy." With practice, a child will internalize the self-control or alternative goal, which will become implicit, activated automatically by entering the supermarket. Moreover, as children mature and learn, they may enjoy participating in selecting alternative goals.

Imitation is the second technique the authors suggest. As influential as a parent's words are, parental actions – responses to challenges, behavior under stress – may be even more powerful teaching tools, in part because they are acquired through osmosis, learned implicitly, imitated without deliberation. Does the parent grab a candy bar while waiting at the checkout counter? Does s/he sit down with a carton of ice cream and a spoon when s/he is upset by something that happened at work? Or does s/he return the candy bar to its place on the supermarket shelf, and in times of stress, comfort herself with a cup of tea?

The third technique the authors recommend that parents teach their children to help them automate self-control is *implementation intentions*. These are "if-then" plans: If a specified condition occurs, then a preselected behavior will follow. For example, "If I see a sugary cookie in the fresh-baked bread and dessert case, then I'll buy a whole grain bagel." While implementation intentions are the products of conscious deliberation, their purpose is to sidestep conscious choice with its concomitant conflicts, by ceding control of behavior to implicit, automatic activation when the condition specified occurs. Büttner et al. (2014) provide this example:

> To illustrate the technique of implementation intentions, think of a child who wants to save his or her pocket money for a higher goal (e.g., a new musical instrument) instead of spending it on sweets. This child might form an implementation intention such as "If I pass a shelf with sweets in the supermarket, I will ignore them." Instead of simply ignoring the distracting stimulus, the then part could also specify a focus on the higher goal: "If I pass a shelf with sweets, I will think about the musical instrument that I will buy with my pocket money." Moreover, the then part could also specify an alternative action. For instance, "If I see a soft drink in the supermarket, I will buy a bottle of mineral water" could be an implementation intention that aims at drinking fewer soft drinks.

The authors suggest that in addition to media literacy education, as outlined above, marketing messages directed at children should be subject to external regulations. Because obesity rates among children and adolescents are at an all-time high, advertising of unhealthy foods has garnered much recent attention from scholars and regulators. The following article explains regulatory initiatives researchers at University of Sydney Law School recommend:

> Around the world, approximately 170 million children under the age of 18 are estimated to be overweight or obese. Childhood obesity can lead to serious health consequences, including an increased risk for heart disease, sleep disorders, cancer, and early death.

The way companies market their food and beverages to children affects what they eat. In a recent paper, two legal scholars show how food advertising regulations in six countries—including the United States—fail to protect children adequately from excessive promotion of unhealthy foods.

Belinda Reeve and Roger Magnusson of the University of Sydney Law School assess the strengths and weaknesses of each country's regulatory schemes. They identify three distinct schemes used to regulate food advertising to children: statutory regulation, where a government entity develops and implements the regulation; co-regulation, where the regulatory process is shared by public and private entities; and self-regulation, where the industry itself writes, monitors, and enforces the rules.

In the United States, food industries self-regulate in the form of an industry pledge. Following the release of a report by the U.S. Federal Trade Commission and the U.S. Department of Health and Human Services recommending an expansion of self-regulatory standards for food marketing to children, U.S. food producers in 2006 established the Children's Food and Beverage Advertising Initiative (CFBAI).

Administered by the nongovernmental Council of Better Business Bureaus (CBBB), the CFBAI sets uniform nutrition standards for the food that participants advertise to children under the age of 12. Eighteen companies, including McDonalds, Kellogg, Ferrero, and Coca-Cola, have signed a voluntary pledge to follow the advertising standards adopted as part of the CFBAI.

According to the CFBAI, "child-directed advertising" includes television, radio, print, and third-party websites where 35 percent or more of the audience includes children under the age of 12. Participants in the CFBAI agree to promote only "healthier choice products" in interactive games targeted at children, as well as to avoid advertising branded foods and beverages in elementary schools. The CBBB sanctions those participants that violate the pledge. Sanctions include expelling participants from the CFBAI and notifying regulatory authorities of breaches.

Reeve and Magnusson note, however, that self-regulation does not necessarily lead to improvements in food advertising aimed at children. Although industry evaluations show high levels of compliance, evaluations by independent contractors offer a different story. In some instances, self-regulation has led to reductions in children's exposure to unhealthy food marketing. Other research, however, has shown that the "vast majority of food advertising seen by children continues to be for unhealthy products." One study even showed an increase in the promotion of unhealthy foods to children.

One of the issues, Reeve and Magnusson note, lies in the fact that public health experts and food industry actors have different ideas about the goals of food advertising regulation. For the food industry, the aim is to reduce the amount of unhealthy food advertisements targeted at children. In contrast, public health advocates argue that the aim is to reduce the overall amount of food advertising children receive—whether targeted at adults or children—because of children's vulnerability to advertising. Self-regulation, according to public health officials, should be replaced by "comprehensive statutory restrictions on food marketing to children, accompanied by effective monitoring and enforcement mechanisms."

To help governments design more "robust and effective" regulatory schemes, Reeve and Magnusson propose an "accountability model" that would enhance advertising regulation's transparency and accountability. The proposed framework addresses three domains of regulatory design: the content of the regulation; the method of administering the regulatory scheme; and how the regulations are enforced. In line with the public health advocates, this "accountability model" presupposes that the government will play a central role in the regulatory scheme.

Reeve and Magnusson first suggest the content of the regulation should contain measurable, clear objectives that can be assessed. Key terms should be clearly defined, and objectives should be achievable.

Second, the regulatory process should incorporate transparency and accountability. An independent body should be responsible for monitoring an advertising scheme and assessing its performance with regular, structured review to ensure objectives are being reached.

Finally, an independent body should enforce the standards by accepting and investigating complaints. That body should be authorized to offer incentives to "encourage and reward high levels of compliance."

Substantial room for improvement exists in the regulation of food advertising to children, Reeve and Magnusson conclude. Their proposed accountability model could assist in reducing children's consumption of unhealthy food and, by extension, reduce rates of childhood obesity.

(Ramirez, 2018)

References

Annie E. Casey Foundation (2020, December 14). "Kids, families and COVID-19: Pandemic pain points and the urgent need to respond". Retrieved from: www.aecf.org/resources/kids-families-and-covid-19.

An, S., Jin, H. S, & Park, E. H. (2014). "Children's advertising literacy for advergames: Perception of the game as advertising". *Journal of Advertising, 43*(1), 63–72. https://doi.org/10.1080/00913367.2013.795123.

Büttner, O. B., Florack, A., & Serfas, B. G. (2014). "A dual-step and dual-process model of advertising effects: Implications for reducing the negative impact of advertising on children's consumption behaviour. *Journal of Consumer Policy, 37,* 161–182. https://doi.org/10.1007/s10603-013-9250-0.

Center on the Developing Child, Harvard University (2022). "InBrief: Executive function: Skills for life and learning". Retrieved from: https://developingchild.harvard.edu/resources/inbrief-executive-function-skills-for-life-and-learning/.

Center on the Developing Child, Harvard University/National Scientific Council on the Developing Child (2011). "Building the brain's 'air traffic control' system: How early experiences shape the development of executive function". Working Paper No. 11. Retrieved from: https://46y5eh11fhgw3ve3ytpwxt9r-wpengine.netdna-ssl.com/wp-content/uploads/2011/05/How-Early-Experiences-Shape-the-Development-of-Executive-Function.pdf.

Centers for Disease Control and Prevention (2022). "Youth and tobacco use". Retrieved from: www.cdc.gov/tobacco/data_statistics/fact_sheets/youth_data/tobacco_use/index.htm.

Clark, H., Coll-Seck, A. M., Bannerjee, A., et al. (2020, February 18). "A future for the world's children? A WHO–UNICEF–*Lancet* commission". *Lancet*. https://doi.org/10.1016/S0140-6736(19)32540-1.

Glass, J. (2017, August 25). "Gendering toys is actually ridiculous as this experiment shows". Retrieved from: www.pinknews.co.uk/2017/08/25/gendering-toys-is-actually-ridiculous-as-this-experiment-shows/.

Jenkin, G., Madhvani, N., Signal, L., & Bowers, S. (2014). "A systematic review of persuasive marketing techniques to promote food to children on television". *Obesity Reviews, 15*(4), 281–293.

John, D. R., & Chaplin, L. N. (2022). "Children as consumers: A review of 50 years of research in marketing". In L. R. Kahle, T. M. Lowrey, & J. Huber (Eds.), *APA Handbook of Consumer Psychology* (pp. 185–202). Washington, DC: American Psychological Association. https://doi.org/10.1037/0000262-007.

Kann, L., McManus, T., Harris, W. A., Shanklin, S. L., Flint, K. H., Queen, B., Lowry, R., Chyen, D. Whittle, L., Thornton, J., Lim, C., Bradford, D., Yamakawa, Y., Leon, M., Brener, N., & Ethier, K. A. (2018). "Youth risk behavior surveillance—United States, 2017". *Surveillance Summaries, 67*(8), 1–114. Retrieved from: www.cdc.gov/mmwr/volumes/67/ss/ss6708a1.htm.

Ladd, A. (2012). "Fresh Impressions on Brand Marks" [Video]. Available at: www.youtube.com/watch?v=N4t3-__3MA0.

Open University of Catalonia (2021, February 11). "Breakfast product ads targeting children contain triple the amount of sugar of those advertised for adults". Retrieved from: https://medicalxpress.com/news/2021-02-breakfast-product-ads-children-triple.html.

Orlando, A. (2020, April 13). "Kids are growing up wired—And that's changing their brains: Smartphones and other tech pose special challenges—And opportunities—For young brains". *Discover Magazine*. Retrieved from: www.discovermagazine.com/mind/screen-time-is-replacing-playtime-and-thats-changing-kids-brains.

Pechman, C., Catlin, J. R., & Zheng, Y. (2020). "Facilitating adolescent well-being: A review of the challenges and opportunities and the beneficial roles of parents, schools, neighborhoods, and policymakers". Retrieved from: https://escholarship.org/uc/item/62t572mr.

Radesky, J. (2018, October 30). "Advertising in kids' apps more prevalent than parents may realize". Retrieved from: www.sciencedaily.com/releases/2018.

Ramirez, S. (2018, August 9). "Regulating food advertising to children". *The Regulatory Review*. Retrieved from: www.theregreview.org/2018/08/09/ramirez-regulating-food-advertising-children/.

The New York Times (2020, October 26). "Are 'Kidfluencers' making our kids fat?". Retrieved from: www.nytimes.com/2020/10/26/well/family/Youtube-children-junk-food-child-obesity.html?/10/181030091452.htm.

Wilmer, H. H., Sherman, L. E., & Chein, J. M. (2017). "Smartphones and cognition: A review of research exploring the links between mobile technology habits and cognitive functioning". *Frontiers in Psychology, 8*. https://doi.org/10.3389/fpsyg.2017.0060. Retrieved from: www.ncbi.nlm.nih.gov/pmc/articles/PMC5403814/.

10 Nonhuman Animals as Special Possessions

Objectives

1. To explore the scope and nature of pet ownership and associated consumer expenditures.
2. To investigate the consumer's journey from petlessness to pet ownership.
3. To propose best practices for marketers at animal adoption agencies and potential pet owners.

Introduction

Companion animals occupy a unique place in our lives: They are legally viewed as our possessions but they are sentient beings with their own cognitions, affect, and behavior. Many consumers are deeply attached to their pets and consider them family members, while others view them as providers of physical or emotional support or as sources of income from breeding and competitions. These roles may and often do overlap.

As our property, companion animals are subject (hence vulnerable) to our decisions about every aspect of their lives, whether those decisions are grounded in species-specific knowledge or well-intentioned but often misguided anthropomorphization, deep love and attachment or affectionate regard, prosperity or harsh, sometimes heartbreaking, economic realities. And yet, as eager or reluctant consumers of the pet-related goods and services we purchase, companion animals have a hand (paw) in shaping *our* consumer cognitions, affect, and behavior.

The vignettes in "A Tale of Two Tabbies" illustrate how even the seemingly simple feeling of love for our companion animals may manifest in divergent consumer cognitions and behaviors:

> A Tale of Two Tabbies
>
> Large-framed and rotund, 19-lb. cat Khilona has always eaten with great enthusiasm. Never a finicky feline, he gobbles up whatever is set in front of him. He has spent the long bright days of his 17 summers out in his catio,

DOI: 10.4324/9780367426897-13

basking in the sunshine. So when the amiable feline stopped eating and spent the day curled up in the small, dark "kitty condo" in the bedroom, his human, Stacie, knew something was wrong. She immediately called her vet, who had recently joined a house-call-only practice catering to well-heeled clients who regard their aging cats and dogs, not as child substitutes, but as their inter-species children. Because cats, natural predators, are hard-wired to hide pain and any other source of vulnerability, it took several in-home exams and a visit to a dental specialist to reveal that the big feline had a very painful dental problem as well as an aggressive and untreatable form of oral cancer. All told, Stacie's vet bills exceeded $4,000 in a week's time. Though she could do little but keep Khilona comfortable until the cancer claimed him, she did not regret the expenditures. In her view, she was responsible for his well-being, and that included the best medical care she could afford.

Stacie's friend Bob loved the cat Moonshine, who hung around his home woodworking shop for years. He kept her well-supplied with good-quality kibble and enjoyed her delight at the occasional treat of human-grade tuna or salmon. In her younger years, the little black feline spent much of her time roaming Bob's rural property, more than once catching and contentedly consuming an unwary starling or mouse. As she aged, Moonshine's outdoor forays grew less frequent and she became a snuggly, snoozing senior kitty Bob contentedly caressed each night as the two drifted off to sleep. In many ways Moonshine's life was idyllic: she had free run of the great outdoors; she was loved, sheltered, and fed well; and perhaps best of all from the feline perspective, she was seldom poked and prodded by the vet. Bob had her spayed and kept up with the required shots, but when she was feeling poorly, he gave her extra treats and lots of cuddles. One day Moonshine disappeared. Bob looked for her every day but after a few weeks he sadly stopped searching, realizing she had likely been killed by one of the coyotes that roamed rural Oregon.

Both Stacie and Bob love their feline friends deeply, derive joy and peace from their companionship, and mourn their passing. But their cat-related consumer behaviors differ dramatically. Stacie displays her love and concern by purchasing premium cat food, seeking advice on nutrition, behavioral issues, and medical concerns from her vet, her cat sitter of many years, and digital sources such as cat-info.org; and having roomy "catios" built to provide her cats safe outside access. Bob manifests his feelings for felines by offering them shelter, food, and affection together with the freedom to roam freely with the other wildlife on his land. In short, the same feeling may result in very different behaviors because of the intervening thoughts. Stacie views her cats as young children for whose well-being she is solely responsible. Bob sees his cats as kindred spirits and wildlife that can choose to take or reject his friendly overtures and offers of help.

Facts about Pet Owners and Their Consumer Behavior

With these complexities in mind, let's turn our attention to what we know about pet ownership and owners. According to a 2016 survey of more than 27,000 internet users in 22 countries, Argentina, Mexico, and Brazil have the largest shares of pet owners, followed closely by the US and Russia (Growth from Knowledge, 2016). Dogs, cats, birds, and fish are the most popular pets, with dogs leading the pack in all these countries except Russia, where consumers show a marked preference for cats. For one of the few in-depth cross-cultural explorations of human views of animal companions, see Gray and Young (2015).

We will focus on the US throughout the remainder of this chapter, in part because it is the leading market for pet food, supplies, and services and in part because research on pets and their owners is most plentiful for the US. Table 10.1 shows the most recent pet ownership statistics from the two organizations that regularly collect such data: American Veterinary Medical Association (AVMA) and American Pet Products Association (APPA). The data were compiled by Humane Society of the United States (n.d.).

The table highlights the following:

1.   Nearly two of every three households include at least one dog or cat.
2.   It is not uncommon for a household to have more than one animal.
3.   Eight in ten pet owners regard their animals as part of the family.
4.   Approximately eight out of ten owned dogs and cats are spayed or neutered.

Note that APPA's estimates consistently exceed those provided by AVMA. We can attribute this to the organizations' different methods of collecting data and to the fact that APPA data are more recent. Both organizations agree that pet ownership is rising.

Humane Society of the United States (HSUS) cautions us that the numbers in Table 10.1 do not tell the whole story:

Pet Ownership Estimates from Underserved Communities

While the figures referenced previously tend to reflect mainstream America, the **Pets for Life** team of the HSUS has spent years working in, and **collecting data** from, our nation's most underserved communities which lack access to affordable and available pet resources. We have found startling differences in pet ownership. People living in underserved communities love their pets as much as pet owners anywhere else in the nation. However, there is extreme inequity in access to veterinary care, spay/neuter providers, and other services most Americans take for granted, and this difference is reflected in the data:

Table 10.1 U.S. pet ownership estimates

Data	2017–2018 AVMA Sourcebook	2021–2022 APPA Survey
Total number of U.S. households	125.819 Million	128.451 Million
Number (%) of households with pet	74.4 Million (59%)	90.5 Million (70%)
Percentage of pet owners who consider their pets		
Family members	80%	
Pets or companions	17%	
Property	3%	
Number (%) of households that own at least one dog	48.3 Million (38%)	69 Million (54%)
Number (%) of households that own at least one cat	31.9 Million (25%)	45.4 Million (35%)
Percentage of owned dogs who are spayed or neutered	69.1%	78%
Percentage of pet cats who are spayed or neutered	80%	85%

- Pets living in underserved communities in the US: 22 million
- Percentage of pets living in underserved communities who are not spayed or neutered: 88%
- Percentage of pets living in underserved communities who have never seen a veterinarian: 69%

(Humane Society of the United States, n.d.)

The need (desire) for animal companionship transcends demographic, lifestyle, and life stage differences. Millennials are most likely to own a pet, accounting for 32% of pet owners, followed closely by Baby Boomers at 27% and Gen X at 24% (American Pet Products Association, 2022). Millennials also tend to spend more on their pets, whom many view as their "fur babies" (Statista, 2020). Those least likely to own a pet are Builders (3% of pet owners), the generation preceding Boomers. These consumers, now in their late 70s or older, are at increased risk of having health, economic, or housing-related limitations that preclude their owning a pet.

Given that a majority of U.S. pet owners view their animals as family members, it is not surprising that sales of pet supplies and services are steadily rising. Expenditures on pet food, supplies, vet care, over-the-counter supplements, and grooming and boarding services climbed from USD 90.5 billion in 2018 to USD 123.6 billion in 2021 (American Pet Products Association, 2022). During the COVID-19 pandemic, pet owners' concerns about their pets' health and wellness resulted in a double-digit (13%) rise in sales of pet medications to USD 10.8 billion in 2020 (Packaged Facts, 2021). This is in large part due to the growth of the senior pet population, as PR Newswire (2021) observes.

Pets are living longer due to advances in veterinary care, and pet owner interest in pet wellness and nutrition is at an all-time high. Growing numbers of aging dogs and cats therefore need health care for obesity-associated conditions including diabetes and joint pain, as well as impaired immune response, heart disease, and cognitive decline. In addition aging pets may need anti-inflammation and pain management products.

At the same time, the priority on protecting health triggered by the COVID-19 pandemic, along with the associated shift to stay-at-home lifestyles, increased pet parent awareness of the health and well-being of their pets. Packaged Facts survey data show that 41% of owners are paying closer attention to their pet's health and wellness because of COVID-19, and 14% have changed the pet health care products they buy, including to address COVID-related pet health concerns, including anxiety/stress and immunity.

In addition to medicines, premium services are also on the rise. Increasing numbers of pet owners are purchasing health insurance for their furry friends (Naphia, 2022), frequenting high-end groomers, consulting animal behaviorists, and seeking luxury boarding accommodations when their animal companions cannot accompany them on trips.

Pets may also influence owners' major purchases that on the surface appear unrelated to companion animals:

> The pet owner and pet have joint consumption experiences in which they interact with other actors such as service providers. The consumer (pet owner) consumes because of the pet, meaning that he or she constantly needs to take the pet into account in choices and activities beyond pet-related consumption, such as what kind of car to buy, where to work, whom to marry and how to live. The co-consumer (pet) also acts as an active agent who experiences, feels, suffers and likes the goods and services that the consumer buys for the pet. Reciprocally, the pet provides the consumer (pet owner) with companionship, support and a boost to wellbeing.
>
> (Kylkilahti et al., 2015)

How do consumers go about "shopping for" and finding a companion animal? What factors contribute to a positive "post-purchase" experience for human and animal alike?

The Consumer's Journey from Petlessness to Pet Ownership

This section takes us back to the paths to purchase discussed in Chapter 4. When consumers are *open to possibility* (i.e., not in the market for a pet but coming across pet-related information incidentally), where might they learn about animal companions? The most prominent and influential offline sources are pet owners among friends and family. They have consumers' trust and may eagerly share anecdotes about their precocious pooches and facile felines, as well as encouraging the petless consumer to interact with their "fur babies."

Those of us who reside in urban areas may also have ample opportunity to observe neighbors walking dogs and cats sunning themselves. We can readily imagine ourselves holding the leash or petting the cat.

Online sources of information and influence are numerous, including the millions of cute animal videos we may while away our time watching, as well as marketing communications from pet rescue organizations. But what triggers the *decision to buy or change*, that is, to adopt or purchase an animal? Friends and family may themselves serve as triggers of the decision to adopt or purchase an animal. Vocal and persistent young children can be especially effective at triggering the decision. Triggers of the decision may be circumstantial as well, for example, a move from renting to owning a home, joining households with a pet-loving spouse or partner, living alone for the first time, or losing a cherished animal companion. An encounter with a stray or knowledge of a pet who needs rehoming may not only trigger the decision to acquire an animal, but also serve to shorten and simplify the journey to pet ownership, as the following anecdote illustrates:

Axel and Annie Find Their "Furever" Homes

Austin Pets Alive is an innovative animal rescue program in Austin, TX that works to find homes for animals most at risk of euthanasia, including older dogs and cats, those with chronic health conditions, and orphaned puppies and kittens whose numbers grow quickly in the absence of high-volume spay-neuter programs. Millennial parents Jenn and Don have a nine-year-old daughter Ayla who had been begging for a puppy.

One evening when Jenn's Baby Boomer parents Judy and Ken came over to visit, the three generations set out on an after-dinner stroll. The first thing they saw as they headed down the sidewalk was two very small puppies playing in the next-door neighbors' yard. They stopped and admired the rambunctious twosome, wondering aloud where they had come from. Neighbor Kaylee approached them to explain, "My husband Brett and I are fostering these little guys for Austin Pets Alive. They were found in a puppy mill and their mother was so badly mistreated that she died before they were even weaned." The puppies were named Axel and Annie.

Young Ayla fell in love with Annie, a tiny but ferocious ball of soft black fur. Jenn's parents Judy and Ken, who had owned dogs previously but had no current plans to adopt one, conferred with each other about Axel: "He's very cute!" Judy commented, "and if we adopt him, maybe we'll get to spend more time with Jenn and her family, since they'll have his sister!"

And so the two households adopted the charming canines. Neither couple evaluated or explored alternatives to the brother and sister. The pups' breed(s) and size when full-grown were unknowns, as were their temperaments and reactions to other dogs and unfamiliar humans. Jenn and Don had been considering adopting a puppy for Ayla, and Annie fell into their hands and hearts. While they had planned to adopt a puppy, adopting Annie was an impulse. Judy and Ken made what appears at first glance to be an impulsive decision to adopt Axel based on their love for daughter Jenn and granddaughter Ayla. In fact, they had enjoyed owning small dogs until their last and especially beloved dog Cristabel had passed just after Jenn left home. In the years after the loss of Cristabel, they had periodically revisited the idea of adopting another dog, but it never felt "right." In other words, Judy and Ken were experienced with dogs and in the open-to-possibility stage for many years. Meeting little Axel just when their daughter was about to adopt his sister seemed fortuitous.

This story demonstrates how the trigger to buy may be unexpected and the decision to purchase may appear to be a leap of faith rather than an informed decision, but deeper understanding of the process and the consumers involved may reveal that experience, intuition, and lengthy openness to possibility work in tandem to drive the purchase. This type of decision process may also occur when a stray animal comes to the attention of a compassionate consumer or when a friend or relative seeks to rehome a pet for any of several reasons including a new baby, a move, or other changes in circumstance.

Table 10.2 indicates that one-fifth to one-third of owned dogs are purchased from a breeder, and the other two most popular sources are shelters or rescues and friends or relatives. Cats, in contrast, are likely to be adopted from a shelter or rescue, taken in as a stray, or acquired from a friend or relative.

Unlike our protagonists and those consumers who take in a stray or acquire a pet from a friend or relative, many potential adopters do go through a more extended and complex version of the **evaluation** stage of the journey. The first part of the evaluation stage may involve deciding whether to adopt an animal from a rescue or shelter or purchase a pet from a pet store or breeder. A common reason for purchasing from a breeder is the popular misconception that breed determines temperament, enabling the purchaser to choose a pet that will meet specifications in that regard. The fallacy in this argument is that while the breed as a whole may have tendencies to behave and respond to humans in certain ways, breed is not the sole predictor of an individual animal's temperament. Environmental factors (likely beginning in utero), some known, others not, also pay a part in shaping behavior, just as they do for humans.

On the other hand, purchasing from a reputable breeder guarantees access to detailed information about the animal based on the parents' qualities, including physical characteristics at maturity, potential health challenges, and ability to compete in shows or athletic events. And many consumers derive deep satisfaction from belonging to a community of like-minded individuals who love and appreciate a specific breed. A consumer committed to buying a pure-bred animal may also adopt from a breed-specific rescue organization. The American Kennel Club

Table 10.2 Where do people acquire pets?

Data	2017–2018 AVMA Sourcebook	2021–2022 APPA Survey
Dogs		
Adopted from a shelter or rescue	28%	40%
Taken in as strays	5%	4%
Acquired from friends or relatives	26%	18%
Purchased from a pet store	6%	9%
Purchased from a breeder	22%	21%
Cats		
Adopted from a shelter or rescue	31%	43%
Taken in as strays	25%	24%
Acquired from friends or relatives	25%	21%
Purchased from a pet store	3%	8%
Purchased from a breeder	3%	4%

Source: Based on Humane Society of the United States (n.d.).

maintains an extensive list of these rescue groups for dog breeds. A few pure-bred and breed-specific cat rescue organizations exist, but dogs are much better represented. Consumers seeking to maximize information available in the evaluation stage of the consumer journey will likely adopt from a breeder.

How do consumers go about *evaluating* the candidates for adoption from a shelter or rescue? Are the evaluation criteria determined before or during the shopping stage? What roles do the "salesperson," "store" atmosphere, and the animals themselves play in their decisions? What roles do consumers' preconceptions/attitudes/beliefs play? The following article describes the ASPCA's research findings:

A more recent study of dog acquisition found that appearance still tops the list of criteria for adoption, and that other criteria include health, behavior, and social trends in popularity of specific breeds (Holland, 2019). It is important to bear in mind that shelters and other rescue organizations typically lack information about the animal's origins and behavior when not stressed. When animals are fostered, as with Austin Pets Alive, their behavior can be more accurately evaluated.

After the adopter brings an animal home, what factors shape the consumer *experience* to be positive or negative? Companion animals offer us several well-documented benefits: They are good company, they love unconditionally, they can be quite entertaining, reminding us to play and laugh, they may help us become more active, and the well-defined caregiving tasks associated with pets may teach children more responsibility. In addition, our nonhuman companions connect us with nature and give us the opportunity to see things from the perspective of a different species. Perhaps most important for many of us, our animals encourage us to be our best, most generous and loving selves. Some would go so far as to say they privilege us with their contented, affectionate presence.

Why Did You Choose Your Pet?

(ASPCA, 2012)

ASPCA Research Uncovers Real Reasons

Study finds appearance and behavior among top reasons for adoption

April 18, 2012

NEW YORK—The ASPCA (The American Society for the Prevention of Cruelty to Animals) today announced that a study of nearly 1,500 adopters from five animal shelters across the country has uncovered the reasons behind why adopters chose the particular pet they took home.

Appearance of the animal, social behavior with adopter, and behaviors such as playfulness were the top reasons for adoption across species and age groups....

Appearance was the most frequently cited reason for kitten adopters (23 percent), while adult cat adopters cited behavior with people as the most important reason (30 percent). In contrast, appearance was the most frequently cited reason for adopters of both puppies (29 percent) and adult dogs (26 percent).

The results of this study give us a glimpse inside of the adopter's mind when it comes to choosing a pet. The information can be used by shelters to create better adoption matches, prioritize shelter resources and staff training, and potentially increase adoptions, said Dr. Emily Weiss, vice president of shelter research and development for the ASPCA....

In addition, a greater number of adopters stated that information about the animal from a staff member or volunteer was important than adopters who found information on cage cards, and health and behavior information was particularly important....

For both cats and dogs, seeing the pet's behavior when interacting with them was more important than seeing the pet behind the cage door or seeing the pet's behavior toward other animals.

But can the benefits possibly outweigh the financial strain of pet ownership among low-income consumers? A recent study of pet-owning versus non-pet owning low-income individuals found that the pet owners reported lower food insecurity compared to the nonowners (Rauktis et al., 2020). How can we explain this?

If owners of pets indicated a willingness to share their own food or go without in order to have pet food in the house, then why would pet owners experience greater food security? The qualitative data clarified this apparent food security paradox. The interviewees were consistent in reporting that having a pet created structure, routine, and an incentive to self-care which includes obtaining food:

The first few days were probably the worst because I had no purpose in life.... And then I realized, oh wait a minute Bobbie needs fed. And that was the first purposeful… And that ray of purposefulness was kind of like, oh it's still there, okay I do have a purpose in life.

On the other hand, the oft-cited mental and physical health benefits of pets are not unequivocally supported by research. The complex connection between human health and pet ownership may be due in part to the challenges of caring for an animal. Older animals may require more expensive medical care, and as noted previously, our animals are now living long enough to manifest health problems associated with old age.

Furthermore, a pet's behavioral condition may lead to undesirable consequences for the owner, including the extra time required for management and training, difficulty exercising the animal, and limitations on the owner's social activities. In addition, relationships with other household members may be affected (Buller & Ballantyne, 2020). Buller and Ballantyne (2020) suggest that "[c]ollaborative relationships between animal health and behavior professionals and human mental health professionals could ensure that both the pet's and the owner's needs are met when managing a pet's behavioral problem." Such collaborations could decrease the number of animals relinquished to shelters. Free behavioral advice offered by specially trained shelter staff has also been shown to decrease relinquishments (Powdrill-Wells et al., 2021).

On the face of it, pet adoption may appear to be a straightforward consumer decision. In fact, taking another sentient being into our home requires much adaptation by all species involved. The following passage from Orzechowski (2016) points out that our animal companions need more than food, shelter, affection, and sporadic play:

> … [C]ats have a fundamental requirement for a safe core zone within their environment to eat, sleep, and play. Within that "core zone" they also need access to "3D space," meaning multiple levels of space that permit "elevation and hiding." Cats also need "safe points of entry and exit from the territory," as well as more nuanced things like privacy (including privacy from other cats) and the ability to express natural behaviors such as hunting and scratching.
>
> For dogs… "the structure and layout of the physical environment is relatively less significant than the social environment." …Spatial requirements vary based on the size, breed, and age of the dog, and there is no one-size-fits-all approach. Still, dogs should be given "as large an area as possible" and all enrichment should be done with an eye towards providing them with choices. "Dogs that are appropriately socialized to humans, other dogs, and other species should be given ample daily opportunities to interact… Social enrichment is a necessity, not a luxury."

Usually a pet dog or cat will predecease the owner. Caring for a beloved animal in the last phase of life requires acute understanding of the pain and stress the pet is experiencing:

[O]ne of the most important parts of the end-of-life process: addressing not only physical pain, but stress, anxiety and fear as well.... Many arthritic or immobile pets appear more agitated by their inability to stand up rather than the pain that standing up elicits. They may not understand why they can't ambulate, which in turn leads to excessive painting, whining, crying and additional physical pain as they attempt to move. Many times, the mental battle is bigger than the physical battle. Euthanasia is not just about ending suffering that's occurring at that moment; it's also about preventing pain from occurring. And with a better understanding of mental and physical pain, clients feel better equipped to make that important decision with the guidance of their veterinarian.

(NcVety, 2017)

Our capacity to love and feel a connection with a member of another species is nowhere more evident than when we lose a cherished animal companion, as the following extract from an article from Faunalytics (2010) shows:

For Makiki resident Joyce Tsuji, Toro was a companion and confidant, a reliable morning alarm clock and an occasional "bedtime hat."

The fawn-colored tabby, a stray who hung out under Tsuji's car and eventually worked his way into her heart, was a beloved pet for more than five years. "Toro became family from the moment he adopted me," Tsuji said.

When her cat was diagnosed with lymphoma about five years ago on top of a bowel syndrome, the animal was too weak for surgery, and Tsuji had to make the heartbreaking decision to euthanize her pet. Losing Toro left a void in her life. She said she cried just as hard when she lost Toro as the day her grandparents died.

Five years later Tsuji still misses him. "If you see a pet as family, the heartbreak is the same," she said....

This kind of grief for pet owners is very real, according to Julie Ann Luiz Adrian, a veterinarian and assistant professor at the University of Hawaii at Hilo who coauthored a study last year on the emotional impacts of the loss of a pet. Of the 106 pet owners surveyed at a vet clinic, about 20% said they experienced significant grief after the death of an animal companion and about 30% said they still felt some grief or sadness over the loss for six months or longer.

Especially challenging for vets are cases of owners seeking euthanasia of an animal for "misbehavior," for example, urinating outside the litter box, or for health problems that could be remedied with costly but routine treatments (e.g., a cat may become very ill because of a tooth infection that could be removed in a dental procedure, but animal dentistry requires great skill and expensive instruments, as nonhumans must be anesthetized for their dental procedures).

All too often, a pet's time with their beloved human is cut short, not by death but through relinquishment to a shelter. While many relinquishments are due to undesirable behaviors that could be resolved with help from an animal behaviorist or counselor, others result from life changes over which the owner has little or no control. These changes include loss of one's home or job, the need to move in order to care for a sick family member whose home does not allow pets, owner illness, and domestic violence. Despite adoption campaigns, many of which are effective to a degree, shelters continue to be filled with homeless animals. Many, especially cats, are strays, while all too many others are relinquished. Below are the most recent HSUS (n.d.) statistics:

- Estimated number of brick-and-mortar animal shelters in the US: 4,404
- Estimated number of rescue groups and animal sanctuaries in North America: 10,000
- Number of cats and dogs entering shelters each year: 6.3 million
- Of the 920,000 cats and dogs euthanized in shelters each year, approximately 750,000 are healthy or treatable and could have been adopted into new homes
- Number of cats and dogs adopted from shelters each year: 4.1 million
- In some regions of the US, 50–75% of the shelter population is cats, and cats and kittens are overwhelmingly more at risk for euthanasia
- Estimated amount spent by humane organizations annually: USD 3 billion
- Estimated amount spent by animal control organizations annually: USD 800 million to USD 1 billion

Taken together, these figures indicate that high-volume spay-neuter programs are essential to overall animal welfare. Many strays are unwanted litters, and left un-fixed, cats and dogs produce kittens and puppies at an amazing rate. "In just seven years, a single pair of cats and their offspring could produce a staggering total of 420,000 kittens" (Animal Rescue Professionals, 2019).

Sterilized animals live longer, happier lives. Spaying eliminates the stress and discomfort that females endure during heat periods, eliminates the risk of uterine cancer, and greatly reduces the risk of mammary cancer. Neutering makes males far less likely to roam or fight, prevents testicular cancer, and reduces the risk of prostate cancer. Altered animals are less likely to contract deadly, contagious diseases, such as feline AIDS and feline leukemia, that are spread through bodily fluids (PETA, 2022).

Given what we know about how consumers travel on the journey from pet-lessness to pet ownership, we are ready to explore a few of the most important (and, we hope, useful) best practices for shelters and rescues "marketing" animals in need of a home and for consumers seeking and caring for animal companions.

Best Marketing Practices for Animal Rescue Organizations

1. To minimize returns or, worse, pets being passed along or sold to unscreened recipients, consider reframing adoption services in terms of matchmaking,

that is, making optimal matches between adopters and adoptable animals. An example of a "matchmaking" organization is the Pixie Project in Portland, Oregon. Below is their adoption philosophy:

Our philosophy at Pixie is simple and unique: find the perfect pet for each person or family. At Pixie we're not about getting animals out the door, we're about getting pets into lifetime homes. Sometimes the "right" pet is waiting for you, and other times you may have to search for a while before your canine or feline soul-mate arrives. We promise, it will be worth the wait!

(Pixie Project, 2021)

After finding the best match possible based on an in-depth questionnaire and interview, the organization offers the potential adopter a two-week "trial adoption," during which Pixie Project retains legal ownership of the animal while s/he and the human consumer get to know each other. The vignette below illustrates the wisdom of this adoption model:

Zoe's Adventure with a Canine

Zoe had always preferred cats and lived happily with her "soul-cat" Gounguroo for all his 14 years. After his death, she grieved for her beloved fe-line, and especially missed his "doglike" behaviors—meeting her at the door when she came home, readily coming when she would call for him, showing curiosity about her activities, etc. She mistakenly concluded that she should adopt a dog, not to replace Gounguroo, but to experience the closeness she had with him.

Zoe feels very fortunate that when she was seeking to adopt a dog, she had the trial period. She learned from living with a very nice dog that canines are not for her. Had she not been absolutely certain that Pixie Project would find the animal a good home, she would have kept him and made the best of it, despite her very unhappy cat companions and the dog's aggressiveness toward other dogs in the neighborhood.

2. Use all data available to make good matches. The *Advertising Age* article be-low describes an innovative adoption drive that targets specific animals to people based on their digital behavior. Rescue organizations are very good at screening potential adopters for general characteristics that would make them less-than-optimal pet owners, for example, plans to keep the animal outside regardless of severe weather. Questions that focus on the poten-tial adopter's goals and expectations of owning an animal may be useful as well:

Programmatic advertising is about to go to the dogs. In a campaign breaking in November, a Beverly Hills, Calif.-based animal shelter will use digital targeting techniques aimed at finding perfect pet-owner matches. The campaign was developed by Saatchi & Saatchi L.A. on a pro bono basis for the Amanda Foundation, a nonprofit that rescues dogs and cats spending their last days at Los Angeles city and county shelters.

The agency will target banner ads for specific pets to people based on their digital behavior. So if someone appears to be athletic, they would be sent an ad for an active breed like a pit bull, including a picture of an actual pooch that is available for adoption. The campaign, called "Digital Pawprint," is "the world's first pet adoption drive that is driven through programmatic media matched up with creative," said Chris Pierantozzi, a creative director at Saatchi L.A. [Below] are some examples.

Human Traits Married, young children
Animal Traits Fun loving, gentle
MEET BROOKLYNNE I love playing with the kids, just like you.
Human Traits Single, reader
Animal Traits Cuddly, domesticated
MEET TIKI I love curling up with a good book, just like you.
Human Traits Homebody, renter
Animal Traits Cuddly, small-compact
MEET CLYDE I love watching the game, just like you.
Human Traits Tech savvy, homebody
Animal Traits Intelligent, mellow
MEET SALLY I love cat videos, just like you.
Human Traits Athletic, hiker
Animal Traits Active, energetic
MEET MANDY I love a good run, just like you.

(Schultz, 2015)

3. Work toward finding foster care for all animals who need a home. Foster "parents" provide a safe and comfortable environment in which they get to know the animal. For example: Does Doogie the cat get along with other cats? How does he respond to dogs? Do children frighten or fascinate him? What does he seek from his foster mom or dad? Is he playful or snuggly, or both? This in-depth information can make all the difference between an excellent permanent match and a disastrous one resulting in the return of the animal. There are increasing numbers of foster-only rescue organizations, usually legitimate nonprofit organizations that survive on private donations and with the help and passionate commitment of local foster parents. An example is the Animal Rescue and Care Fund in Portland, Oregon. Furry Friends, a rescue in Vancouver, Washington, has an innovative model, sheltering homeless cats in a large, comfortable house that offers plenty of space for them to roam and segregates cats who need their own space in separate rooms rather than in small cages. The volunteers who care for them come to know each cat as well as a foster parent would.

Potential or Current Pet-Owner Best Practices

1. Educate yourself about your current or potential animal's species. There are many excellent resources online, for example, www.catinfo.org and Best websites, for pet tips. Offline sources abound as well, including vets, animal behaviorists, and trainers.

2. Don't adopt an animal because s/he physically resembles a beloved deceased pet. You will surely be disappointed that the look-alike is not a replica in temperament or behavior patterns, and your disappointment will color your ability to love and enjoy the animal for who s/he is. The unrealized expectations may then affect the new pet in detrimental ways. Even a clone is not a copy, as this story "If by Chance we meet again" from the public radio program "This American Life" illustrates.

3. Dig deep to surface your most dearly held expectations, beliefs, and goals that are pushing you toward adopting an animal.

4. Know your emotional, physical, and financial limits, but tap into your generosity of spirit and your wise intuition that assures you that you – and all other humans – thrive on changes that enrich, educate, and edify!

5. There are many ways to help animals without adopting one. Here are seven from petfinder's website:

DONATE YOUR TIME
Volunteering for a shelter is one of the most impactful ways to get involved. Many shelters need help with cleaning and caring for the animals, and keeping the facility in good condition.

DONATE YOUR SKILLS
Do you have a special talent or hobby like photography or creating video? Photographing shelter pets or highlighting one in an adoptable pet video for his Petfinder profile can bring attention to a pet who's often overlooked.

DONATE YOUR PETS' GENTLY-USED ITEMS
Shelters can always use some extra supplies. Often a shelter's wish list will include water and food bowls, toys, leashes and collars, brushes/grooming tools, and pet beds.

DONATE A PLACE IN YOUR HOME
Fostering a pet is not only a rewarding experience, but it's a great way to help out your local shelter from the comfort of your own home.

DONATE PART OF YOUR WEDDING OR EVENT REGISTRY
Getting married or throwing a big party? …[H]ave your shelter set up a registry page so guests can donate to the shelter rather than purchasing a customary wedding gift.

DONATE HOUSEHOLD ITEMS
Pet supplies aren't the only supplies shelters need. Some other things that come in handy for shelters include cleaning supplies, paper towel and toilet paper rolls, old towels and blankets, hand sanitizer, and office supplies.

DONATE PET FOOD AND LITTER

Shelters and rescue groups go through a lot of pet food and cat litter every day. You can buy pet food in bulk at wholesale stores.

(Petfinder, 2022)

Best Practices for Communities

Owners should be supported in accessing resources to mitigate any issues that may jeopardize the human–animal bond and increase the risk of relinquishment or abandonment. Especially important are resources and solutions that will be accessible and feasible to people who may be suffering from job loss, economic uncertainty, and housing insecurity. Considering positive relationships with pets may buffer the deleterious effects of stressful or adverse circumstances; pets could be a source of comfort and normalcy during the pandemic and any resulting fallout, economic or otherwise. Communities can support families and individuals with pets by forming partnerships between human and animal social services in order to meet the needs of the holistic family unit; hence, pet relinquishment prevention is in service of healthy communities (Applebaum et al., 2020).

We end this chapter with a story about how pets can change lives:

> Remember Zoe and Gounguroo? In December, 2000, Zoe's big orange tabby Gounguroo kept her from quitting a good job to go back to school and train for a profession that (she realizes now) would have made her miserable. She was enjoying a few days of vacation from her position as a financial analyst for a large telecommunications firm in Atlanta, GA. After more than a decade in her current position, each time she entered the office she was filled with trepidation about the challenges and stresses she faced as a woman in an industry that was still predominately male, and she yearned to do something that would improve the lives of those most oppressed by society. After much reflection, she had a brainstorm: "If I become an attorney, I can be a child advocate or public defender, and really make a difference in the world!" she thought, and began to feel renewed optimism about her future as she excitedly arranged to take the LSAT and began to explore law school programs.
>
> Zoe's best and oldest friend Ravi kept telling her, "We are too old to be poor students! Don't you remember what graduate school was like? We could barely feed ourselves and pay the rent some months!" Knowing Zoe as he did, he also observed, "You'll want justice and that doesn't always happen in the courtroom. You'll be very frustrated most of the time." The more he protested Zoe's decision, the more she embraced it.
>
> So there she was, breathing a sigh of relief that she could soon quit her job and do something more meaningful, enjoying an evening of reading with her cats lying nearby. She noticed before long that her alpha cat Sheroo was staring intently at her young cat Gounguroo, who was uncharacteristically still and quiet. So she went over to Gounguroo and touched him lightly. He

screamed and bit her hard. Zoe knew then that something was very wrong. She bundled him up and rushed him to the nearest emergency clinic. The doctors there filled him with painkillers, which made him manic, a scared little cat hurling himself at the cage bars. An X-ray, blood work, and urinalysis gave no hint what was causing him so much pain.

After two days of monitoring and medicating Gounguroo, the vets said the only thing they could figure out was that he had swallowed a foreign object which had gotten stuck in his intestines and didn't show up on the x-ray. "We'll have a surgeon on site tonight and then not again till after Christmas," they said. "Do you want him to do exploratory surgery?" There was no other alternative given his level of pain, so Zoe jumped at the opportunity. She sat in the dreary waiting room for what seemed like hours, heart pounding, thoughts made incoherent by fear and anxiety.

When at last the doctor came out, he was holding a little brown medicine bottle. "This is what I found inside him," he said, giving Zoe the bottle. Inside it was a tiny rubber gasket that clever and foolhardy Gounguroo had pulled off the plunger part of a syringe for giving oral medications. Zoe figured out that he must have leapt up onto the kitchen counter, grabbed the plunger from the dish drainer where she had put it after washing it, jumped down to the floor, and somehow held onto the base of the plunger while working the little gasket off the tip. One downside of being a cat is that once you start swallowing something, you can't stop and spit it out even if you don't want it. The gasket, tiny as it was, couldn't get through Gounguroo's even narrower intestines, and so got lodged there. The blockage would have eventually killed him since he would've been unable to keep food down even if he had felt well enough to eat.

The entire incident cost Zoe about $2,000. When she brought her boy home, it dawned on her that if she were in law school living on a scholarship that barely covered lodging and food, her beloved soul cat would have died. And so it was that her sweet, clever, foolhardy orange tabby brought Zoe to her senses. In the 15 years since then, Zoe has learned a lot about how to navigate the "man's world" in which she works, and she has been mentoring young women majoring in finance at her alma mater, Georgia State University. This activity adds purpose and richness to her life.

The author is certain there are many more accounts of the significant ways companion animals can influence their humans' lives. The more stories we can document and disseminate, the greater respect we can engender for the human-animal bond, and the deeper the care and compassion we can elicit for our animal friends.

References

American Pet Products Association (APPA) (2022). "Pet industry market size, trends & ownership statistics". Retrieved from: https://humanepro.org/page/pets-by-the-numbers.

Animal Rescue Professionals (2019, May 10). "Two cats can turn into 420,000 kittens". Retrieved from: www.animalrescueprofessionals.org/animal-facts/a-single-pair-of-cats-could-produce-a-staggering-total-of-420000-kittens/.

Applebaum, J. W., Tomlinson, C. A., Matijczak, A., McDonald, S. E., & Zsembik, B. A. (2020). "The concerns, difficulties, and stressors of caring for pets during COVID-19: Results from a large survey of U.S. pet owners". *Animals, 1*(10). https://doi.org/10.3390/ani10101882.

ASPCA (2012, April 18). Why did you choose your pet? ASPCA research uncovers real reasons. Retrieved from: www.aspca.org/about-us/press-releases/why-did-you-choose-your-pet-aspca-research-uncovers-real-reasons.

Buller, K., & Ballantyne, K. C. (2020). "Living with and loving a pet with behavioral problems: Pet owners' experiences". *Journal of Veterinary Behavior, 37*, 41–47.

Faunalytics (2010, November 9). "Coping with pet loss: The death of a household pet often amounts to a significant absence in a family". Retrieved from: https://faunalytics.org/wp-content/uploads/2015/05/Citation1520.pdf.

Gray, P. B., & Young, S. M. (2015). "Human – Pet dynamics in cross-cultural perspective". *Anthrozoös, 24*(1), 17–30.

Growth from Knowledge (2016, May 23). "International average: What pets do you have living with you?". Retrieved from: International pet ownership data.

Holland, K. E. (2019). "Acquiring a pet dog: A review of factors affecting the decision-making of prospective dog owners". *Animals, 9*(4): 124. https://doi.org/10.3390/ani9040124.

Humane Society of the United States (2022). "Pets by the numbers". Retrieved from: https://humanepro.org/page/pets-by-the-numbers.

Kylkilahti, E., Syrjälä (Jyrinki), H., Autio, J., Kuismin, A., and Autio, M. (2015). Understanding co-consumption between consumers and their pets. *International Journal of Consumer Studies.* https://doi.org/10.1111/ijcs.12230.

Naphia (2022). "Pet insurance in North America". Retrieved from: https://naphia.org/industry-data/.

NcVety, D. (2017). "Fear is worse than pain in veterinary patients". *DVM 360, 32* (September/October).Retrievedfrom:www.dvm360.com/view/fear-worse-pain-veterinary-patients.

Orzechowski, K. (2016). "Cat and dog enrichment for every context". Retrieved from: https://faunalytics.org/cat-and-dog-enrichment-for-every-context/.

Packaged Facts (2021, June 1). *Pet Medications in the U.S.* (7th edn). Retrieved from: https://www.packagedfacts.com/Pet-Medications-Ed-14658187/.

PETA (2022). "Spay and neuter". Retrieved from: www.peta.org/issues/companion-animal-issues/overpopulation/spay-neuter/.

Petfinder (2022). "Surprising ways to donate to an animal shelter". Retrieved from: www.petfinder.com/helping-pets/information-on-helping-pets/unusual-donations-for-shelters-rescue-groups/.

Pixie Project (2021, August 23). "Pixie update!". Retrieved from: https://www.pixieproject.org.

Powdrill-Wells, N., Taylor, S., & Melfi, V. (2021). "Reducing dog relinquishment to rescue centres due to behaviour problems: Identifying cases to target with an advice intervention at the point of relinquishment request". *Animals, 11*, 2766. https://doi.org/10.3390/ani11102766.

PR Newswire (2021, June 8). "Pet medications market thrives in wake of pandemic". Retrieved from: www.prnewswire.com/news-releases/pet-medications-market-thrives-in-wake-of-pandemic-301308028.html.

Rauktis, M. E., Lee, H., Bickel, L., Giovengo, H., Nagel, M., & Cahalane, H. (2020). "Food security challenges and health opportunities of companion animal ownership for low-income adults". *Journal of Evidence-Based Social Work, 17*(6), 662–676. https://doi.org/10.1080/26408066.2020.178172.

Schultz, E. J. (2015, October 29). "Programmatic goes to the dogs in Saatchi pet-matching effort: Campaign for nonprofit group breaks in November". Retrieved from: https://adage.com/article/digital/saatchi-launches-pet-matching-effort-nonprofit-group/301106.

Statista (2020). "Do you consider your pet as your 'fur baby'?". Retrieved from: www.statista.com/statistics/1128358/perceptions-of-pets-as-fur-babies-by-generation-us/.

Part 4
Shifts in Technology and Consumer Values

11 The Rise of Collaborative Consumption and the Sharing Economy

William Barnes and Greg Hill

Objectives

1. To investigate and understand collaborative consumption practices contrasted to traditional consumer-brand relationships.
2. To explore the appeal and the evolution of collaborative consumption and the sharing economy.
3. To examine consumer behavior and experience in industries and cases where collaborative consumption is occurring.
4. To examine the relationship between collaborative consumption and sustainability.

Introduction

"Owning a car is a pain – it's expensive to buy, insure, and maintain – but it's unavoidable in the US where public transit is terrible" (a familiar refrain from a certain father, circa 1983).

This particular father wasn't wrong back then and is at least partially right today: The American love affair with their vehicles is still an expensive one. According to the 2021 AAA Driving Costs study, a typical U.S. car costs a total of USD 11,000 dollars a year to own and to operate (AAA, 2021).

Yet the point for many is to go from A to B (and back again) reliably. After the trip, or between legs of the trip, the car sits, sometimes expensively in an urban parking space. In fact, the average car sits unused for about 22–23 hours a day. Is there another way?

Well, yes......and millions are exploring these transportation alternatives – including Zipcar, Turo, BlaBlaCar, Lyft, and Uber.

But wait. Consider all the *other* underused assets that you own, just sitting around your property:

That lovely but lonely back corner guest room?
That sleek, expensive dress, so far used just twice?

DOI: 10.4324/9780367426897-15

That fancy crosscut saw in the garage, on top of a storage shelf?

How about that unused corner of your back yard, perfect for gardening?

Wasteful, right? Do we all individually really need to *own* these things, particularly those things that we use sporadically? Or is it swift and convenient *access* that we need? And if we own these things already, can we find an easy (and maybe remunerative) way to amp up their use when they are sitting around? Or how about an easy way to sell or give them to the buyer/borrower who needs them most? And along the way as we develop these "peer-to-peer" possibilities, can we cultivate exchanges that are more personal, trust-building, and societally beneficial as we continue to grapple with pressing global issues like the increasing inequality and climate change?

Many of us are in the process of answering these questions with the help of the evolving tools and platforms associated with what is variously known as the sharing economy, collaborative consumption, and peer-to-peer economy.

What Is the Sharing Economy...and What Is the Appeal?

But what exactly is the "sharing economy"? What is the difference between the transactions that occur in "collaborative consumption" and those that occur in "more traditional" consumer-brand relationships?

For the purpose of keeping terminology to a minimum, we will primarily use the terms "sharing economy" and "collaborative consumption" below. Both of these terms, and other terms, do not perfectly capture all activity that is commonly portrayed. For instance, if we use Zipcar as a primary example of the "sharing economy," where is the "share" – with all its altruistic implications – in renting a Zipcar? In fact, much of the activity that occurs in the sharing economy is actually renting access, as many have pointed out. To put it in the words of an NPR broadcast: "What's mine is yours (for A price) in the sharing economy" (NPR, 2013).

Here are two definitions developed by Rachel Botsman[1]:

- *Collaborative consumption*: Systems that reinvent traditional market behaviors – renting, lending, swapping, sharing, bartering, gifting – in ways and on a scale not possible before the internet.
- *Sharing economy*: Systems that facilitate the sharing of underused assets or services, for free or for a fee, directly between individuals or organizations.

So what are these terms trying to capture?

At their core, these terms are about much easier *access* to pre-owned and underutilized goods through distributed networks of individuals – whether we get access temporarily as a "service" or ownership changes hands. In both cases, we might pay money or receive temporary access or ownership for free. Botsman, one of the first high-profile evangelists on the collaborative economy along with April Rinne (2022), originally illustrated many of these points in this Ted Talk. Technology is central in her story because it radically reduces the time and expense needed to obtain access to what we need (Botsman, 2010).

Of course, peer-to-peer renting, sharing and borrowing, and bartering are not new concepts. What is new is the internet-based technology that has reduced the transactions costs of sharing goods (for free or in exchange for a fee) or selling or giving your goods permanently to another person. It has also dramatically scaled the possibilities.

In other words, it's no longer a hassle to match peers who want stuff with those who have the stuff – either for temporary use or to buy as a used product. (Imagine, for a moment, no Internet. Now, find a quick way to rent a private room in a stranger's house in a strange new city for two nights, next week.) But when you can quickly and inexpensively find and utilize spaces and products without buying them new or even without owning them at all – that bike in great shape on Craigslist; that car from Turo or Getaround; a surfboard from a local; a saw from the local tool library – then buying and owning *new* begins to look much less attractive. Combine this with the fact that *you* can also lease out your own back bedroom on Airbnb, and toss in the proposition that the sharing economy is better for the planet (15 people sharing one car seemingly has less environmental impact than 15 people owning 15 cars) and the sharing economy begins to look attractive indeed, at least in theory. Own a car? Who, me?

But can we break all this activity down in a way that captures some of the subtleties above?

Collaborative consumption is often broken down in three primary ways.

Product-Service Systems

Easy access to the benefit of a product (the service) is provided.

In product-service systems, tangible goods are shared or rented through peer-to-peer or business-to-consumer platforms. The key point is that ownership does not transfer from the sharer/seller to the borrower/buyer – the product is essentially leased as a service and the good itself is eventually returned if needed (e.g., a car is returned to a private owner). For products that sit unused for much of the time (like our car above, idled for 95% of a day, or, for that matter, the nice dress), these systems can be a great way for a peer owner to make some money and for a renter to avoid the expense and the hassles of ownership. Examples include Turo (cars), Tulerie and Rent the Runway (clothing), and Peerby (tools, electronics, many household goods). Need a pet for a time (or need your pet out of your life for a week)? Try BorrowMyDoggy.

Redistribution Markets

Underutilized, pre-owned goods are redistributed.

In this case, ownership does transfer, for example, used goods are transferred from one buyer to the next. Goods are passed from someone who doesn't want them to someone who does – and the rise of the internet has made it much more likely that givers/sellers will find takers/buyers. (Think of the sheer numbers on both sides of an eBay search for a Patagonia down jacket.) Redistribution markets may be primarily free (Freecycle, Buynothingproject) or not (eBay, uSell, Etsy).

Collaborative Lifestyles

Non-product assets like space, skills, and money are exchanged in new ways.

Many exchanges are not typical "products"; instead, they may involve spaces, labor, money, and even love. Airbnb, utilizing underused bedrooms and entire homes, is an example. Taskrabbit, which typically matches those who need errands and work done around the house with those willing to do it (often close by, in the neighborhood), is another example. Need to fund a creative idea that standard markets or the bank might not finance? Try Kickstarter, which matches those with ideas with those willing to provide the money – by 2022, over USD 6.6 billion have funded about 220,000 projects. Want to garden, but don't have the land? Try Sharedearth, which pools landowners with those willing to work a plot. How about sharing your culinary chops and enthusiasm with those from other cultures? Try matching up in Eatwith. Speaking of matching, yes, Tinder and Tawkify certainly qualify as sharing platforms.

(The three definitions above are all adapted from an article authored by Rachel Botsman, 2013.)

A central proposition in all of these exchanges is that we are using our goods, our spaces, and our skills more efficiently with the help of technology. In a seminal *Harvard Business Review* article in 2010, Botsman and Rogers developed an initial tripartite typology of such exchanges and provided examples of the innovative solutions each offers to reduce resource waste:

1. Product-service systems
   Example problem/solution:

   Half of U.S. households own power drills, but most are used for only 6 to 13 minutes during their lifetime. Zilok.com offers peer-to-peer daily rental of tools…

2. Redistribution markets
   Example problem/solution:

   Americans discard 7 million tons of cardboard annually. UsedCardboardBoxes. com 'rescues' and resells boxes to movers.

3. Collaborative lifestyles
   Example problem/solution:

Millions of houses and spare rooms around the world are sitting empty and have "idling capacity". AirBnB.com, the "Match.com for travel," allows anyone from private residents to commercial property owners to rent out their extra space.

It is worth pointing out that since 2010, a large number of startups associated with the sharing economy hit roadblocks or have completely gone under, including Zilok itself. Hint: Is it worth the trouble to one-time-rent a USD 50 drill when you can have one delivered to your door quickly through Amazon Prime, to be used forever after? It may depend on the details. And do you really want to share an instrument/car/your labor/you name it when there is a global pandemic raging? From early hyperbolic enthusiasm about the unstoppable rise of the sharing economy to the inevitable declarations of its death (Kessler, 2015), one thing is certain – the sharing economy is still here, and it is resiliently evolving and growing despite some unexpected developments. We discuss this in further detail below.

First, let's discuss a broad initial appeal of the sharing economy and collaborative consumption. What are some of the key potential economic and environmental advantages of the sharing economy? And on top of economic and environmental advantages, how is sharing economy exchanges potentially an improvement on traditional exchange?

Economic Advantages

In a study titled "The sharing economy and consumer protection regulation: The case for policy change," Koopman et al. (2014) argued that the sharing economy creates economic value in five basic ways. Here they are, with italics added for emphasis:

1. By giving people an opportunity to use others' cars, kitchens, apartments, and other property, *it allows underutilized assets or "dead capital" to be put to more productive use.*
2. By bringing together multiple buyers and sellers, it makes both the supply and demand sides of its markets *more competitive and allows greater specialization.*
3. By lowering the cost of finding willing traders, haggling over terms, and monitoring performance, *it cuts transaction costs and expands the scope of trade.*
4. By *aggregating the reviews* of past consumers and producers and putting them at the fingertips of new market participants, it can significantly *diminish the problem of asymmetric information between producers and consumers.*
5. By offering an "end-run" around regulators who are captured by existing producers, it allows suppliers to *create value for customers long underserved by those incumbents that have become inefficient and unresponsive because of their regulatory protections.*

To the extent that these five points are true, the sharing economy seems like it has many distinct economic advantages, and a quick Google search will reveal that these advantages are frequently brought up in arguments for the superiority of the sharing economy.

There are some assumptions built into realizing these five advantages, including: (1) the internet-based technology that brings together buyers and sellers works seamlessly enough (and is not more trouble than it is worth), (2) information collected on sharing economy platforms is reliable, and (3) the positives of "end-running" current regulation outweigh any negatives. However, this raises some questions. Is the time cost of accessing rather than owning goods actually low enough? And does it depend on what kind of good is involved? Are the reviews of past consumers and producers accurate and trustworthy – how do we ensure that feedback is not fake? Is end-running regulation truly net positive for the consumer (and for other stakeholders, like employees) – what are the true costs and benefits of this kind of regulatory-end-running behavior?

Environmental Advantages

Another possible advantage of the sharing economy is that it has the potential to lower damaging environmental impact, including the impact associated with greenhouse gas emissions. If consumers are exchanging existing goods and services between themselves, this means less need for the production of new products and services. For every new good not produced, resource needs and pollution impacts are reduced. Less take, less make, less waste. Hotels not built because of Airbnb rentals instead, extra new cars not bought because of car sharing and ride-hailing services, tools not bought because of a great neighborhood tool library – all can theoretically reduce impact because of a reduction of the need for new products. To the extent that the sharing economy truly encourages the three Rs in Reduce, Reuse, and Recycling, the environment benefits. Related, leasing and borrowing helps to ensure that products last as long as possible, because it reduces costs for the lender. Are you making profits by selling as many new goods as possible (e.g., through products that are intentionally designed to break down or marketed as obsolete every year)? How about making profits through leasing/renting products in an access economy, keeping the product in service as long as possible (e.g., through an easily repairable high-quality car, copy machine, musical instrument, scooter, bicycle, and...wait for it...cell phone)?

There are some assumptions built into the above as well, including (1) the level of production of new goods and services will go down as the sharing economy grows, because sharing economy goods and services truly substitute for new goods and services, and (2) the decreased resource use associated with relatively less production of new goods and services will not be more than offset by any increased use of existing products. But, is the production and consumption of new goods and services truly going down as the sharing economy evolves and grows? (Or....is the sharing economy growing along with increased production of new goods and services, e.g., to what degree are car sharing and hailing services like Zipcar, Uber, Lyft, and Turo truly preventing the buying of new cars?). Related, is the use of our products the same as before? Or has use increased? Noting that use is often the biggest contributor to a product's greenhouse gas footprint, it might swamp the benefits of any reduced production of new products and services. Consider the overall greenhouse gas emissions associated with a car. Whether electric or internal combustion based, the lifetime greenhouse gas emissions of a car is still associated with use, not production, of a car (Bieker, 2021, Figure ES.1). Now think about whether Uber and Lyft drivers have piled into the streets in big urban settings, increasing traffic and the use of existing cars, circling for customers.

Given the urgency of the climate change issue and the need to mitigate cataclysmic risk, the "metric that matters" for greenhouse gas emissions is whether the world's current per capita emissions (roughly five tons of CO_2, less than one-third of a typical U.S. citizen, which is still far too high) actually goes down substantially. How much do we need to reduce CO_2 and other greenhouse gas emissions to keep global warming to within 1.5–2 degrees centigrade? Down to the equivalent of 2.3 tons by 2030 and less than 1 ton of CO_2 emissions per person by 2050 given predicted population and consumption growth over the next decades (World Bank Group, 2020). To get that to happen, reduced per capita consumption of low-impact goods and services is the surest way to do it. On the demand side and the supply side, if the sharing economy encourages relatively less demand for new products *and* supply of products and services that is less damaging in use, that's significant. Fewer and cleaner cars, each car driven less? Clear progress.

Social Advantages

Finally, an often-noted advantage of the sharing economy is that it has the potential to provide an experience that is relatively more satisfying and societally beneficial than traditional exchanges. Examples include the psychological benefits of the greater agency and variety afforded in peer-to-peer exchange formats, the increased fulfillment that might come from a higher level of trust in exchanges, the appreciation of deeper connections and even friendship facilitated through peer-to-peer exchange, possibilities for increasing local coherence through community building opportunities, opportunities for cultural exchange, and the broader societal benefits realized through any sharing-economy-inspired altruistic behavior.

Realizing social advantages like the above implies that certain conditions exist. A few obvious ones are: (1) higher trust does build up in any given sharing economy platform, presumably through successful interactions often founded on reliable information and the ability to build reputation, (2) the platform and customer support associated with a platform is personal and reinforces values emphasized above, including trust, human contact, inclusiveness, and creativity, (3) a critical mass of consumers actually want the direct peer-to-peer (and often more time-intensive) interaction available in sharing economy platforms, (4) consumers actually want the eclectic variety with these platforms and are willing to tolerate any quirks or relative risks associated with them, and (5) sharing economy platforms do not have the effect of magnifying conflict; rather, the net effect in online and associated local communities is collaborative and more unifying than divisive. Consider, however, a few questions. Do buyers/borrowers really have the time and interest in more intense peer-to-peer interaction, some of which involves an element of risk/unpredictability (and how do introverts weigh in? And... what about human apathy in the face of easy alternatives like a dependable purchase on Amazon or a Hilton Hotels website?). How meaningful and collaborative is any peer-to-peer contact, and is the experience smooth, authentic, safe, and reliable enough to encourage repeat interactions with "peers"?

It's also important to keep in mind the big picture. Here are some framing questions to keep in mind as we investigate the growth and evolution of the sharing economy.

Does the sharing economy represent a more inclusive and participatory economic model? Is it a new model of production and property?

How can the sharing economy help us to solve some of our most pressing environmental and social problems, including the rising risks of climate change, escalating autocratic and tribalist tendencies, and increasing income and wealth inequality? Can the sharing economy help us to accelerate a needed transition to a more sustainable economy? What's happened in practice and what should happen going forward?

Drivers: Consumers (Internet-Powered and Financially, Socially, and Environmentally Savvy)

To help us further frame our exploration of how the sharing economy has evolved and where it should go, it's instructive to review some early predictions on how the sharing economy would shake up the status quo.

In 2013, the consulting firm Altimeter authored a report that was typical of the time, titled "The Collaborative Economy" (Owyang et al., 2013), targeted to traditional firms. The authors open with this theme, posed as a warning of industry disruption in the works: *Customers don't need you* (Unless you adapt!). Here is an excerpt:

> From a Social Media-Driven Era to the Collaborative Economy Era, Customers Are Increasingly Empowered.
>
> We are witnessing early indicators of an important shift. Hundreds of startups like Airbnb and Lyft have emerged to enable people to share goods and services. An influx of venture capital funding is accelerating this trend. Customers are not just using social technologies to share their activities, opinions, and media, but also to share goods and services. In this evolution, companies risk being disrupted as customers buy from each other. We see the evolution of these market relationships in three phases, in part, driven by new technologies:
>
> • First Phase—Brand Experience Era (Web): The internet makes information broadly accessible, but the ability to publish remains in the hands of

media and corporations. This is a "one-to-many" model in which companies speak "at" customers through corporate websites. The power lies with a few, though many are impacted.

- Second Phase—Customer Experience Era (Social Media): New tools empower customers to publish themselves. This is a "many-to-many" model in which customers share their opinions, activities, and media, requiring brands to listen to and speak "with" customers. Customers and companies share power.
- Third Phase—Collaborative Economy Era (Social, Mobile, Payment Systems): Fueled by social, mobile, and payment systems, customers are now empowered to share goods and services. Companies are *disrupted* as consumers *buy from each other* over traditional institutions. *Power shifts to the consumer* [italics added].

(Owyang et al., p. 5)

In another section, the authors also write: "Companies risk becoming *disintermediated* by customers who connect with each other" (p 1, par 4, italics added). "Disruption" translates to radical change of the status quo within industries. It is often applauded by economists as "creative destruction" – an inherent and positive component of a dynamic market capitalist system evolving through time. "Disintermediation" translates to "cut out of the transaction" as parties directly go "peer-to-peer." It is often celebrated as more efficient and thus laudable. Both terms imply "code red" emergencies for traditional firms: adapt or risk obsolescence.

The report then turns to drivers of the collaborative economy and why change was imminent. The figure on the companion web site nicely captures three main drivers, in turn further broken into sub-drivers.

How has this report aged, which reinforces many of the potential advantages of the sharing economy that were listed above? The authors (and many others at the time) conducted surveys of consumers and other stakeholders to determine the impetus for change, finding high interest in climate change, building community, social networking, service/access instead of ownership, and the financial opportunities for peer-to-peer buyers and sellers. An overarching central thesis of the report was this: the sharing economy trend clearly provides more choices and more power for consumers, not to mention noncorporate "peer" sellers. In other words, a growing sharing economy represents progress.

An article put out by the Wharton School shortly after the Altimeter report, "The sharing economy spills into new markets" (2015a), echoed these points and emphasized the momentum of the sharing economy. An excerpt:

The genie is not going back in the bottle. Despite all the resistance, virtually no one thinks the sharing economy is going anywhere but up. Gilles Duranton, a Wharton real-estate professor, said it is probably too late to stop the sharing economy with regulation. 'Banning Uber or Airbnb after people have actually experienced them and decided they liked them a lot, will make many consumers unhappy. The elected officials that block these services will pay a heavy price.' While many will lament the changes wrought by the new economy, 'there are only very few cases of successful bans on real progress,' he said. 'The Tokugawa shoguns in Japan managed that but from what I've read this is a rare example.'

(Wharton School, 2015a)

So, what has happened since this point? If we fast forward to the present day, a simple thought experiment is useful. Imagine:

(1) Students deprived of online opportunities to buy used textbooks or rent texts for a semester from University bookstore competitors (back to USD 250+ new textbooks at the local University bookstore monopoly!)

(2) Travelers deprived of the web-based opportunity to rent/provide unique entire houses (back to the Marriot)

(3) City dwellers deprived of app-based ride hailing/car sharing (back to cab companies, taking public transportation, or buying a car to get around)

(4) Consumers deprived of the opportunity to scour online (nationally) for used goods, delivered to the door within days (back to local newspaper ads and slogging to yard and estate sales)

(5) The curious among us deprived of the shared wisdom available in free on-line encyclopedias edited by all (back to paying for a hard copy encyclopedia?). Would we collectively tolerate this deprivation? Common sense tells us no.

Seen from a growth perspective, early analysts and proponents of the sharing economy were onto something – consumers and citizens, empowered through platforms like Chegg, Airbnb, Lyft, eBay, and Wikipedia, have been a part of disrupting entire industries. From this perspective, the genie is bottle-free and thriving.

On the other hand, if we are serious about impactful and positive change, it's important to critically analyze how the sharing economy is evolving and where we want it to go from here (Sands et al., 2020).

The Growth and Evolution of the Sharing Economy

One thing is clear as we take stock of the past decade: Many initial sharing economy platforms and organizations have failed or have hit major roadblocks, from Botsman's Zilok above to WeWork – still very much alive but under new leadership (Namaste, 2022). However, industry consolidation is common as industries and new business paradigms evolve. In the case of the sharing economy, one reason why this is the case might be at least partially traced to "network effects" (Currier, 2018) – which can help a platform/organization quickly gain value and build on any first mover advantage as more and more people use the platform. There is also evidence that other factors are absolutely critical for competitive advantage, including the importance of building and maintaining stakeholder trust and loyalty (Wirtz et al., 2019).

Another thing is clear: Despite the churn within industry and a variety of exogenous shocks, including a global pandemic, survivors have managed to grow robustly, with many garnering more and more market share within their respective industries relative to traditional businesses. A prime example of this is Airbnb, which has already bounced back robustly from a pandemic-induced drop in revenue. We explore Airbnb in further detail below as model of resilience and an example of a best practice case.

Furthermore, recent research indicates that earlier projections on sharing economy growth are likely to be accurate, if not an underestimate. In a 2014 report that is often cited even today, PwC estimated that the revenue in five key sharing sectors (finance, online staffing, accommodation, car sharing, and music/video streaming) was about USD 15 billion in 2014 and will grow to USD 335 billion by 2025 (this is growth of more than 22 times or 2,100%) (PwC, 2014). They contrasted this to growth of revenue for traditional firms in the five sectors, predicting growth from USD 240 billion in 2014 to USD 335 in 2025 (a multiple of less than 1.5 times or less than 50%). Just looking at one of these five sectors through more recent research, a recent ride sharing global market study predicts estimated 2021 revenue of USD 85.8 billion to increase to USD 185.1 billion by 2026, meaning just one of these five important sectors is now projected to rise to half of USD 335 billion within a year of 2025 (Markets and Markets, 2022). Given that the other sectors in the PwC study are also significant (think accommodation and finance), it is likely that the original 2014 PwC analysis underestimates the growth of the sharing economy by 2025 in these five sectors.

In the US, evidence suggests that familiarity and use of sharing platforms is increasing dramatically. For example, according to a 2022 Statista publication, sharing economy services are increasingly well known by the U.S. population, with familiarity with at least one sharing platform increasing from 47% of consumers in 2015 to 83% by 2018 (with obvious growth past 2018). Furthermore, Statista estimates the number of adults using sharing economy services to be 44.8 million in 2016, forecasted to rise to 86.5 million by 2021 (Lock, 2022). For more statistics on the rise of the sharing economy, see Statista (2022).

Table 11.1 includes a variety of current examples of sharing economy organizations within particular sectors. Many, but not all, of the listed organizations have significant market shares within their respective industries within nations and even globally, and have become widely recognized brands by consumers worldwide, whether fee-based (Airbnb) or accessible for free (Wikipedia).

In addition to the rise of particular winners within the sharing economy and the growth overall of sharing platforms, many have argued that the shape of the sharing economy is changing, sometimes attributing this to factors like the pandemic. The following *Economist* article titled "The sharing economy will have to change" (2020) represents a common perspective that the sharing economy is evolving from its original roots in collaborative "what's mine is yours" frugality

Table 11.1 Sharing economy examples

Sector	"Sharing" Category	Platform/Organization
Spaces/land	Accommodation/travel	Airbnb, Couchsurfing, Vrbo, Homeexchange
	Gardening	SharedEarth
	Work space	Sharedesk, Coworking, Wework
	Storage	Stashbee, Neighbor
Transportation	Ride sourcing	Uber, Lyft, drivers.coop
	Ride sharing	Blablacar
	Car sharing	Turo, Getaround
Skills/labor	For home/household	Taskrabbit
	For employer	Fiverr, UpWork
Goods	Used/unused goods	Craigslist, Ebay, *Buynothingproject.org*
	Clothing	RenttheRunway, Threadup
	Food/meals	Eatwith
Pets	Petting sitting/access	Rover, Borrowmydoggy
Finance	Crowdfunding	Kickstarter, Gofundme, Indiegogo
	Lending	Lendingclub, Prosper, SoFi
Learning	Homework, textbooks	Chegg
	Open courses	Coursera, Khan Academy
	Teaching	Superprof
	General learning	Wikipedia
Love	Matchmaking	Tinder, Tawkify

Source: Author research.

and volunteerism toward a new sharing economy model – one that is more transactional and driven by profit. An excerpt:

> The Great Recession in the wake of the financial crisis of 2007–09 did much to create the ideological impetus to use technology to build an economy in which consumption would be more social, frugal and sustainable. Instead of owning things, the thinking went, people should share access to them using apps and other online services. "I don't want stuff, I want the... experiences it fulfils," said Rachel Botsman, one of the champions of the trend.
>
> Using peer-to-peer services to share and barter things, from books and CDs to power tools and cars, never took off. Most of these businesses did not generate enough cash to sustain themselves. But they paved the way for

another sharing economy that seeks to make money by creating online marketplaces to match supply and demand. Startups of that sort could, in the lingo, be "blitz-scaled" into large global businesses. Such size promised big profits, attracting oodles of venture capital.

(*The Economist*, 2020)

The article then goes on to note how three "poster children" of the well-funded new sharing economy, Airbnb, Uber, and Bird, struggled to adapt to COVID, laying off staff and cutting costs in the face of consumer fear about safety, and notes how these three organizations creatively adapted to the safety demands of the virus even as they positioned for a recovery in demand for access (which has begun to happen).

One subtext in some of these "original" versus "new"/"other" sharing economy arguments is that (1) evolved, for-profit sharing economy platforms have effectively replaced platforms that are more altruistically inclined (depending on the author, often portrayed as positive "efficiency" progress (Kessler, 2015) or a negative reversion to business as usual (Scaraboto & Figueiredo, 2022) – in effect a supplanting substitute for original intent in sharing platforms), and (2) for-profit sharing economy organizations are less motivated and maybe less effective at delivering on noneconomic outcomes, including social and environmental ones. However, can't both versions of sharing economy platforms coexist together? (think Airbnb and Wikipedia). Related, is it not possible for sharing economy stakeholders (customers, citizens, shareholders, regulators – all of us) to push for what we want out of all forms of sharing economy organizations and platforms? How do we collectively push the current "portfolio" of all sharing economy actors to do what is best for the greater (international) public good?

What Kind of Sharing Economy Do We Want?

Noting the "portfolio approach" above, we briefly discuss some thoughts on how to achieve the sharing economy that we want. Cultivate:

1. **Proper regulation**. Regulators, representing the collective interests of citizens, still need to protect consumers from unscrupulous platforms and/or unskilled unethical suppliers and customers, whether in traditional industries or in the sharing economy. Bad things are always going to happen, but risks should be appropriately minimized. How do we ensure that the risks for consumers are not relatively elevated in the sharing economy? How can we be sure Uber drivers are adequately trained and have been adequately vetted, culture by culture? And how do we ensure that Airbnb services are safe and as advertised? Are the feedback mechanisms in any sharing economy context sufficient to cull bad apples? Is the regulation appropriate? Sharing economy organizations should collaborate with regulators in all settings to ensure appropriate agreed upon protection for all (Moore, 2021).

For a deeper dive on sharing economy regulation, see this downloadable paper: "Does sharing mean caring? Regulating innovation in the sharing economy" (Ranchordas, 2014). A common theme is risk. Are sharing economy companies appropriately taking on risk or are they offloading too much of it onto other actors? How do we "share" risks appropriately and fairly with the various stakeholders involved? How do we anticipate problems proactively? And when unanticipated problems do crop up, are sharing economy businesses willing to work closely and authentically with customers and regulators to make it right?

2. **High trust**. Related, in a now infamous case in the summer of 2011, Airbnb reactively added insurance coverage for all hosts after one of its hosts in San Francisco came home to an extraordinarily ransacked apartment, complete with holes in the walls where the customer broke into a locked closet to steal jewels and identification papers (EJ, 2011). Airbnb's existing policies and reaction were initially criticized as inadequate. The company did much damage control over the following weeks, with the CEO penning apology notices with titles like: "We screwed up and we're sorry" (Parr, 2011). They also implemented a retroactive USD 50,000 insurance guarantee for apartment damage to all customers. Over the past decade, Airbnb has proved to be attentive in situations like this because their core business model – heavily reliant on trust and the assumption that providers and buyers on their platform will have integrity – was in extreme danger.

As the victimized host herself put it:

> I would be remiss if I didn't pause here to emphasize that the customer service team at airbnb.com has been wonderful, giving this crime their full attention. They have called often, expressing empathy, support, and genuine concern for my welfare. They have offered to help me recover emotionally and financially, and are working with SFPD to track down these criminals. I do believe the folks at airbnb.com when they tell me this has never happened before in their short history, that this is a one-off case. I do believe that maybe 97% of Airbnb.com's users are good and honest people. Unfortunately I got the other 3%. Someone was bound to eventually, I suppose, and there will be others. For this reason, I felt compelled to get my story out as soon as possible – as a warning to travelers and renters everywhere – even though this case remains under investigation, and the final chapter of this story remains unwritten.
>
> (EJ, 2011)

At the beginning of their journey, Airbnb, Uber, and other startups were arguably quick to expand their businesses first and ask questions later, ignoring regulation and often initially offloading the risk on the service supplier (the apartment host, the driver, the car provider). The true tests for sharing economy platforms come when inevitable problems, including crimes and accidents, occur. Consumers such as the above pay attention in these moments, and perceived integrity helps. On this score, Airbnb has arguably fared better than Uber (Siddiqui, 2019).

3. **Science-appropriate ESG/sustainability goals and transparency.** Can sharing economy platforms truly deliver superior environmental and social outcomes (Zhifu & Coffman, 2019)? To get there, sharing economy platforms need to be transparent about their impacts, set appropriate performance metrics, and then transparently disclose whether the goals are being achieved. Is there truth in advertising? Do ride sourcing platforms really take cars off the road (Szymkowski, 2021) or does home sharing really save CO_2 through greater efficiency (see Airbnb's [2014b] claims on the benefits of home sharing)? To what extent are sharing economy organizations serious about delivering on meaningful environmental and social performance? (For more, see the Wharton School piece in collaboration with Rubicon: "How green is the sharing economy?" [2015b]).

4. **Well-treated platform suppliers/workers.** Are sharing economy, aka "gig" economy (Lutkevich & Gillis, 2022), workers more vulnerable, more exploited, underpaid due to misclassification, subject to the whims of parasitic sharing economy platforms (Viswanath, 2020)? What do suppliers ("workers") want from the platform and are they satisfied? Are sharing economy workers "employees" of sharing economy "employers" or are they "independent contractors" not subject to standard rules, regulation, and benefits for regular employees, including health and retirement benefits? A critical question revolves around control – many sharing economy platforms are built around the premise that they are merely intermediaries, connecting providers/suppliers and users. In the case of Uber, drivers own their cars, set their own hours, and can provide their labor to other companies at will. This allowed Uber to initially avoid rules and regulations revolving around employee safety, pay, and benefits. However, Uber sets rates, sets minute requirements for the care and cleanliness, and monitors driver performance – all typical forms of control that a normal employer engages in. Erring on the side of taking the "high road," treating suppliers/workers as employees, may help to avoid headaches like Uber's current court woes in both the US (Bloomberg Law, 2022) and Europe (Haeck, 2021).

In this final section below, we further reflect on the case of Airbnb to illustrate how a sharing economy platform might be seen as an evolving model, centered on some of the best practices hinted at above.

Airbnb takes flight – and is still flying

To illustrate how rapidly some startups have grown and the threat to existing companies, it is instructive to briefly look at the experience of Airbnb more closely. In December 2020, Airbnb went public, and was instantly worth more than the top three hotels in the sector combined (Sonnemaker, 2020). According to the US-based report by PwC, by 2015 Airbnb had an average of 425,000 guests per night, which translates to 155 million guest stays per year. It has only grown since then.

In a midstream rebranding (Carr, 2014a), Airbnb proved savvy in seizing on multiple consumer needs. First, reassure the consumer through a reliable and familiar experience in terms of booking and basic amenities. Second, provide a unique experience that delivers more than just a room, complete with a fuller form of hospitality and an opportunity for connection that goes beyond a typical hotel experience.

Airbnb's introduction of a much discussed "Bélo" logo (viewable on YouTube) might be seen as a test case for sharing economy organizations as they seek to distinguish themselves from traditional institutions. The campaign directly taps into the idea that urban consumers are seeking connection with others all over the world and that they want to share and belong. In the words of the release: "At Airbnb, we imagine a world where you can belong anywhere. Introducing the Bélo."

Video transcript:

> The world is full of cities and towns
> constantly growing larger
> But the people within them are less connected.
> Yet we are all yearning for a sense of place.
> we are all seeking to
> Belong.
> We all want to connect and share.
> To feel accepted and feel safe.
> Imagine having that anywhere.
> Airbnb stands for something
> much bigger than travel
> We imagine a world where you can...
> Belong Anywhere.
> This needs its own symbol.
> One that can be drawn by anyone
> and recognized anywhere.
> A symbol of belonging.
> We call it the Bélo.
> The Bélo represents all of us,
> and it stands for four things:
> People
> Places
> Love
> Airbnb
> Wherever you see it, you'll know you belong
> My home
> San Francisco Los Angeles Tokyo Barcelona London Buenos Aires Helsinki Mumbai Rome Sydney Paris New York Bangkok Rio De Janeiro

Shanghai Dubai Vancouver Casablanca Berlin New Delhi Copenhagen
Amsterdam
   Airbnb
(Source: "Airbnb introduces the Bélo: the story of a symbol of belonging"
     (2014a) at https://www.youtube.com/watch?v=nMITXMrrVQU).

Airbnb's CEO and Cofounder Brian Chesky elaborated on rationale for the logo
and the rebranding in a lengthy blog post the day of the release. At the core of his
blog is this section on belonging:

Belonging
   We used to take belonging for granted. Cities used to be villages. Everyone knew each other, and everyone knew they had a place to call home.
But after the mechanization and Industrial Revolution of the last century,
those feelings of trust and belonging were displaced by mass-produced and
impersonal travel experiences. We also stopped trusting each other. And
in doing so, we lost something essential about what it means to be a community. After all, our relationships with people will always be the most
meaningful part of our lives. You just need to get to know them. That's
why Airbnb is returning us to a place where everyone can feel they belong. Like us, you may have started out thinking you were just renting out
a room to help pay the bills. Or maybe you were just booking a bed for a
night on an unexpected layover. However we first entered this community,
we all know that getting in isn't a transaction. It's a connection that can
last a lifetime. That's because the rewards you get from Airbnb aren't just
financial—they're personal—for hosts and guests alike. At a time when new
technologies have made it easier to keep each other at a distance, you're
using them to bring people together. And you're tapping into the universal
human yearning to belong—the desire to feel welcomed, respected, and
appreciated for who you are, no matter where you might be. Belonging is
the idea that defines Airbnb, but the way we've represented Airbnb to the
world until now hasn't fully captured this.

Is Airbnb tapping into something that enough consumers in the sharing economy
truly want in a travel experience: Connection, not "distance," trust, not mistrust –
to be welcomed, respected, and appreciated – by strangers in new places? Do consumers want this kind of sharing and belonging, this kind of "social"? Or do they
simply want the access to relatively inexpensive hotel-like experiences with extra
perks and conveniences (full kitchens, laptops available with free internet service,
good locations in hip areas)? Or both?

   In a *Harvard Business Review* article by Eckhardt and Bardhi (2015), the authors
argue that consumers generally are much more interested in the access component
of the sharing economy and not the social component. In their words:

By this logic, Airbnb's rebranding, which highlights 'people, places, love and community,' will be a misstep. AirBnB wants its new logo to be a universal symbol of sharing, yet the reason why most consumers use AirBnB is the value they can get for their money, especially in expensive cities. Additionally, when choosing a place to stay, most consumers opt to have the entire place to themselves, meaning they don't share the space with the owner at all. AirBnB provides the means for travelers and owners to engage in a market transaction of short term access, and their brand should reflect this.

(Eckhardt & Bardhi, 2015)

The authors hold up Uber as an example of a company that gets this – stressing pricing, reliability, and convenience ("Better, Faster and Cheaper than a Taxi") – and not sharing. Are they right?

The comments section contained significant pushback from readers of the article. For example, there was this comment:

Every time I use Airbnb.. My friends too....We share that person's life through his neighbourhood... We share information and experiences through whatsapp with the host. We develop a relationship before, during and maybe after... We often share each others lives for a while....So i strongly feel the sharing economy does exist and or goes beyond access, where it is just about the physical exchange, but it is also about the practical and emotional one. I very much feel part of an airbnb community of people who makes travelling in a social way possible. So I do not agree with you that airbnb Is only about physical access to reasonably priced accommodation. I also pick an apartment based on look, yes, location yes and price of course... But a fundamental factor in my choice is the relationship I develop with the host when searching. To me it is sharing their lives either physically or virtually (both = relationship) while I am there that makes my stay so much more special than accessing a hotel, or as it seems to you...

(Eckhardt & Bardhi, 2015)

It is safe to say this: The sharing economy is providing consumers with an amazing array of new choices, including the degree of connection and sharing they want to engage in. Uber may be more about efficient access, and Lyft (with its fist bumps) may be more about sharing and connection, and perhaps there is room for both. In the case of Airbnb, in addition to the variety of particular spaces, users can dial up or down the degree of contact they want with their local hosts. The businesses that can empower consumers by providing users with efficient, intuitive, and trust building interfaces for sorting through and making satisfying choices – tailored to needs and personalities – will likely do better in the long run.

And therein lies the challenge with many sharing economy startups – the complexity of variety. This is captured in a series of questions that Austin Carr asks in a piece for Fast Company on Airbnb's "Grand Hotel Plans":

How do you strike the right mix of host and guest amenities for 550,000 disparate listings in 192 countries?

How do you manage the thorny legal and regulatory hurdles raised by governments eager for new tax revenue?

How do you get into those other areas of the trip, like the car ride from the airport and exploring the neighborhood where you're staying?

Perhaps most important, and of most immediate concern: How do you overcome the nagging perception that staying in someone's spare bedroom is unpredictable, awkward, and a far cry from what mainstream travelers know they'll receive at traditional hotels?

(Carr, 2014b)

Not easy. But then again, going forward there will probably be enough consumers and peers demanding idiosyncratic new realities like this one in the hospitality industry. And yes, entrepreneurs will continue to try to create and expand these new realities (*The New York Times*, 2016).

Note

1. For one take on the wide range of terms being used and an attempt at interpreting their differences, see *The Sharing Economy: A Dictionary of Commonly Used Terms* (https://medium.com/@rachelbotsman/the-sharing-economy-dictionary-of-commonly-used-terms-d1a696691d12) available at a key sharing economy website www.collaborativeconsumption.com, or work through the slide presentation.

References

AAA (2021). "How much does it really cost to own a new car". Retrieved from: https://newsroom.aaa.com/wp-content/uploads/2021/08/2021-YDC-Brochure-Live.pdf.

Airbnb (2014a). "Airbnb introduces the Bélo: The story of a symbol of belonging". Available at https://www.youtube.com/watch?v=nMITXMrrVQU.

Airbnb (2014b). "New study reveals a greener way to travel: Airbnb community shows environmental benefits of home sharing." Retrieved from: https://www.airbnb.co.uk/press/news/new-study-reveals-a-greener-way-to-travel-airbnb-community-shows-environmental-benefits-of-home-sharing.

Bloomberg Law (2022, January 4). "Gig economy companies brace for crucial year as challenges mount". Retrieved from: https://news.bloomberglaw.com/us-law-week/gig-economy-companies-brace-for-crucial-year-as-challenges-mount.

Botsman, R. (2010). "The case for collaborative consumption". TED talk at TEDxSydney. Retrieved from: www.ted.com/talks/rachel_botsman_the_case_for_collaborative_consumption#t-89425.

Botsman, R. (2013, November 19). "The sharing economy lacks a shared definition: Giving meaning to the terms". Retrieved from: www.slideshare.net/CollabLab/shared-def-pptf.

Botsman, R., & Rogers, R. (2010). "Beyond zipcar: Collaborative consumption". *Harvard Business Review*. Retrieved from: https://hbr.org/2010/10/beyond-zipcar-collaborative-consumption.

Bieker, G. (2021). "A global comparison of the life-cycle greenhouse gas emissions of combustion engine and electric passenger cars". White paper, International Council on Clean

Transportation. Retrieved from: https://theicct.org/sites/default/files/publications/Global-LCA-passenger-cars-jul2021_0.pdf.

Carr, A. (2014a, July 16). "Airbnb unveils a major rebranding effort that paves the way for sharing more than homes". Retrieved from: www.fastcompany.com/3033130/airbnb-unveils-a-major-rebranding-effort-that-paves-the-way-for-sh.

Carr, A. (2014b, March 17). "Inside Airbnb's grand hotel plans". Retrieved from: www.fastcompany.com/3027107/punk-meet-rock-airbnb-brian-chesky-chip-conley.

Currier, J. (2018, January 9). "The network effects manual: 13 different network effects (and counting)". Retrieved from: https://medium.com/@nfx/the-network-effects-manual-13-different-network-effects-and-counting-a3e07b23017d.

Eckhardt, G., & Bardhi, F. (2015, January 28). "The sharing economy isn't about sharing at all". *Harvard Business Review*. Retrieved from: https://hbr.org/2015/01/the-sharing-economy-isnt-about-sharing-at-all.

EJ (2011, June 29). "Violated: A traveler's lost faith, a difficult lesson learned". Blog. Retrieved from: https://ejroundtheworld.blogspot.com/2011/06/violated-travelers-lost-faith-difficult.html.

Haeck, P. (2021, September 20). "Uber risks death by a thousand court cases". Retrieved from: www.politico.eu/article/uber-platform-employees-workers-benefits/.

Kessler, S. (2015, September 14). "The sharing economy is dead, and we killed it". Retrieved from: www.fastcompany.com/3050775/the-sharing-economy-is-dead-and-we-killed-it.

Koopman, C., Mitchell, M. D., & Thierer, A. D. (2014). "The sharing economy and consumer protection regulation: The case for policy change". *SSRN Electronic Journal*. https://doi.org/10.2139/ssrn.2535345.

Lock, S. (2022, January 7). "Number of sharing economy users in the U.S. 2016–2021". Retrieved from: www.statista.com/statistics/289856/number-sharing-economy-users-us/.

Lutkevich, B., & Gillis, A. S. (2022). "What is the gig economy?". Retrieved from: www.techtarget.com/whatis/definition/gig-economy.

Markets and Markets (2022). "Ride sharing market by type (E-hailing, station-based, car sharing & rental), car sharing (P2P, corporate), service (navigation, payment, information), micro-mobility (bicycle, scooter), vehicle type, and region (2022–2026)". Retrieved from: www.marketsandmarkets.com/Market-Reports/mobility-on-demand-market-198699113.html.

Moore, M. (2021, January 25). "Uber has a wild new plan for global ride-hailing domination". Retrieved from: www.wired.co.uk/article/uber-ride-hailing-future.

Namaste, J. (2022, March 18). "How WeWork rebounded after its controversial IPO". Retrieved from: www.bustle.com/entertainment/does-wework-still-exist-who-owns-it-now.

NPR (2013, November 13). "What's mine is yours (for a price) in the sharing economy". Broadcast. Retrieved from: www.npr.org/sections/alltechconsidered/2013/11/13/244860511/whats-mine-is-yours-for-a-price-in-the-sharing-economy.

Owyang, J., with Tran, C., & Silva, C. (2013, June 4). "The collaborative economy". Retrieved from: www.slideshare.net/Altimeter/the-collaborative-economy.

Parr, B. (2011, August 1). "Airbnb: 'We screwed up and we're sorry'". Retrieved from: https://mashable.com/archive/airbnb-ransackgate#uGegWMWY3iqW.

PwC (2014). "The sharing economy: How will it disrupt your business?". Blog. Retrieved from: https://pwc.blogs.com/files/sharing-economy-final_0814.pdf.

Ranchordas, S. (2014). "Does sharing mean caring? Regulating innovation in the sharing economy". *Minnesota Journal of Law, Science & Technology*. Retrieved from: https://papers.ssrn.com/sol3/papers.cfm?abstract_id=2492798.

Rinne, A. (2022). "Thriving in a world of flux". Retrieved from: https://aprilrinne.com.

Sands, S., Ferraro, C., Campbell, C., Kietzmann, J., & Andonopoulos, V. V. (2020). "Who shares? Profiling consumers in the sharing economy". *Australasian Marketing Journal, 28*(3), 22–33. https://doi.org/10.1016/j.ausmj.2020.06.005.

Scaraboto, D., & Figueieredo, B. (2022, April 7). "Airbnb's Ukraine moment is a reminder of what the sharing economy can be". *The Conversation*. Retrieved from: https://theconversation.com/airbnbs-ukraine-moment-is-a-reminder-of-what-the-sharing-economy-can-be-180506.

Siddiqui, F. (2019, August 29). "Internal data shows Uber's reputation hasn't changed much since #DeleteUber". *Washington Post*. Retrieved from: www.washingtonpost.com/technology/2019/08/29/even-after-ubers-ipo-long-shadow-deleteuber-still-looms/.

Sonnemaker, T. (2020, December 11). "Airbnb is worth more than the 3 largest hotel chains after its stock popped 143% on its first day of trading". Retrieved from: www.businessinsider.com/airbnb-ipo-valuation-tops-three-hotel-chains-combined-opening-day-2020-12?r=US&IR=T.

Statista Research Department (2022, February 7). "Sharing services in the U.S. – statistics & facts". Retrieved from: https://www.statista.com/topics/4694/sharing-services-in-the-us/#dossierKeyfigures.

Szymkowski, S. (2021, February 4). "Yet another study says Uber and Lyft are worse for traffic congestion". Retrieved from: www.cnet.com/roadshow/news/uber-lyft-traffic-congestion-car-ownership-study/.

The Economist (2020, June 4). "The sharing economy will have to change: But that will help it survive the pandemic and thrive". Retrieved from: www.economist.com/business/2020/06/04/the-sharing-economy-will-have-to-change.

Viswanath, K. (2020, September 14). "How Uber and Airbnb created a parasite economy". Retrieved from: https://marker.medium.com/uber-and-airbnb-are-parasites-but-they-dont-have-to-be-36909355ac3b.

Wharton School, Knowledge at Wharton staff (2015a, December 11). "The sharing economy spills into new markets". Retrieved from: https://knowledge.wharton.upenn.edu/article/the-sharing-economy-spills-into-new-markets/.

Wharton School, Knowledge at Wharton Staff (2015b, December 11). "How green is the sharing economy". Retrieved from: https://knowledge.wharton.upenn.edu/article/how-green-is-the-sharing-economy/.

Wirtz, J., Fung So, K. K., Mody, M. A., Liu, S. Q., & Chun, H. H. (2019). "Platforms in the peer-to-peer sharing economy". *Journal of Service Management, 30*(4), 452–483. https://doi.org/10.1108/JOSM-11-2018-0369.

World Bank Group, Climate Watch (2020). *GHG Emissions*. Washington, DC: World Resources Institute. Retrieved from: https://data.worldbank.org/indicator/EN.ATM.CO2E.PC.

Zhifu, M., & Coffman, D. M. (2019). 'The sharing economy promotes sustainable societies". *Nature Communications, 10*. Retrieved from: www.nature.com/articles/s41467-019-09260-4.

Index

Note: **Bold** page numbers refer to tables; *italic* page numbers refer to figures.

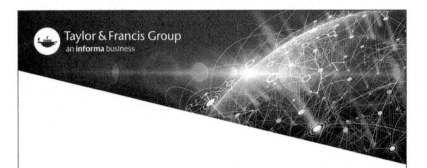

Printed in the United States
by Baker & Taylor Publisher Services